SMALL AND MINIATURE TURNING

a complete guide

SMALL AND MINIATURE TURNING

a complete guide

Ron Hampton

Guild of Master Craftsman Publications

First published 2005 by
Guild of Master Craftsman Publications Ltd
Castle Place, 166 High Street,
Lewes, East Sussex BN7 1XU

ISBN 1 86108 384 X

A catalogue record for this book is available from the British Library.

Managing Editor: Gerrie Purcell
Production Manager: Hilary MacCallum
Project Editors: Rachel Netherwood and Stephen Haynes
Cover design: Andy Harrison
Book design: Fineline Studios
Additional photography: GMC Publications/Anthony Bailey (front cover and pages 2, 6, 36, 50, 59 (Fig 24), 70, 80, 92, 106, 109 (Fig 1), 125 (Fig 45), 126, 129 (Fig 1), 145 (Fig 46)); photographs of other turners' work by courtesy of the artists concerned
Illustrator: Simon Rodway
Drawings on pages 39 and 41 by courtesy of PSI Woodturning Products

Set in Myriad and Hiroshige Book

Colour origination by Wyndeham Graphics
Printed and bound by Sino Publishing House Ltd, Hong Kong, China

Contents

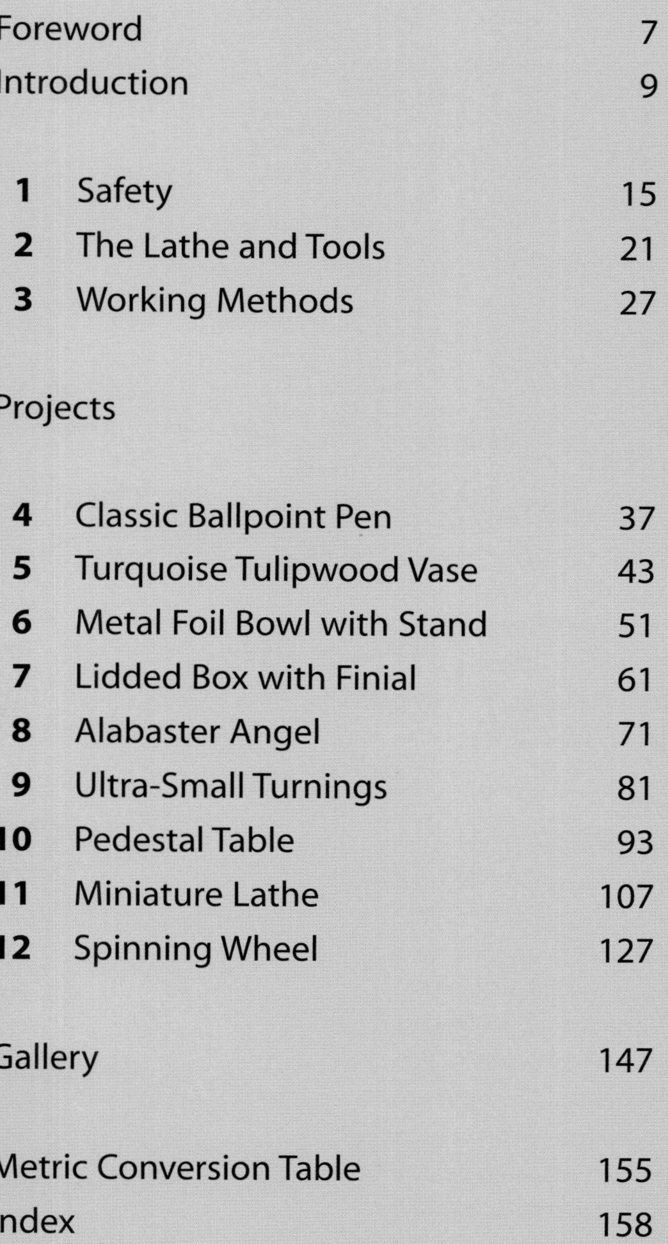

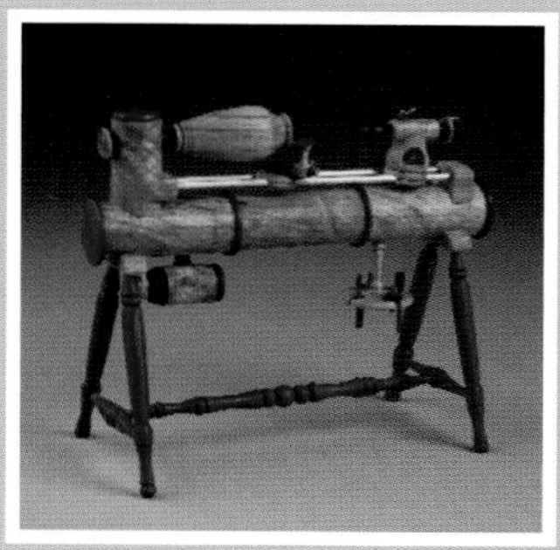

To Barbara, my wife.
You are the most important person
in my life. Thank you!
You can never know how much your
love and support mean to me.

Acknowledgements

Very few people are self-made; I certainly am not a self-made man. Most of us have learned from a long list of people. Like most turners I have been influenced and taught by many who have gone before me.
In particular, Ray Key and Richard Raffan have made a tremendous impact on my turning life through their books and videos, though until recently I had never met either of them in person.

I would like to thank my friend Delbert Dowdy for his tremendous assistance in solving computer software problems. Another friend, Buddy Rose, has given me invaluable help with building workshop equipment. My editor, Stephen Haynes, has been a delight to work with. Also I want to thank my office staff: Barbara Hampton, Lynne Peavy and Sarah Whitten-Morris. They have put up with me these last 13 months when the only thing I talked about was miniature turning and 'the book'.

Measurements

Although care has been taken to ensure that the metric measurements are true and accurate, they are only conversions from imperial. They have been rounded up or down to the nearest whole millimetre, except in some instances where greater precision is needed. In cases where the imperial measurements themselves are only approximate, they have been rounded to the nearest convenient equivalent. **When following the projects, use either metric or imperial measurements; do not mix units.**

Above and opposite: Examples of ultra-small turnings, made using the techniques described in Chapter 9. The smallest goblet is $^{11}/_{64}$in (4.3mm) high.

Foreword

There is a special fascination with working on a small scale. We admire the dexterity of those who work metal into jewellery, or carve small lumps of hardwood into exquisite netsuke. Or we're grateful for the skills of a dentist like Ron Hampton, who clearly likes to work small-scale in his leisure hours as well – and then to pass on what he's learned.

Turning wood on a lathe is an ancient craft that for the most part has provided us with mass-produced components for all manner of trades and industries. And in addition to all the millions of round tool handles, doorknobs and chair parts, for centuries our ancestors ate from turned plates and bowls.

Over the past thirty years there has been a phenomenal renewal of interest in turning wood – but this time as a hobby rather than a trade. And from the hobby base, professional studio turners and a lathe-art movement have emerged. Amongst contemporary woodturners there's a tendency to work on a grand scale, creating imposing works of apparent virtuosity. But when working large-scale, ineptitude and blunders are easily concealed, whereas – as Ron Layport has pointed out – 'In small work, every wrong decision is huge.' He's right: considerably more skill is required when working small-scale, which may be why we see so few small turnings. This makes Ron Hampton's book all the more timely.

Kip Christensen has said that 'If you don't find woodturning to be fun, you're probably not doing it right.' This book opens a whole world of woodturning, and should certainly help you to do it right – and to use up all those little offcuts that you always knew would, one day, be useful.

Richard Raffan
August 2005

Introduction

Small and miniature turning is an unusual and exciting artform within woodturning. Miniature turnings are scaled-down reproductions of full-sized objects, often made using a plan of the full-sized object to work from. Small turnings, on the other hand – usually defined as being around 6in (150mm) or smaller – are generally not miniaturizations of full-sized pieces, and are judged on their artistic merits alone. With many forms of woodworking it can take months to complete a project. However, a beautiful small-scale turning can often be produced within several days or a couple of weeks. This short production time is a tremendous advantage to those of us who are less than patient, as well as to the artist who wants to make a living as a turner. Many more people can afford a two-day project than those who can afford to take three months. The projects in this book are ideal both for the professional who needs to earn money from turning and for the hobbyist who wants to create beautiful items which also make fantastic presents.

If you've never turned wood before, I'm sure you'll enjoy it. Shapes develop in seconds as the shavings fly away, and I have the hunch that the ability to remove so much wood so quickly satisfies some basic destructive urge and gratifies the vandal in us all.

Richard Raffan, Turning Wood

Other advantages

Small and miniature turning offer many other advantages over full-size turning. These include:

Ease of construction

This should be a major consideration for the beginner turner. Starting off on a project that is too difficult is discouraging and can slow down development. This book contains projects that will get the beginner started and challenge the intermediate to advanced turner; it starts with simple projects and then moves to progressively more challenging turnings and in this way the beginner turner will not be left behind. Likewise the more advanced turner will learn new techniques that will develop his turning skills.

Savings on equipment

A significant advantage of small and miniature turning is that the necessary equipment is far less expensive than that for full-size turning. Good mini (or midi) lathes can be purchased for a third of the price of most top-of-the-range lathes (such as the Oneway lathe used for this book); and even the best small lathes are about a quarter of what you might pay for an equivalent large lathe (Fig 1).

However, small and miniature turning does require a very good four-jaw chuck with several different-size collet jaws. These collet jaws allow you to mount and hold many different-size turning blanks quickly and easily. A good collet system on a four-jaw chuck will save you an incredible amount of time (Fig 2). There are many areas in woodturning where you can save money, but you should not skimp on your four-jaw collet system.

Economy of turning materials

The small-scale turner has a tremendous advantage over the full-size turner when it comes to the cost of turning materials. Admittedly it is not unusual for professional turner Ron Fleming to spend a couple of hundred dollars on a turning blank for a small-sized turning (Fig 3), but it is quite possible for the small-scale turner to use even exotic wood without spending large sums of money on the turning blank.

Ease of sale

There are many more places in a home to put a small turning than there are to put a large turning, which is a tremendous advantage to the small turner. It is far easier to sell small turnings because customers will have many more places in which they can display their new piece of art. Small turnings are also usually less expensive and because you can make and sell many more small items, you can make just as much, or more, money than if you sold only a few large items.

1 The Oneway 1224 (seen here from the back rather than the operator's side) is an excellent lathe for miniature and small turning

2 A good chuck system with interchangeable collets is a worthwhile investment

3 Ron Fleming, *Ivory Rose*, 6in tall by 4½in diameter (152 x 114mm). For small-scale projects you can use beautiful wood without breaking the bank

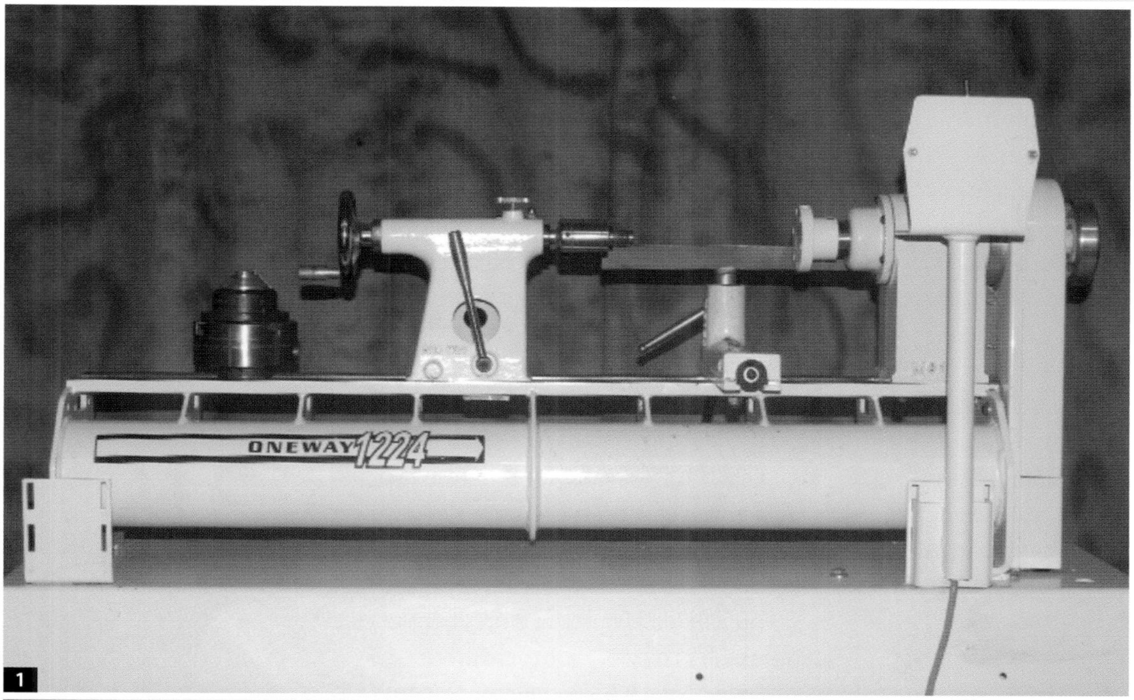

Getting started

Form, colour, grace, style and contrast are important components of woodturning, and indeed of all art. Usually an artist will not be trying to create something that is just 'pretty' and while it is true that he or she will often create pieces that are pleasing to the eye, the art should always carry a message within it. This can be a personal vision of the artist, or it may be an expression of what he or she is going through at a particular time in their life. Likewise, when an art patron purchases a piece of art, they are not just purchasing an object. The patron is moved by the artistic insight of the artist and wants to share part of their creation.

Goals of the turner

Your first goal as a turner is to learn the basics of the lathe and tool control. Once you have mastered these basics, your next task is to master the wood. Always look for new ways to express its richness, beauty, warmth, and texture. Turning is not simply making a piece of wood round; real artistic turning creates something far more than just a nice piece of wood with a pretty finish on it. The form (or shape) of the turning is of paramount importance. Some turning artists, such as Richard Raffan and Ray Key, have developed their technique to such a high level that their forms are instantly recognized as exquisite pieces of art (Figs 4 and 5). Spend time thinking about how you can use different materials. Keep your mind open, and always look for ways to do things better and differently from everybody else.

When we copy someone else's work, we tell ourselves that our own ideas are not good enough… We put ourselves down and it's no wonder we have no confidence in ourselves. The more we copy, the worse it gets.

Frank Sudol

Inspiration

The Gallery at the end of this book has examples of turnings by some of the top turners in the world. Study these beautiful pieces of art for inspiration, and use this to help you create a distinctive style of your own. You can learn and develop your technique by copying another turner's style, but once you have developed some basic skill, you should begin to create your own artistic voice. This is not as hard as it might sound. Look at work that you like. Then think about new and different ways you might 'improve' a piece that you have been studying. Nature provides an endless supply of beautiful shapes that can be translated into your turnings.

A final thought

Above all else, the main reason we do small and miniature turning is because it is a lot of fun!

4 Richard Raffan, *Citadel* boxes. Richard's box profiles are instantly recognizable

5 Ray Key, selection of knobbed boxes in yew, olivewood and kingwood, largest 4in high by 2¾in diameter (100 x 70mm). Ray Key's boxes are some of the very best in the world. Photograph by the late Tony Boase

4

5

1 Safety

Turning is a lot of fun and can be done safely. However, it is necessary to pay attention and follow some safety rules. All tools can be dangerous! There are numerous ways that an accident may happen, and if one does occur it is very important that you are wearing your safety equipment so that you do not get hurt.

Turning accidents happen to beginners and experienced woodworkers alike. Beginners have accidents because they do not know the rules for safe turning. Experienced turners have accidents because they ignore the rules, work too fast, or lose their concentration. So to have fun, and be safe at the same time, it is necessary to follow some basic guidelines.

You must be mentally alert and paying full attention at all times. If you are compromised by fatigue, alcohol, or medication you must quit; any one of these factors will affect your judgement and reflexes. Remember that the lathe does not care if you are tired or in a hurry. So pay attention!

*If you don't find turning wood to be fun,
you are probably not doing it right.*

Kip Christensen

Lathe safety

Speed kills

This is true for cars, and for machinery. The speed of your lathe must be slow enough not to cause vibration. High speeds can cause pieces to come apart from excessive centrifugal force, which is very dangerous. You must always wear a face shield because you never know when your turning might come apart, and a thick lab apron can give you some chest protection should this happen.

No loose clothing

Do not wear any long or loose clothing, or have untied hair: it will eventually get caught in moving machinery. Lathes are especially dangerous because you are working close to a rotating shaft.

Line of fire

Position your toolrest between you and the turning so that if your turning comes apart, the toolrest will give you some protection. With the toolrest in place between you and the turning, any flying object will almost always travel in a straight line away from the lathe or straight up. Be aware that if your turning goes straight up, it will eventually come back down. Also make sure anyone else present is not in the line of fire.

No unattended machines

If you leave the machine, turn it off. Never walk away from, or across the path of, a running lathe.

No vibrations

Make sure that your turning is balanced and not causing the lathe to vibrate. Whenever possible, hold the turning at both ends, using your tailstock.

Sharpness of tools

Keep your tools sharp: use sharp tools and a light touch when cutting. Dull tools require that you use more force pushing the tool into the wood, and excessive force may cause your turning to come apart.

Correct body position

Do not stand in the line of fire when you turn a lathe on. Do stand or sit in a comfortable position that does not fatigue you.

Safety zone

Always keep your fingers behind the toolrest. If you allow your finger to be caught between the toolrest and the turning, you can suffer a serious injury. Keep your fingers away from the danger zone while the lathe is moving (Fig 1).

1 A view of the lathe from above, showing the danger zone between the toolrest and the turning. If you allow your finger to be caught here, you can suffer a serious injury. Always keep your fingers in the safe area behind the toolrest. Remove the toolrest before starting to sand

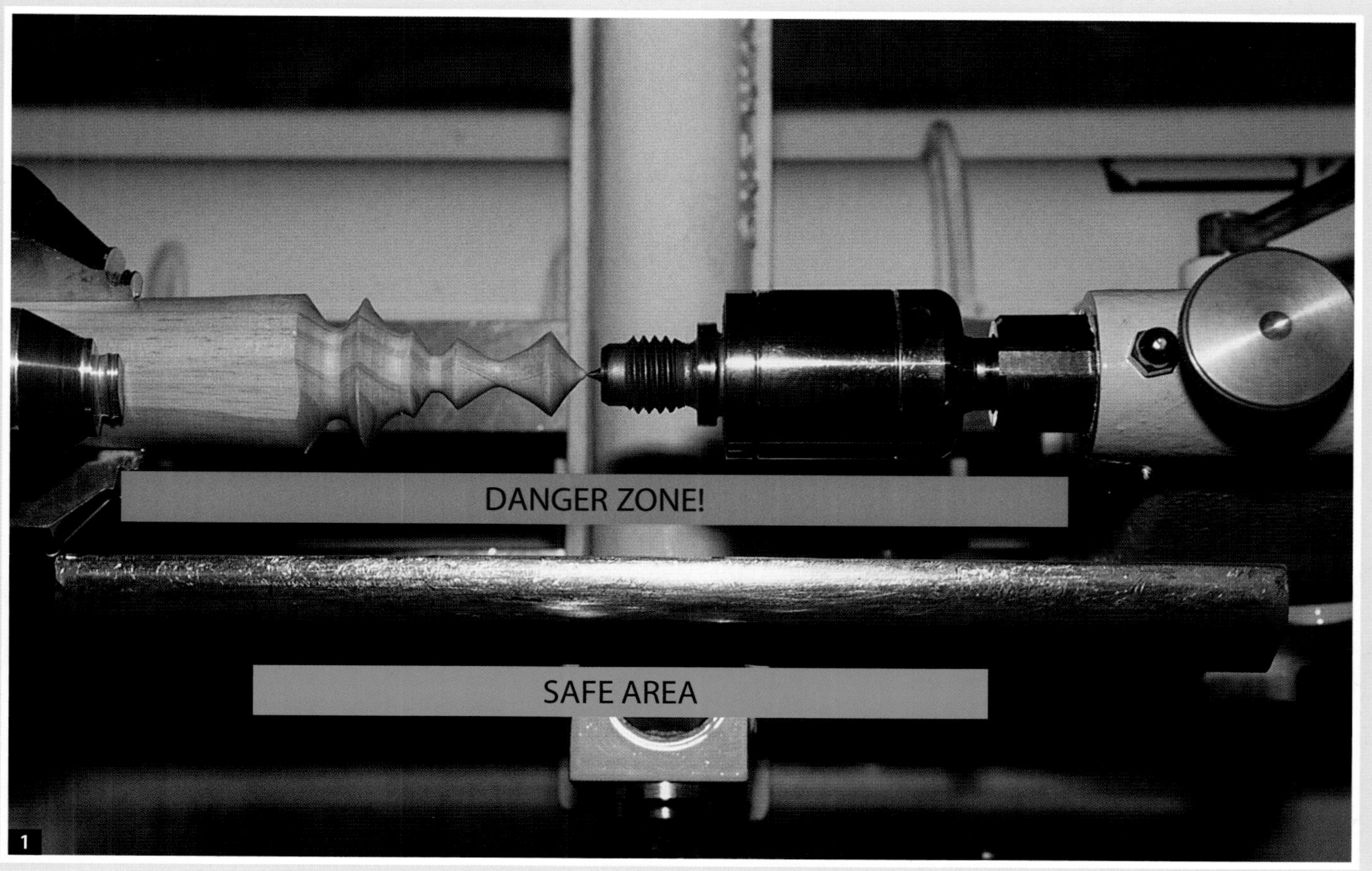

1

General safety

Sober and alert

When working in the shop you must always be sober and alert. If you are too tired, or in too much of a hurry, to do something the correct way, then it is time for you to quit and go home. You cannot work well if you are compromised.

Safety equipment

Always wear the proper safety equipment. This means that before turning on the lathe you must *always* put on a face shield (Fig 2), which must fully cover your face.

A plastic full-face shield gives you a tremendous amount of head protection during turning. There are many types available; just make sure that it is made of high-impact-resistant plastic. My preference is to wear a face shield that has automatic air filtration in the mask. It is fairly common to hear stories where a turning comes apart at a late stage. If the turner is wearing a face shield, it is just a story of a turner losing a beautiful turning. If the turner is not wearing a face shield, then it becomes a story about a trip to the hospital.

Use a shop apron that ties at the back so that there are no loose sleeves or strings. A heavy apron will give you considerable protection if the turning comes apart.

Lung protection

Always use some sort of dust filtration system. All sawdust is a lung irritant, and some kinds can even cause cancer, so avoid breathing sawdust at all times. Lung protection involves the following:

- Wear a respirator (Fig 3). There will be many different types of respirators available from your local woodworking supply store.

- Use one of the dust vacuum systems that pick up dust as it is made (Fig 4). Your system may be attached to an inexpensive shop vacuum or a larger and more expensive central vacuum system.

- Shop air-filtration systems pick up any dust circulating (Fig 5). There are many good brands available and they do an excellent job of collecting dust.

- Box fans behind and to the side of the turner deflect dust out of the way (Fig 6). Box fans are inexpensive and the filter holder is easy to make. I have two of these in my shop.

- Use your common sense. Do not work with wood that you are allergic to.

● Pay attention

Think how you need to do the job, so that you do it safely. Try to anticipate any situation that could cause you an accident. Wear your safety equipment at all times, and control your speed. Turning is fun and safe when done properly. If you are a beginner it is a good idea to get some instruction from an expert; there are many good videos that can help get you started safely.

2 Always wear a face shield when turning on the lathe. The face shield must cover your full face and be made of high-impact-resistant plastic. Better still is one that has an automatic air filtration system built into the mask

3 There are many different types of face masks and respirators available from woodworking supply stores

4 A simple shop-made holder can easily position your dust vacuum system just where it is needed. This system may be attached to an inexpensive shop vacuum or a larger and more expensive central vacuum system

5 A commercial air filter; there are many excellent brands available

6 Box fans can make excellent dust filters for the shop if they are placed in a shop-made box that has a slot for air filters. The fan is placed to one side, behind the user

2
3
4
JDS AIR-TECH 2000
HIGH EFFICIENCY AIR FILTRATION SYSTEM
THE JDS COMPANY COLUMBIA, S.C.
5
6

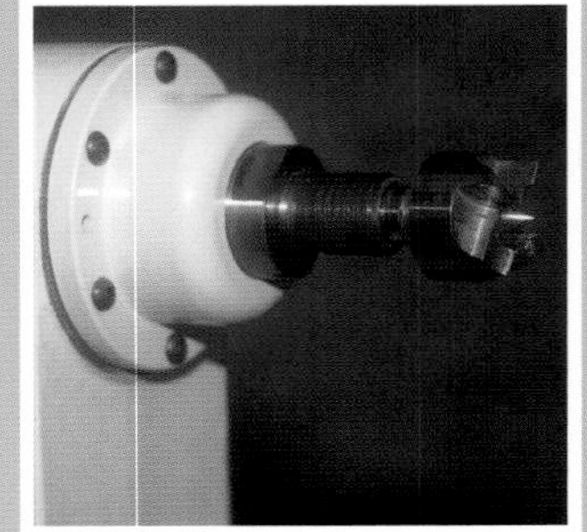

2 The Lathe and Tools

The wood lathe is a wonderfully enjoyable machine to work with. With a little instruction and practice you can have fun while making beautiful turnings. In this chapter we will go through the parts of the lathe and how to use it, as well as the tools used with the lathe.

Historically, the lathe was one of the first of the modern woodworking machines made by man. The ancient Chinese used hand-powered lathes to make beautiful teacups, and the Egyptians used a lathe to make a very ornate chair for one of their Pharaohs. English 'bodgers' of the eighteenth century used pole lathes to turn green wood chair legs with an incredibly high speed of production. With the modern electric lathe we can make beautiful turnings without tiring ourselves out pushing a treadle.

To impart my concepts of man upon a surface is to leave my fingerprint in time. From the mind to the hand to the form – it is personal, because it is most about the passion I can convey.

Ron Fleming

Lathes

Lathes are often described with two numbers. The first number is the height of the spindle over the bed of the lathe, in inches. This determines the radius of the biggest bowl you can turn (Fig 1). For example, if your lathe is 12in (305mm) above the bed, then in theory you could turn a bowl of 24in (610mm) diameter; but in practice, the largest bowl you can turn has about a 22in (560mm) diameter. The second number is a measure of how long the bed of the lathe is. The longer the bed, the longer your turning can be. The lathe used in this book is the Oneway 1224 (shown on page 11), which means that the height of the spindle is 12in (305mm) and the bed is 24in (610mm) long.

For small and miniature turning it is not necessary to have a large lathe. Large lathes are good for large turning, but they do have some distinct disadvantages: they take up more space and cost a large amount of money. On a day-to-day basis, the biggest disadvantage of a large lathe is that the parts are heavy and a lot of work to move. The tailstock of my heavy lathe weighs 66lb (29.9kg), while the tailstock of my Oneway 1224 weighs only 9lb (4kg). Fighting a heavy tailstock is a lot of unnecessary work when working with small turnings.

Lathe parts

Headstock

Wood is mounted on the headstock end of the lathe. Faceplates and four-jaw chucks may be attached to the headstock by screwing them onto the spindle (Fig 2). A spur drive or cup drive may be inserted into the spindle for initial turning of rough stock (Fig 3).

Tailstock

The tailstock is used to support the turning from the opposite end to the headstock when turning between centres (Fig 4), and is of vital importance for the safe operation of the lathe. The tailstock is brought forward and locked in position using a cam lever. A live centre is advanced into the wood by turning a handwheel at the back of the tailstock. The tailstock should be used whenever possible, to steady the work and minimize vibration.

Toolrest

The toolrest (or banjo) is moved into position and locked in place by means of a cam lever (Fig 5). It is important that the toolrest slides easily when the cam is released but locks down firmly when the cam is engaged. When cutting, the toolrest must be as close to the work area as possible without fouling the work.

Faceplates

Screwing wood to a faceplate is a common way to hold it when turning (Fig 6). When using a faceplate it is important that the screws used are big enough for the job, and penetrate far enough into the wood to hold it securely.

Four-jaw chuck

A good four-jaw chuck with a good collet set is invaluable for small and miniature turning (Fig 7). This system allows you to mount your wood and turnings quickly and securely. The tremendous amount of time you will save with the jaw-and-collet system will quickly pay for itself many times over.

1 The height of the spindle over the bed of the lathe determines how large a diameter your turning can have

2 A four-jaw chuck (shown resting on the lathe bed) or a faceplate can be screwed onto the headstock to hold the turning.

3 A spur drive mounted in the headstock

4 The tailstock is shown here from the back so that its locking lever can be seen

5 The toolrest must be positioned close to the turning, but not so close that the wood touches it

6 Faceplates are a versatile way to mount wood on the lathe

7 The four-jaw chuck and collets are essential accessories

Spindle height
1
2
3
4
5
6
7

Tools

Turning requires an assortment of basic tools (Fig 8). You can do a lot of small turning with the set listed below.

● A basic set of turning tools

- $^5/_8$in (16mm) bowl gouge (Fig 9 bottom)
- $^3/_8$in (10mm) spindle gouge (Fig 9 middle)
- $^3/_8$–$^1/_2$in (10–13mm) round-nose scraper (Fig 9 top)
- small $^3/_{32}$in (2mm) parting tool (Fig 10 bottom and Fig 11)
- regular-size $^3/_{16}$in (5mm) parting tool
- $^3/_8$in (10mm) beading tool (Fig 10 middle)
- $^3/_4$in (19mm) square-end scraper (Fig 10 top)
- $^1/_4$in (6mm) round skew chisel (Fig 11 middle)

A set of commercially made miniature turning tools can be a nice addition. Henry Taylor and Robert Sorby, among others, make excellent miniature tool sets for turning (Figs 12 and 13).

Home-made tools

For miniature turning you will often make some of your tools. This is really not as complicated as it may sound. Masonry nails are hard enough, and can easily be purchased from your local hardware store. It is a simple procedure to insert the pointed end of the nail into a home-made handle and then grind the end of the nail to suit your needs. If you need to bend the nail so that your tool has a curve, then you might want to consider using a regular nail; the steel in a regular nail can easily be bent to the shapes that you might need.

Magnification

Some form of magnification is very useful, as well as good lighting. I like a fairly inexpensive head-mounted magnification system with an attached light (Fig 14).

● Tip

Practice is an essential component of improving your turning ability. Daily practice and inspiration are two major factors in becoming an artist.

Great woodworking is a marriage between good design, the technical expertise to create the item out of raw wood and a great finish. The finish is the crowning glory to your work and I strive for a great finish in every piece I make. It makes the wood cry out to be touched and admired.

Caroline Harkness

8 A mobile cart with a support rack will help you organize your tools. Over time we seem to collect more and more tools to try to make our work a little simpler or easier

9 The three tools I use most
- round-nose scraper: excellent for finish cuts on the inside of a bowl
- $^3/_8$in (10mm) spindle gouge: excellent for detail work, it is a forgiving tool, with little tendency to dig in
- $^5/_8$in (16mm) bowl gouge

10 Three very useful tools
- square-end scraper: ideal for cutting square tenons and shoulders
- beading tool: excellent for making beads and cutting square shoulders
- $^1/_{16}$in (1.5mm) thin parting tool. The Robert Sorby thin parting tools save a lot of wood

11 Four more very useful tools
- $^3/_{16}$in (5mm) parting tool, which can also cut small beads in the process
- $^1/_4$in (6mm) round skew, used for much of the detail work in this book
- Robert Sorby $^1/_{16}$in (1.5mm) thin parting tool
- Chris Stott model thin parting tool

12 and **13** Miniature tool sets by Robert Sorby and Henry Taylor

14 Good magnification is very useful for miniature turning. This unit has a built-in light and is fairly inexpensive

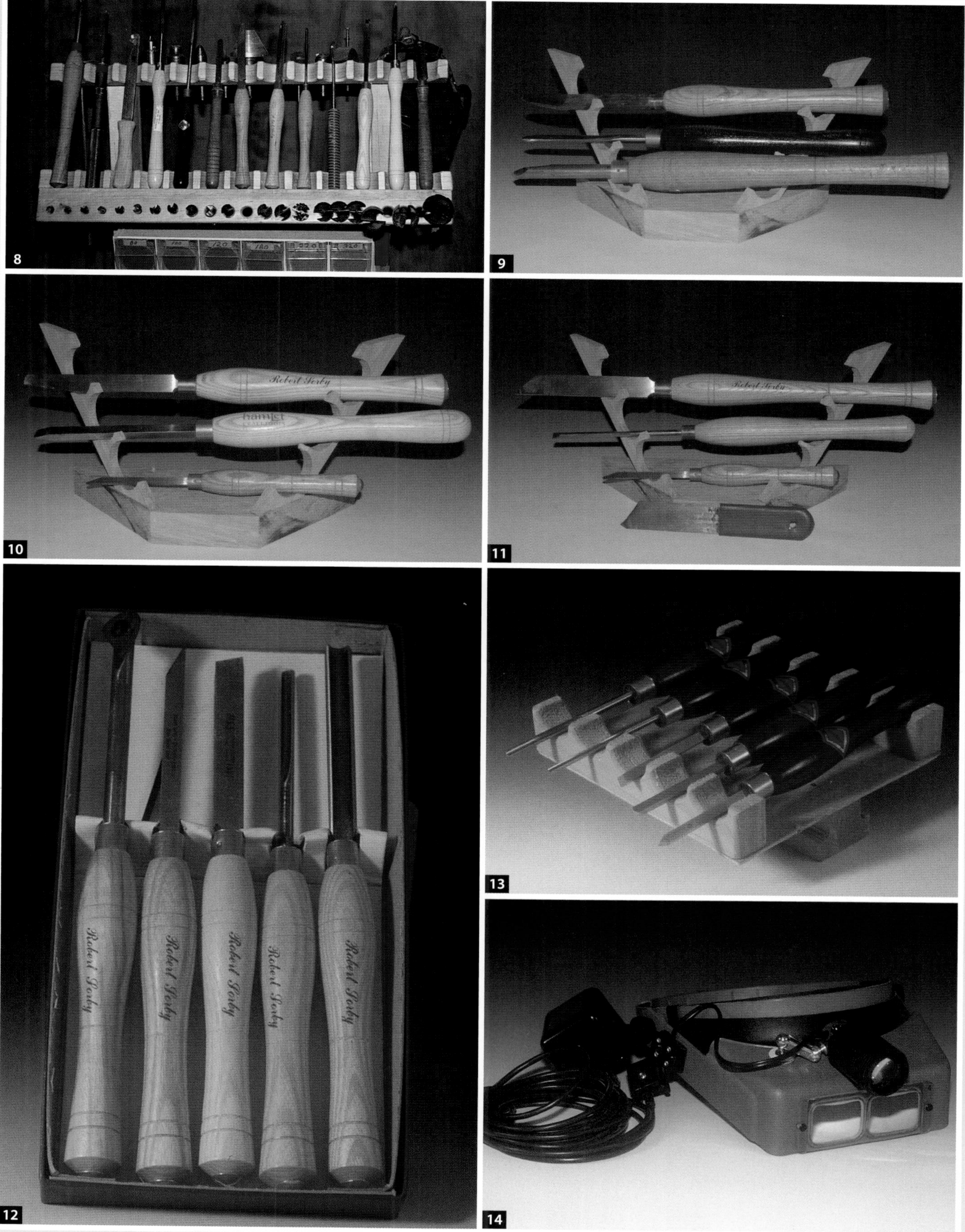
8
9
10
Robert Sorby
hamlet
11
Robert Sorby
12
Robert Sorby
Robert Sorby
Robert Sorby
Robert Sorby
Robert Sorby
13
14

3 Working Methods

To master any art or craft it is necessary that we understand the material we are working with and know how to control it. Woodturning is both an art and a craft, and there are some basic principles of wood and machinery that we need to understand if we are to be successful – and, above all, safe.

Woodturning has many requirements. We work with a beautiful material that shrinks, cracks and warps as it dries. It is necessary for us to be able to dry wood successfully and control these changes that it goes through. We must know how to mount the wood on the lathe, and then remount the rough bowl accurately once it has dried. We need to know how to cut with the grain of the wood, but also against the grain when the need arises. Finally, we must know how to refine the surface to a satisfactory standard and apply a beautiful and durable finish to our work of art.

By mastering the concepts in this chapter you will be much closer to your goal of becoming a master woodturner.

To work and produce any object efficiently you must have mastered a wide range of techniques.

Ray Key

Principles of cutting with the grain

Long grain

Cutting in the long direction of the tree is called cutting with or along the grain (Fig 1). It is much easier than cutting across the grain, and produces a much smoother cut.

Let's assume that you mount your turning blank with the grain running lengthwise from the spur drive in the headstock to the live centre in the tailstock. If you think of the grain lines as contour lines, all cuts should be made 'downhill' (Fig 2). This will produce a clean, shearing cut because each wood fibre is supported by the underlying fibres. It is possible by this method to make a cut so fine that sanding is unnecessary. On the other hand, cutting uphill – against the grain – will tear the fibres and produce a rough cut, as shown by the enlarged detail in Fig 2.

When turning between centres with the grain running lengthwise, you can easily cut downhill, so you should always be able to make a very fine finish cut (Fig 3a). Notice that the profile in this drawing looks a bit like a chess piece; if you want to have very fine detail in a chess set, cut all of the pieces with the grain oriented lengthwise.

Bowls or vases with their grain arranged in this way are often described as 'end-grain' vessels, because you must cut into the end grain of the wood to hollow the inside. One complication is that many end-grain bowls may have the pith (the heart of the tree) in the middle. This part of the tree is much more likely to shrink and crack as the bowl dries out. There are some ways around this problem, but you need to be aware that you may have a cracking problem if you leave the heart of the tree in the centre of your bowl.

Cross grain

There will be many times when the natural beauty of the wood will require you to orient the grain in a different direction, at right angles to the axis of the lathe. When cutting the same chessman, this time using cross-grain wood, it is much more difficult to get a fine finish cut (Fig 3b). This time the finish cut should be made uphill, so as to have the wood fibres supported. However, there are often some areas (marked red in Fig 3b) where it is not possible to do this, because there is no access for the tool. Here you will have to cut downhill with a sharp tool slowly and carefully, to achieve the best finish cut possible under the circumstances.

A cut across the grain will leave open cell pores that appear rough; you may want to fill these pores with wood filler to make the wood look and feel smooth.

Long grain or end grain?

When the final cut and finish are of utmost importance – as in a chess set or an elegant small box – cut along the grain. However, Fig 4a shows that a natural-rim bowl can also be cut from cross-grain wood. Ray Key is well known for his natural-edge bowls, and bowls of his, cut from cross-grain wood, are shown in Figs 5 and 6.

An end-grain bowl can also be produced with a natural edge, or with light-coloured sapwood all the way around the edge (Fig 4b). Ron Layport produced a world-class work of art called *High Cirrus* by end-grain turning and carving a full log (Fig 7). By exploiting the natural break in the colour between sapwood and heartwood and turning the vessel to the point that best revealed the break, he was able to separate the white bird from the dark heartwood.

1 Grain direction in a living tree and a crosscut log

2 Section through a workpiece mounted long-grain between centres. The enlarged detail shows the rough surface produced by cutting against the grain

3 (a) The correct cut for spindle-mounted long-grain wood is always downhill
(b) The correct cut for spindle-mounted cross-grain wood is always uphill, but the red arrows indicate areas where this may not be possible

4 Natural-edge bowls with (a) cross grain and (b) long grain

5 Ray Key, natural-edge footed bowl in African blackwood, 7 x 4in (180 x 100mm), cut cross-grain. Ray Key also produces some of the most beautiful long-grain boxes in the world (photograph: Ray Key)

6 4in (100mm) laburnum branch and bowls by Ray Key, showing how a natural-edge bowl can be cut from cross-grain wood (photograph: Ray Key)

7 Ron Layport, *High Cirrus*, black walnut, 14½ x 8½in (370 x 215mm), turned and carved from a log mounted long-grain

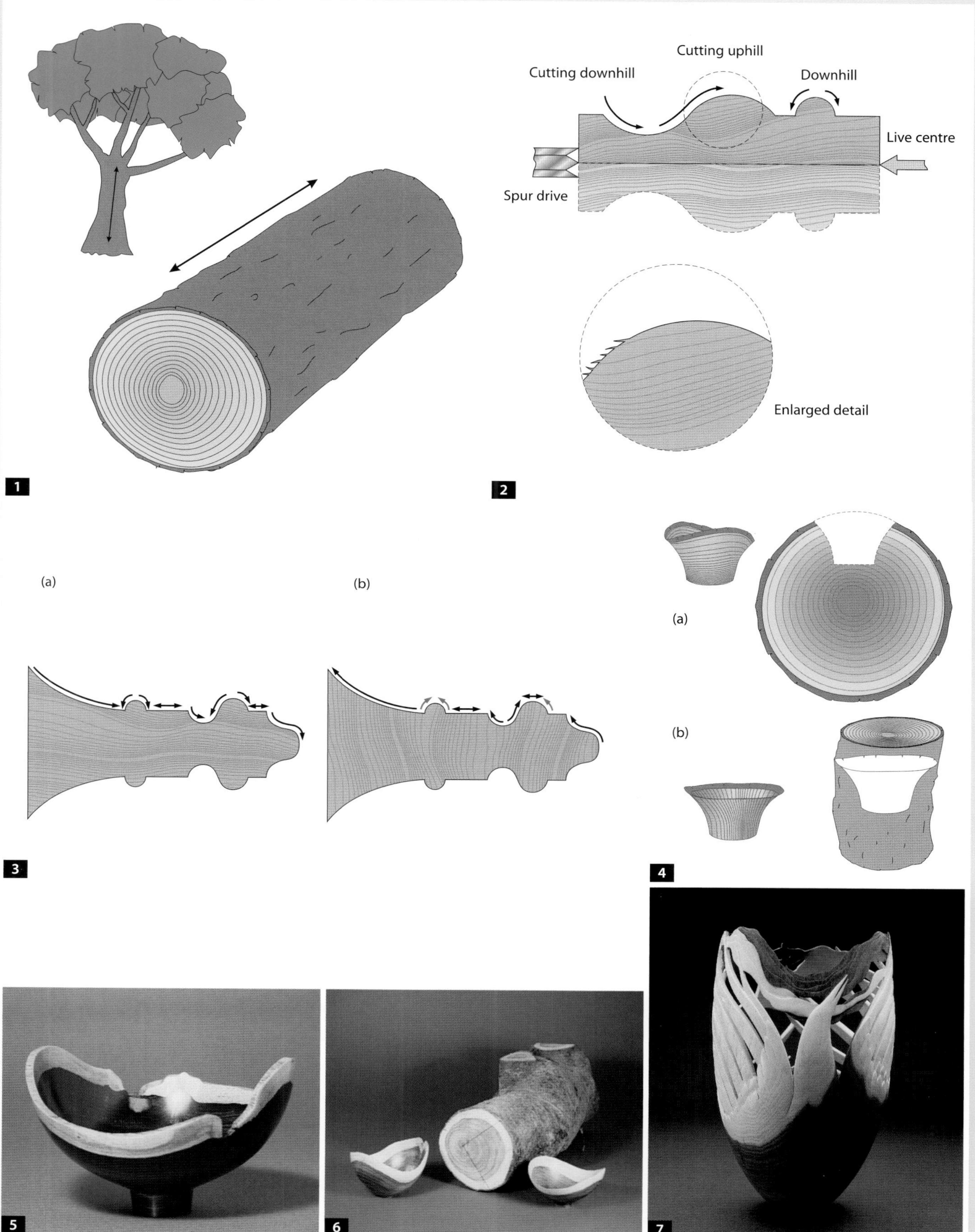
1
Cutting uphill
Cutting downhill
Downhill
Live centre
Spur drive
Enlarged detail
2
(a)
(b)
3
(a)
(b)
4
5
6
7

Preparing wood

Woodturners get wood from many different sources. I encourage beginner turners to use free, locally grown wood whenever possible – there is a fairly big learning curve to turning and it is therefore best to learn using free or inexpensive materials. Professional tree trimmers or tree surgeons are a good source for locally grown wood; they will usually be glad to give you logs from a tree they have just cut.

Drying wood

Wood is living tissue and accordingly has water in it. Living wood has a moisture content of 100%. To be successful in woodworking we usually need to bring the moisture content down gradually to about 10 or 12%, to suit the conditions in which the finished item will be kept. Seal the ends of your logs to help prevent the wood from cracking. Sealing wood slows down the drying process, which means the wood will crack less. The best and easiest way to seal wood is to dip the ends in paraffin or candle wax, melted with an electric heating element in a large pie pan or wide bucket.

Drying techniques

The slower the process of drying, the more gentle it is to the wood. Rapid drying greatly increases the risk of cracking. There are several reliable methods of slowing down the process.

In small work, every wrong decision is huge.

Ron Layport

Air-drying

This traditional way of drying wood is extensively used among professionals and amateurs alike. It is an inexpensive and simple technique, but it is also very slow.

The wood is cut into slabs and stacked with spacers between the boards. The spacers allow air to circulate around the wood and dry it slowly (Fig 8). The rule of thumb for air-drying is that it takes one year of drying for each inch (25mm) of thickness of the wood. If possible, dedicate an area of your shop to storing and drying (Fig 9). When air-drying a bowl, rough-turn it first to approximately 1in (25mm) thickness for an 8in (203mm) diameter bowl. Place the rough-turned bowl in the storage area of your shop and allow it to dry until it stops losing weight, before turning to final shape. This technique usually requires about four to six months.

Retarding the moisture loss

A variation of the air-drying technique is to cover the work with a bag (paper or plastic) once the rough-turning is completed. The bag is then turned inside out once a day, and in this way the moisture loss is very slow and controlled – it is the most gentle of all the drying techniques. On a bowl 1in (25mm) thick, this technique will usually take about six to eight months.

8 Commercial lumber stacked for air-drying. In Texas, where I live, this wood will be dry within six months

9 Shelves for wood storage are a must in the wood shop. Unfortunately there is often not enough room!

8

9

Kiln-drying

Kiln-drying is a rapid process; most commercially purchased wood is kiln-dried. The wood is stacked in a chamber where dry air is heated and circulated around the wood. The moisture is removed at a slow, controlled rate to minimize cracking. This process takes several months. Many professional woodturners, like Trent Bosch, make kilns to dry their rough turnings (Fig 10). Old refrigerators, light bulbs, fans and dehumidifiers are often components of a homemade kiln.

Boiling wood

The rough turning is placed in boiling water for about 30 minutes. The boiling water dissolves a lot of the resin that clogs the pores of wood so that it can then dry more quickly. Then allow the bowl to air-dry in your shop until it stops losing weight. This usually takes about four to six weeks. I have used this technique and it works well – it seems to stop some wood from cracking that would normally crack.

Microwave oven

Heat the bowl until it is warm to your hands; usually about 20–30 seconds for a small bowl and 45–60 seconds for a large bowl. Allow the bowl to cool and then re-heat. Repeat the process for several hours. I do not like this technique because although the microwave is good at heating the water in the wood, it is not good at expelling the water, which is why I developed the following two techniques:

Double-baked drying

This technique uses both the microwave oven and the regular kitchen convection oven. Start by warming your rough-turned bowl in the microwave. The bowl should be warm, but not hot. Set your regular oven to just above 'warm' (225°F/110°C). Place the bowl in the oven and leave the oven door open 1in (25mm). Allow the bowl to sit for an hour, then re-heat the bowl in the microwave and return it to the regular oven – do this every hour. In about six hours you can usually reduce the moisture content of the wood to about 7–10%.

The microwave oven heats the water, and the regular oven drives the water out of the wood. The two ovens together give a very rapid drying of the wood, but will cause some woods – such as oak and holly – to crack excessively. However, this is the drying technique that I use most of the time; I find it very useful for burl wood when I want to accentuate the flaws in it.

Baked drying

This is the technique to use when you have a glue block on the bowl, as the higher heat used for double-baked drying will make your glue joint come apart. To protect the glue joint, a lower temperature is used on the kitchen oven. Set the oven to its lowest setting – about 180°F/80°C. Warm the rough-turned bowl and glue block in the microwave, not so hot that you cannot hold it in your bare hands. Place the bowl with glue block in the kitchen oven and leave the door open as before. Keep the bowl in the oven a full 12 hours (overnight is ideal). This technique will bring the moisture content down to about 7–10%.

Baked drying is a little gentler to the wood than double-baked drying; it also takes twice as much time. It is invaluable when you have a glue block attached to the work and you want to dry the wood overnight. Every project in this book was dried using either the baked or the double-baked method.

10 Rough-turned bowls drying in Trent Bosch's kiln

11 Turning stock can be cut using a bandsaw

12 A turning blank rounded using a bandsaw. Notice that my 1in (25mm) bandsaw blade will not really cut a curve; a narrower blade would allow you to cut an actual circle

Tools for wood preparation

Chainsaw

A chainsaw is very useful for the woodturner. It allows you to cut the timber to size quickly so that you can manipulate it with ease.

● Warning!

The chainsaw can be very dangerous. Always wear the recommended safety gear and follow all safety instructions provided by the manufacturer. Take an approved training course if you possibly can.

Bandsaw

The bandsaw is a handy saw for the woodturner, useful for cutting stock so that it can air-dry (Fig 11). It is also ideal for cutting your stock round before it goes on the lathe (Fig 12). As a general rule buy the biggest bandsaw you can afford, that will fit into your shop.

10

11

12

Remounting the work

It is often necessary to take the wood off the lathe and then remount it later. It is possible to remount with almost no loss of accuracy if you take a few simple precautions.

In a four-jaw chuck

Turn spigots on the workpiece so that your four-jaw chuck closes down to within 3/8–5/8in (10–16mm) of full closure. This gives the jaws the maximum gripping power. Tighten the jaws firmly, but not excessively. Number the jaws and use a pencil or knife to mark exactly where each jaw goes (Fig 13). Remount the spigot back into the same location and tighten down with the same force originally used. If done correctly you should be able to remount without any perceptible loss of accuracy.

After drying

The spigot must be re-turned after drying, as it will no longer be accurate. Mount the bowl between centres and turn the shoulder and spigot true again (Fig 14).

Sanding

Sanding is an important part of a good finish. After making your best finish cut with your turning tool, sanding is required to smooth over the tool marks that are left in the wood.

All sanding is done with the work revolving slowly on the lathe. If the lathe is running fast, the sandpaper will bounce off the turning and leave rough spots. Progress gradually from coarser to finer grades. The first sandpaper used – the coarsest – takes the most time because it has to remove the uneven marks created by the turning tool. All subsequent grades only have to take out the cut marks left by the previous paper.

Padded hook-and-loop sanding discs on an electric drill are a very efficient way to sand the inside of a bowl (Fig 15). Because the rotating sanding disc is travelling perpendicular to the rotating wood, the sanding action is much more efficient than hand-sanding. Be sure to have a vacuum close to the sanding area (Fig 16).

● Tip

If you find yourself spending more than a couple of minutes sanding with your roughest sandpaper, then it is time to try something different. You need either to make a finer finish cut with your turning tool, or to switch to an even coarser grade of paper.

Final finish

All finishes on the market today should give nice results if used properly. I usually use a lacquer because they dry quickly. Water-based finishes are very good nowadays – and much safer to breathe – and have the advantage of being easy to clean up.

My basic principles of finishing are set out on the next page. You can stop whenever you choose, but you cannot skip a step and still achieve the desired high-quality results. Each step you complete will take you towards a higher quality of finish.

13 Marking the exact placement of the jaws around the spigot will ensure that remounting is very accurate

14 After drying, the spigot must be turned true. Here I am using a square-ended scraper

15 An electric drill with padded hook-and-loop sanding attachments

16 A vacuum system next to your sanding position is a must for lung protection

Principles of finishing

- To achieve a good finish, you must begin with a pleasing shape that has been cut and sanded properly. All turning flaws must be removed, either with good finish cuts or with sandpaper. Use sandpaper to smooth all uneven areas. Sand to at least 220 grit. Soft finishes, such as wax or oil, can be applied at this stage and look excellent. They should be well buffed with a soft rotating buffing rag.
- If using lacquer or varnish, apply numerous coats in thin layers and build them up gradually. You can use a spray gun, spray from a can or apply the finish with a brush. Allow the finish to dry well before applying the next coat.
- Lightly sand the finish with 1000–1200-grit sandpaper after the first two to three coats have been applied.

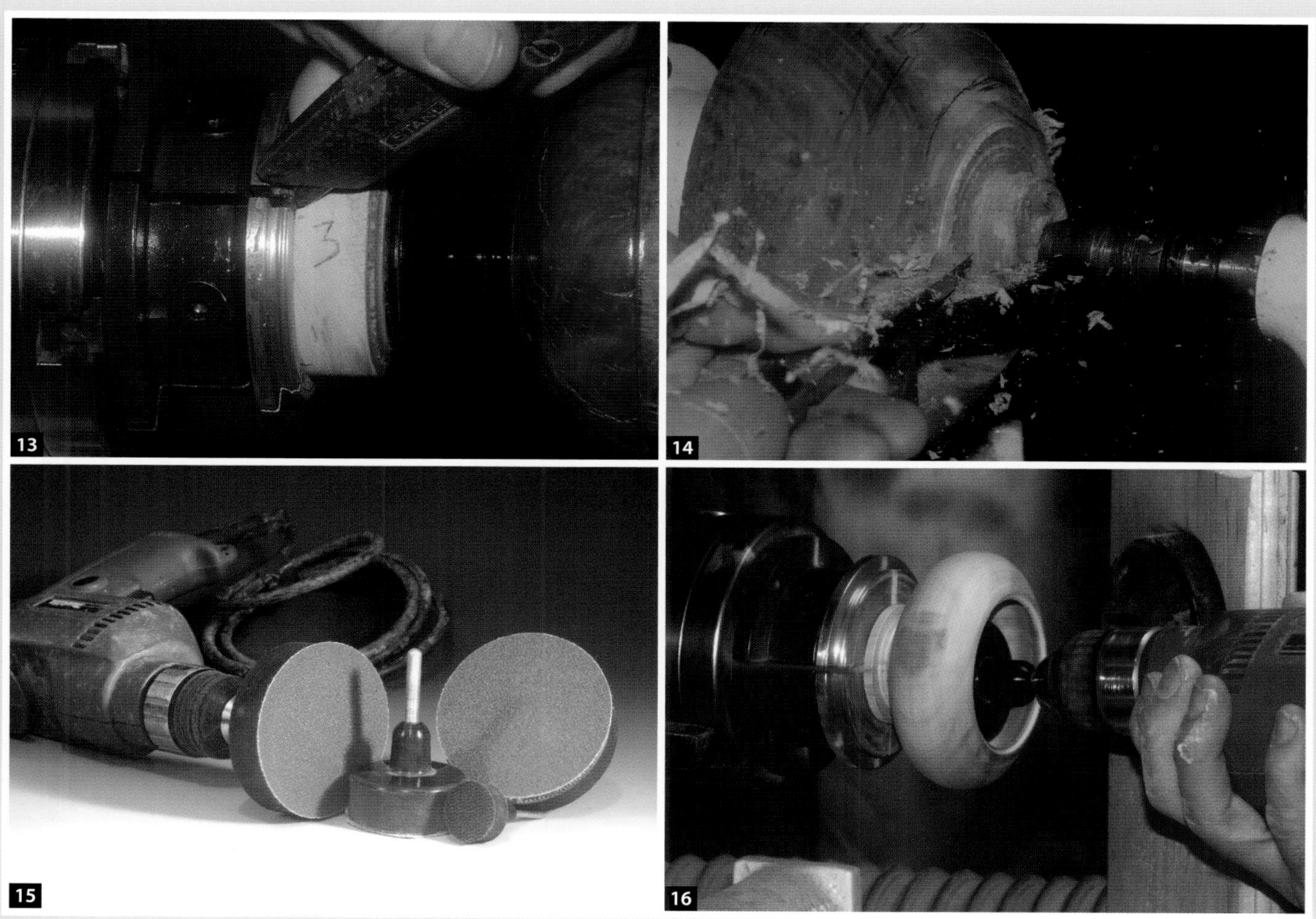
13 14 15 16

4 Classic Ballpoint Pen

Turning a writing pen is something that almost all turners do eventually, and makes a terrific first project for a beginner. Pens make good presents and are always popular items at craft shows. In this first project we will turn a classic 'click'-type ballpoint pen, similar to the famous Parker pen design of the 1920s. Many turning supply stores carry pen-turning kits. Mine came from Penn State Industries (www.pennstateind.com), and if you are using a different make you may have to modify the process slightly, by reference to the manufacturer's instructions.

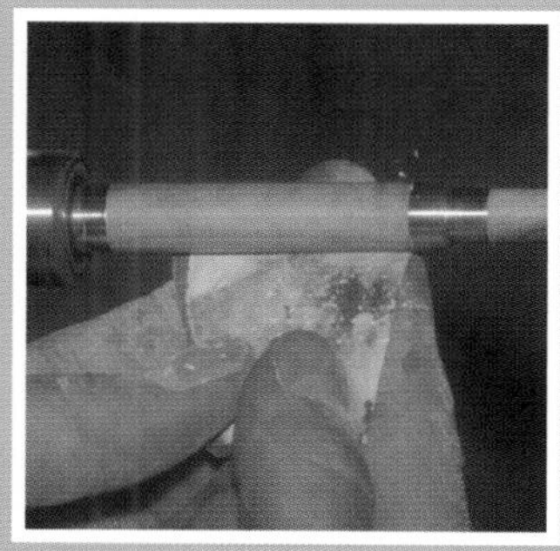

Simple forms
are never as simple
as they look.
Richard Raffan

Bill of goods

- South African olivewood, or other attractive wood, $^5/_8$ x $^5/_8$ x 8in (16 x 16 x 203mm)
- Ballpoint pen kit
- Pen mandrel with bushings to fit the pen tubes
- Drill bits: $^{27}/_{64}$in (or the slightly larger 11mm) and $^5/_{16}$in (8mm)
- A $^5/_{16}$in (8mm) barrel trimmer
- Cyanoacrylate glue (superglue) or epoxy cement

Preparation

Check to make sure that all parts have been included in your pen set. It is usually best to order an extra set in case you have a problem either with the mechanism or with following the procedure. My kit came with a helpful diagram showing all the parts required (Fig 1).

A pen mandrel consists of a Morse taper to fit in the headstock (on the left in Fig 2), with a steel rod and screw-on nut; it is made specifically to be used with the correct-size bushes so that when the brass tube and the wood are placed on the mandrel they can be turned to the correct diameter. The bushes can be purchased to suit the size of pen you are making, and the mandrel, complete with bushings, is not particularly expensive. The live centre from your tailstock fits into the opposite end of the mandrel (the right end in Fig 2).

Getting started

The first step is to cut two $^5/_8$in (16mm) square blanks using a tablesaw. I used South African olivewood for this project, which turns nicely and smells wonderful. The blanks should be about $^1/_{32}$in (1mm) longer than the two brass tubes that come with the kit. Mark the centres of the turning blanks. Hold the square blanks using a carpenter's handscrew while you drill them. Check to make sure that the blank is square to the drill bit (Fig 3). The upper (larger) wooden tube needs a $^{27}/_{64}$in hole drilled down the centre for the brass tube to fit into. (The manufacturer's instructions called for an 11mm drill bit, but for me this produced a loose-fitting hole.)

Gluing the tubes

Glue the tubes in the wood blanks using either cyanoacrylate glue (superglue) or epoxy cement. Very lightly sand the outside of the tube before applying the glue; the light sanding will make for a better glue joint. Apply glue to the outside of the brass tube. Insert the tube and seat flush to the wood blank. If any glue has got into the brass tube, use a cotton swab (cotton bud) to clean it up as soon as possible (Fig 4).

Trimming to length

Trim the wood blanks to the exact length of the brass tubes. Sand the larger wood blank flat to the brass tube using a belt sander. The smaller brass tube may be trimmed flat using a $^5/_{16}$in (8mm) barrel trimmer (Fig 5).

1 Contents of Penn State Industries' Classic Click Pen kit (not to scale)

2 In addition to the pen parts, you will need a mandrel, correct-size bushings and drill bits

3 Use a handscrew clamp to hold the wood blanks under the drill press

4 Apply glue to the brass tubes and then insert them into the wood blanks. Wipe off excess glue immediately with paper towels and cotton swabs (buds)

5 Trim the wood flush to the brass tubes, using a belt sander for the larger blank. You can use a barrel trimmer for the smaller blank

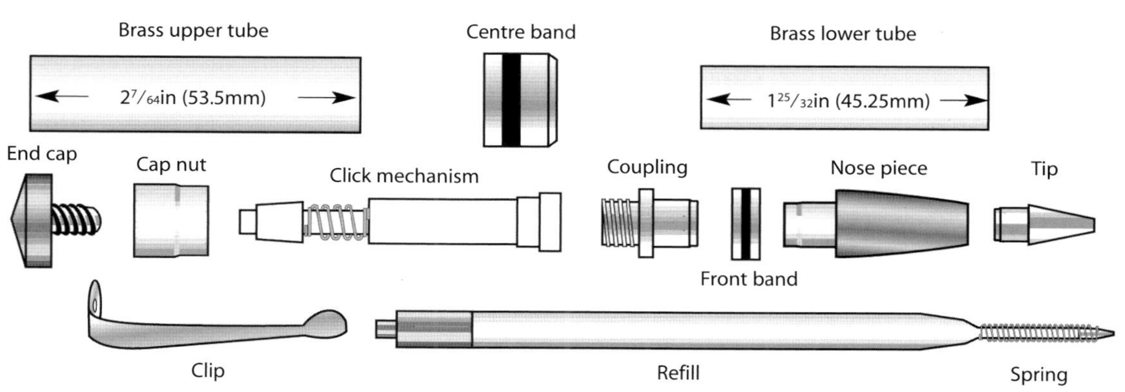

Brass upper tube
2 7/64in (53.5mm)
Centre band
Brass lower tube
1 25/32in (45.25mm)
End cap
Cap nut
Click mechanism
Coupling
Nose piece
Tip
Front band
Clip
Refill
Spring

1

PSI WOODWORKING PRODUCTS
1 EACH ITEM #PKPARK-6MM
6MM DRILL BIT

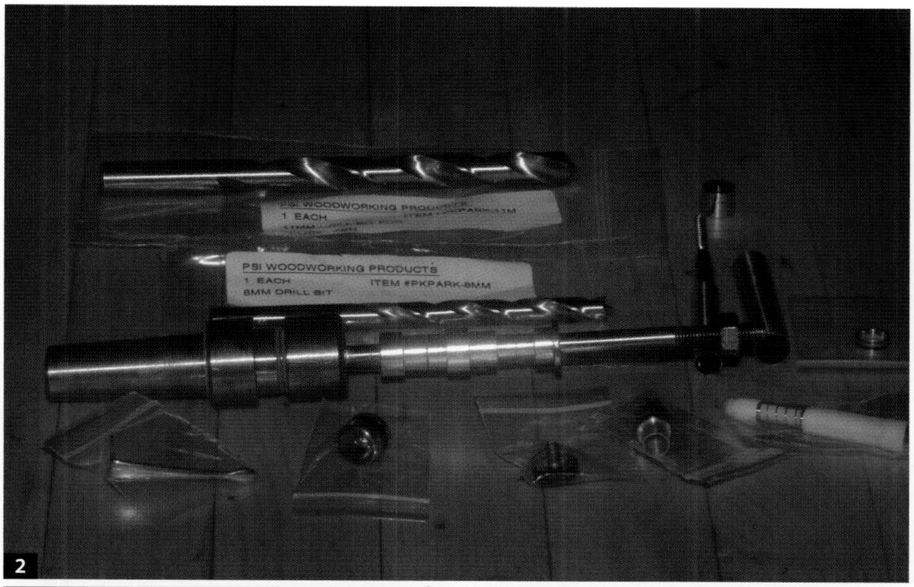

2

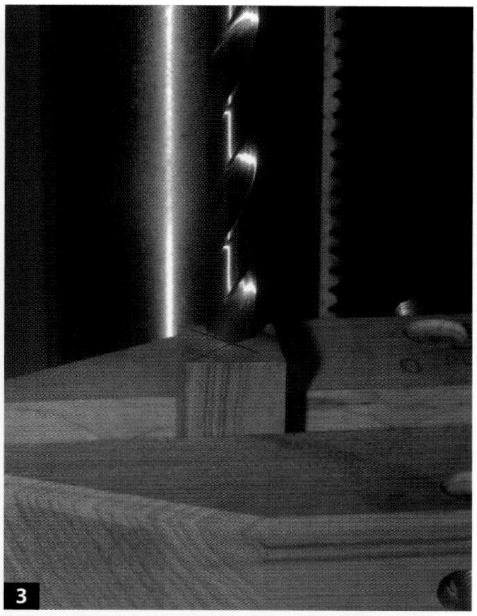

3

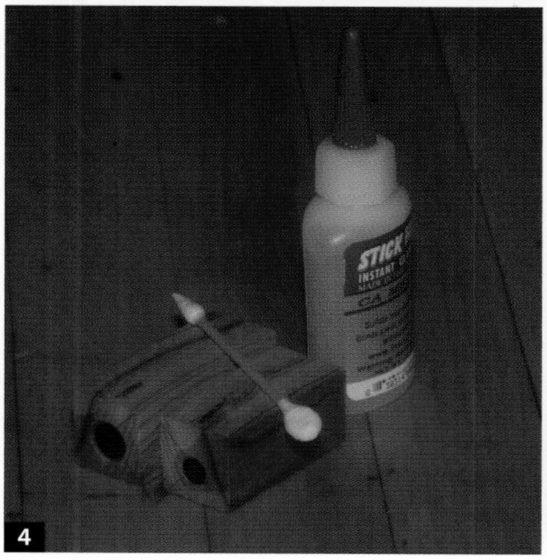

4

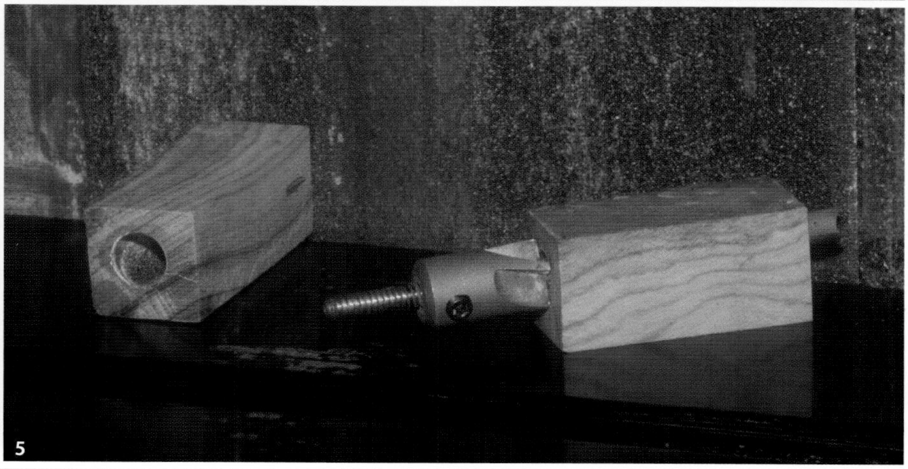

5

Mounting on the lathe

Place the wood blanks and bushings onto the pen mandrel as shown in Fig 6. Mount the mandrel on the lathe with the Morse taper fitting into the headstock; the tailstock end of the mandrel is held by a live centre (Fig 7). Apply very light pressure on the tailstock – heavy pressure will make the mandrel flex.

Turning the pen blanks

The wood blanks are turned down flush with the two bushings at each end of the blank. The large-diameter blank must be trimmed flush with the large-diameter bushing (on the left and centre in Fig 8), and the small blank must be flush with the small-diameter bushings (centre and right). It is critically important for the wood on the small blank to be no larger in diameter than the small bushing. This wood tube must slide smoothly into the larger brass tube.

Finishing the blanks

Sand the two blanks exactly flush with the adjoining metal bushings (Fig 9). Sand to approximately 800-grit sandpaper – which may sound a bit extreme, but remember that everybody will be looking closely at your artwork. Take the two wood blanks off the pen mandrel at this time and make sure that the small wood/brass tube slides smoothly inside the large wood/brass tube. If the small tube does not slide smoothly, remount it on the lathe and turn or sand it down to the correct dimension.

Applying finish

Apply finish while the wood blanks are still on the lathe (Fig 10). I used Deft cellulose finish diluted 50 : 50 with lacquer thinner, but a hard wax will also make a nice finish.

Trimming the large wood blank

Carefully measure 1⅞in (48mm) from the left end of the larger blank. Use a sharp parting tool very gently to cut through the wood at this point and expose the right end of the brass tube (arrowed in Fig 11). At assembly time the centre band will be pressed onto this exposed length of brass.

Assembly

Most parts of the pen are pressed together with an ordinary workshop vice or a one-hand clamp. Apply slow, gentle pressure, making sure that the parts are properly aligned. The nose piece is pressed onto the lower tube and then the coupling is pressed onto the other end (Fig 12).

The cap nut is pressed onto the upper end of the upper blank, then the centre band is pressed onto the exposed brass tube. Insert the screw thread of the cap through the hole in the clip, and screw the cap into the cap nut (Fig 13).

Place the refill cartridge into the bottom section of the pen and screw on the click mechanism. Finally, screw the bottom section onto the top assembly. Pressing the top of the pen will allow the bottom part to slide inside the top and thus activate the clicking mechanism.

I wish to thank PSI Woodturning Products for kindly allowing me to reproduce their drawings in this chapter.

6 The wooden blanks and metal bushings assembled on the mandrel

7 The mandrel assembly on the lathe, with the Morse taper mounted at the headstock (left) and the tailstock end supported by a live centre, using only light pressure

8 Turn each wood blank down level with the adjacent bushings

9 Bringing the wood level with the bushings

10 Applying finish; make sure that the lower blank still slides smoothly into the top blank

11 Expose part of the large brass tube, leaving 1⅞in (48mm) of wood on the left side of the tube

12 Press the pen parts together with a shop vice or a hand-held clamp

13 An exploded view of all the components ready for assembly

Headstock
Stop bushing
Upper wooden blank
Sharp corner here
Lower wooden blank
Locknut
Tailstock live centre
Mandrel
Upper cap bushing
1⁷/₈in (48mm) wood retained
Wood removed to brass
Centre bushing
Outline of wood after turning
Lower cap bushing

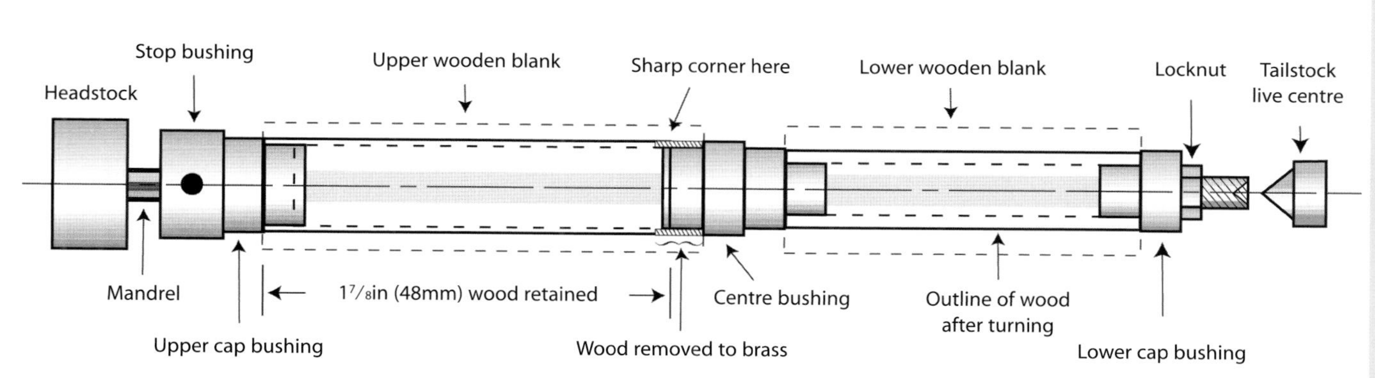

6

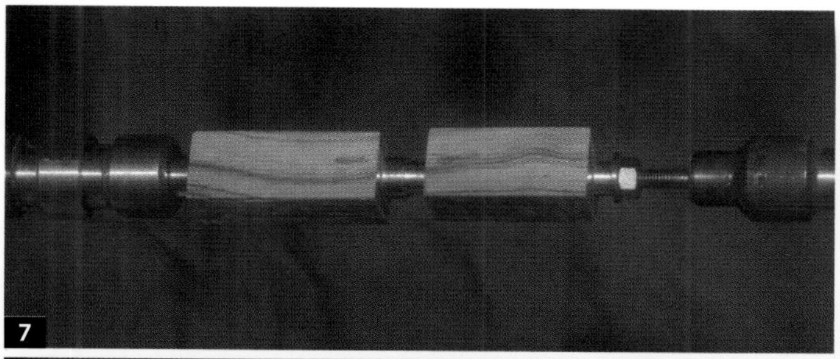

7

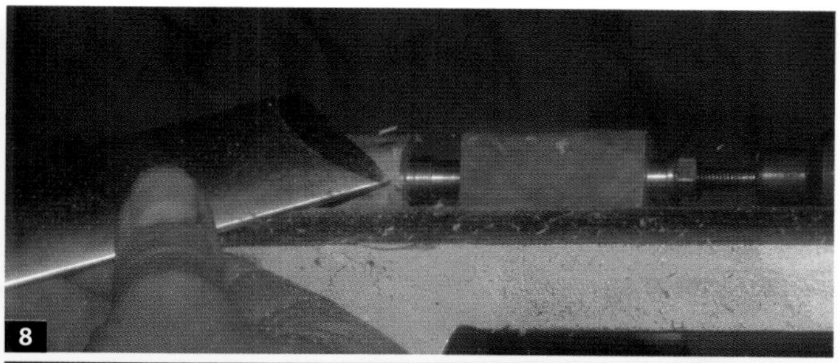

8

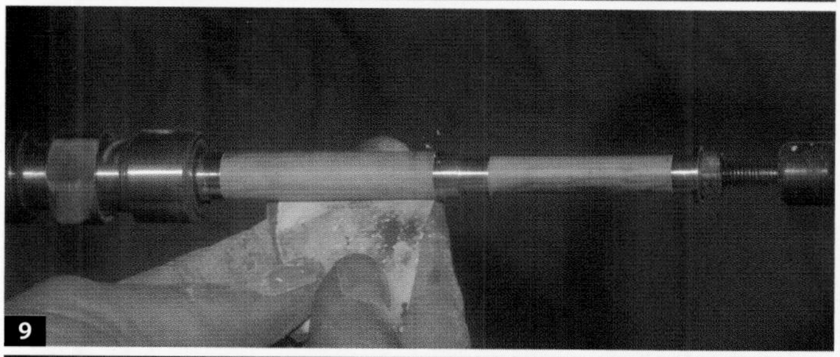

9

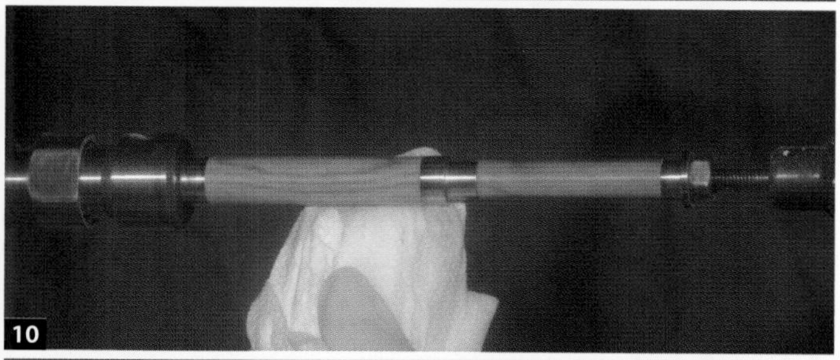

10

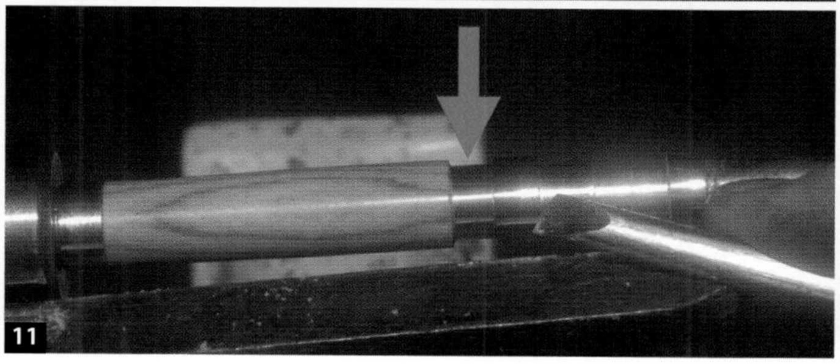

11

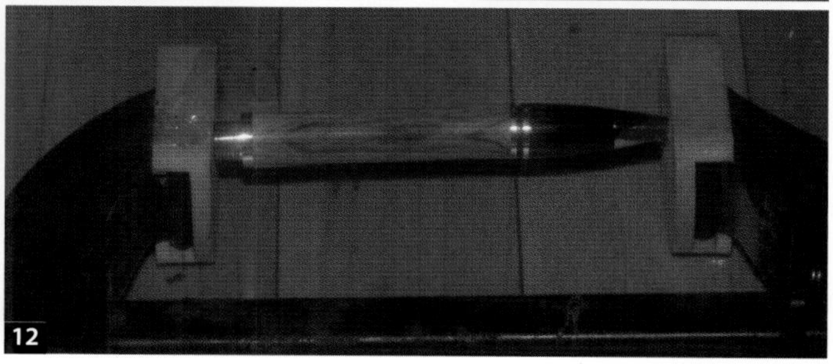

12

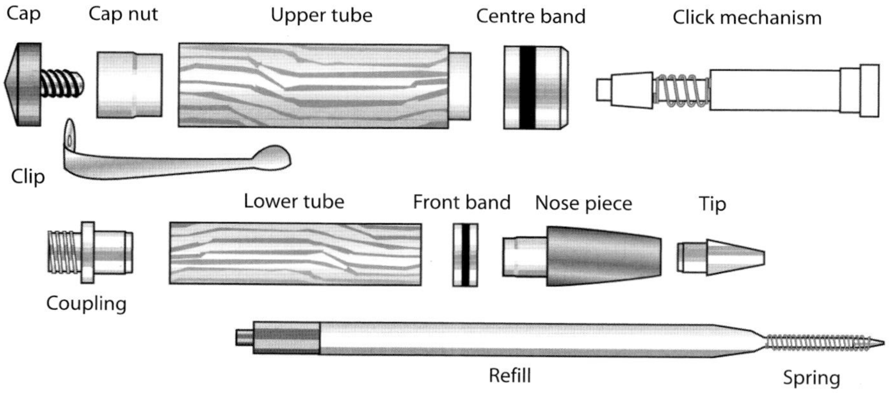

Cap
Cap nut
Upper tube
Centre band
Click mechanism
Clip
Lower tube
Front band
Nose piece
Tip
Coupling
Refill
Spring

13

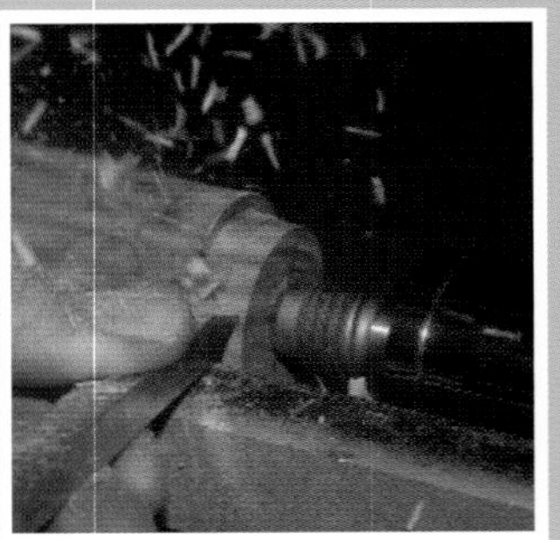

5 Turquoise Tulipwood Vase

In this chapter we will turn an elegant tulipwood vase decorated with inset turquoise beads. I was introduced to this unusual technique by Kip Christensen, Professor of Industrial Design in the School of Technology at Brigham Young University in Provo, Utah. Kip is an accomplished and internationally famous woodturner whose small turnings are among the most beautiful I have seen.

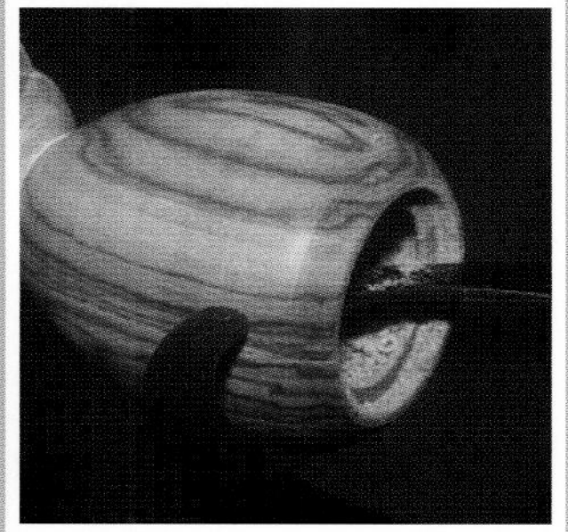

There is something inherently satisfying in making an item of lasting beauty or utility out of a piece of wood from your neighbour's firewood pile.

Kip Christensen

Bill of goods

- Fully seasoned tulipwood, or other attractive dried wood, 6 x 2 x 2in (150 x 50 x 50mm)
- Half-round turquoise beads, ⅛in (3mm) diameter, enough to make a row about 8in (200mm) long
- Cyanoacrylate glue (superglue)

Getting started

The construction of the vase is shown in Fig 1. I chose tulipwood because it makes a pleasing contrast with the half-round turquoise beads, which came from the local hobbycraft supply store.

Cut the blank to size, mark the centre of each end with a centre finder and mount the wood between centres.

Roughing out

On small work, I usually rough out with a skew chisel or a beading tool (Fig 2). This gives me some practice before I start doing fine detail work with the same tool.

Cutting spigots

Cut spigots to fit your four-jaw chuck on both ends of the turning blank (Fig 3).

Mounting in a four-jaw chuck

Most projects in this book use a four-jaw chuck and spigot jaws. It is possible to use a faceplate and a jam-fit chuck, but making jam-fit chucks requires much more time.

Mount the piece in the four-jaw chuck by the spigot, positioning the top end of the vase toward the tailstock.

Initial shaping

Use a thin parting tool to mark the locations of the bottom and top, and of the junction between the two sections of the vase (Fig 4). The parting marks will help you get the proportions correct. You might find it helpful at this stage to use a pencil to actually draw the shape of the vase onto the turning blank.

Carry out the initial shaping of the lower part of the vase (Fig 5), but be sure to leave the bottom end thick until after the inside has been hollowed out – otherwise it will be hard to make a clean cut on the inside because of vibration.

Use a thin parting tool to part off the upper part from the main body (Fig 6). The top section must also be left oversized at this stage.

Refining the main body of the vase

Refine the shape of the main body at this time, still erring on the large side until the inside has been hollowed. Use the tool of your choice to develop a pleasing curve which flows smoothly from top to bottom (Fig 7).

1 The two components of the Turquoise Tulipwood Vase

2 Rounding the blank between centres

3 Use a beading tool or skew to cut spigots at both ends of the work

4 Using a parting tool to mark out the lengths of the two sections of the vase

5 Rough-shaping the base of the vase

6 Separating the top from the base

7 Shaping the base; the beading tool is considerably easier to master than the skew

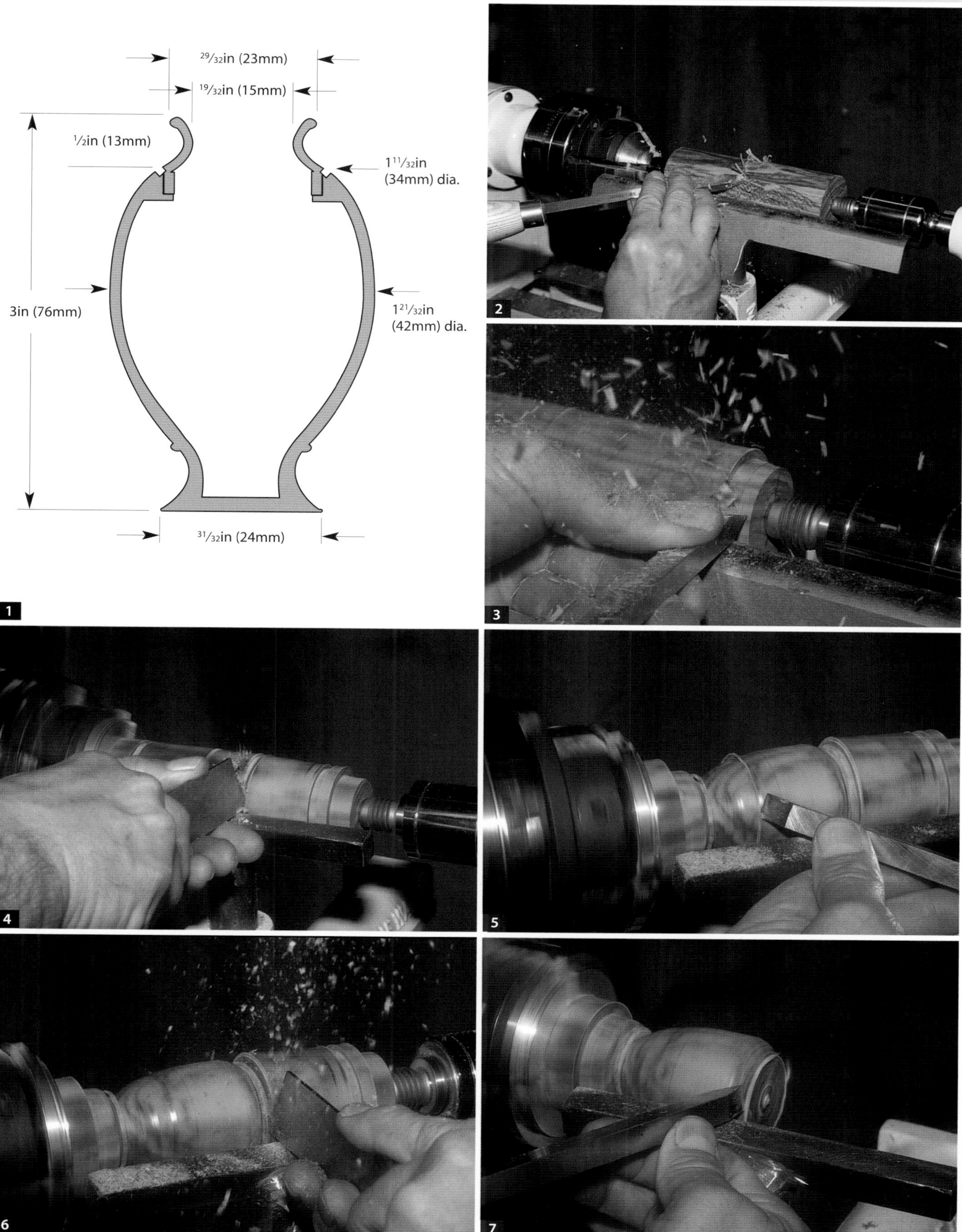
29/32in (23mm)
19/32in (15mm)
1/2in (13mm)
1 11/32in (34mm) dia.
3in (76mm)
1 21/32in (42mm) dia.
31/32in (24mm)
1
2
3
4
5
6
7

Hollowing the inside

Use a Forstner bit to drill out the inside of the vase to the correct depth (Fig 8). Mark this depth on the bit with electrical tape.

Use a skew or a bedan (a beading tool, ground on one bevel only) to cut a rebate 1⁄8–3⁄16in (3–5mm) deep in the top of the vase body (Fig 9). The neck of the vase will fit into this rebate, and the beads will conceal the joint. Leave enough material at the shoulder to ensure that the channel in which the beads sit will not cut through the bottom of the rebate.

A 3⁄8–1⁄2in (10–13mm) round-nose scraper works very well for cutting the inside of the vase (Fig 10). Stop often to check the wall thickness (Fig 11); aim for 1⁄8–3⁄16in (3–5mm). This should be fairly easy if you make slow, careful cuts and check your progress often.

Sand the inside and apply finish; I use cellulose diluted 50:50 with lacquer thinner. Apply using a paper towel and wipe off excess while the lathe is turning slowly.

Taking the vase body off the lathe

Use a pencil or knife to mark where the jaws grab the spigot. This will allow you to remount the base accurately on the chuck in the same location, after you have turned the inside of the top section of the vase.

Turning the top of the vase

Mount the top turning blank on the four-jaw chuck, using the spigot you cut earlier. Use a pair of vernier or dial callipers to measure the exact diameter of the rebate in the top edge of the vase body, and transfer this measurement to the bottom edge of the upper section (Fig 12). Cut a short tenon on the top section to fit the rebate in the body of the vase. The base should fit snugly onto the tenon without excessive force (Fig 13).

Refining the shape of the top

Use a parting tool to cut the demarcation line for the top of the vase, then refine the shape of the vase top. A sharp 3⁄8in (10mm) bowl gouge or spindle gouge works well for cutting the cove or hollow below the rim, and a small skew or beading tool for refining the rounded lip (Fig 14).

Hollowing the inside of the top

Drill out the inside using a 5⁄16in (8mm) drill bit (Fig 15), and then hollow it out further with turning tools; a small skew or a beading tool works well for this cut (Fig 16). Make the finish cut using a round-nose scraper. Sand the work and apply your chosen finish.

8 Drilling out the lower section

9 Use a skew or a beading tool to cut the rebate for the top

10 Hollow out the inside of the vase using a round-nose scraper

11 Use callipers regularly to measure the wall thickness

12 Use vernier callipers to measure the correct size for the tenon on the vase top

13 The tenon of the top section should fit snugly into the rebate of the base

14 Use small, sharp gouges and a small skew to shape the top of the vase

15 Drill out the centre of the top using a 5⁄16in (8mm) drill bit

16 Hollow out the inside of the top using either a small skew or a small round-nose scraper

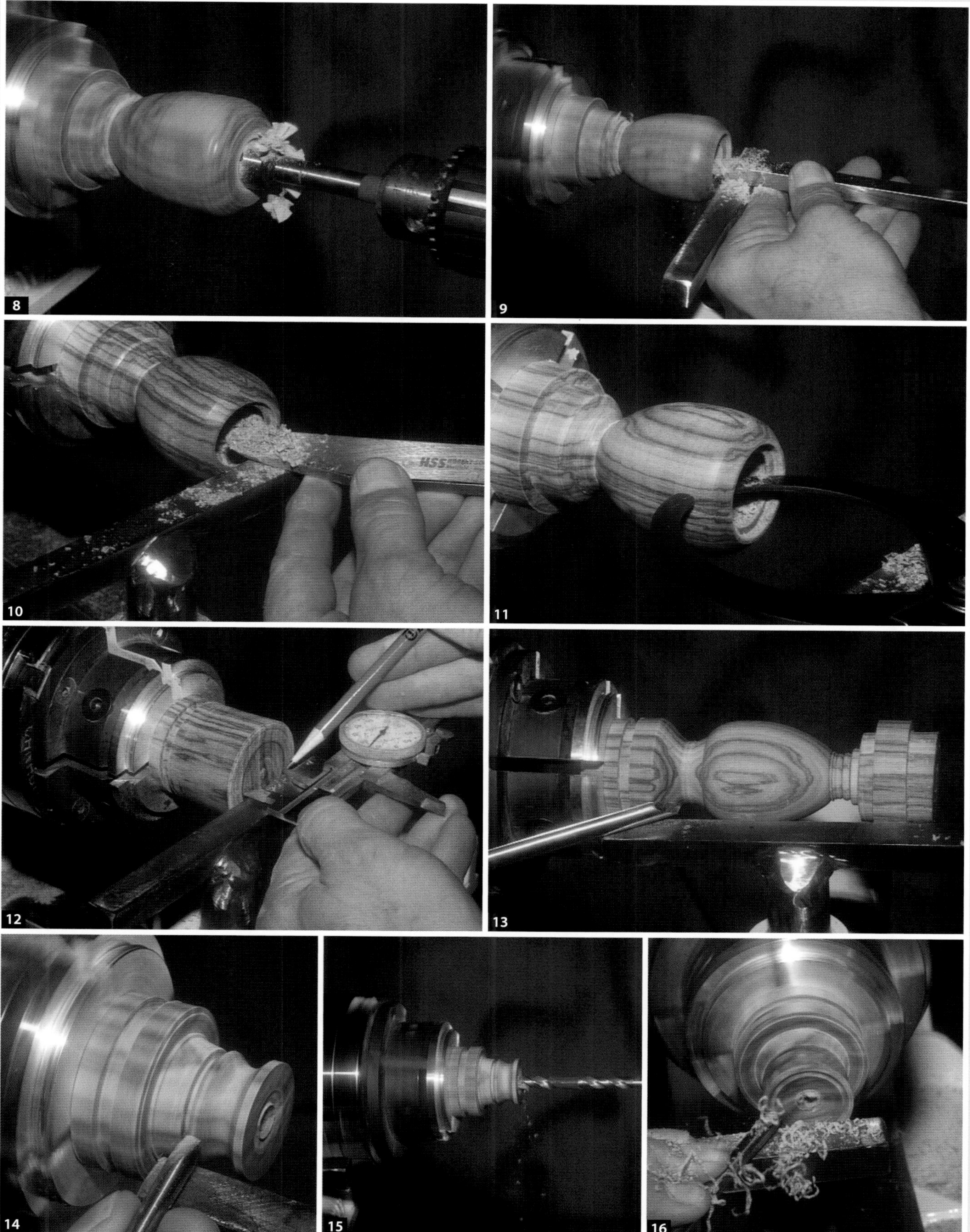
8
9
HSS
10
11
12
13
14
15
16

Joining the vase and top

Part the top off from the turning blank. Remount the vase body onto the four-jaw chuck and carefully align the spigot into the same position it was in when you did the original turning.

Test-fit the top onto the main body of the vase, being sure to align the grain of the wood correctly. Use a small amount of cyanoacrylate glue to join the top and the bottom. When set, carefully blend in the shapes of the top and bottom.

Cutting the bead rebate

Carefully cut the rebate for the beads, which must cover the joint line. Use a small skew to make the initial penetration cuts to mark the location of the rebate.

You may want to make a miniature square-nose scraper to clear out the centre of the rebate. I made one using a nail that had a ⅛in (3mm) head (Fig 17). This worked so well that soon after the photograph was taken, I mounted the nail into a custom-made handle for future use.

Final shaping of the base

You can now safely shape the base of the vase. Start by using a parting tool to demarcate the end of the turning. I used a 3⁄16in (5mm) shallow bowl gouge to cut the small cove which forms the foot. Use a small skew or bedan to cut the fine beads on the base (Fig 18).

Finishing touches

Complete the shaping and sanding of the entire turning at this time. Sand the surface to at least 400 grit. Apply an initial finish to the turning while it is still on the lathe (Fig 19). You can now part the vase off. Sand the base by hand and apply finish.

Placing the turquoise beads

Placing the beads accurately requires a certain amount of patience. Work in a clean, clutter-free environment. You can use small tweezers to pick up the beads, or a nail with double-sided sticky tape attached to it (Fig 20). Place the beads into the rebate around the neck of the vase. Choose a thin, slow-setting cyanoacrylate glue, and place a small drop into the area where you will start working. Use a small, sharp-pointed tool, such as a small nail, to manipulate the beads into the correct position. You will need to adjust the last few beads by eye to make the spacing come out correctly.

Apply the final finish of your choice and buff the whole vase to the desired degree of gloss.

If, as a turner, you are lucky enough to have your work become a hit, you will have developed work that will be called your signature work. Hopefully the demand will last your lifetime. To me, the really lucky turners are those whose work is different with each piece, yet recognizable as theirs.

J.Kelly Dunn

17 Cutting the rebate for the beads using an improvised parting tool

18 Refine the body of the vase using a small gouge and a small skew

19 Sand and apply an initial finish while the turning is still on the lathe

20 Applying the beads using double-sided tape on the head of a nail

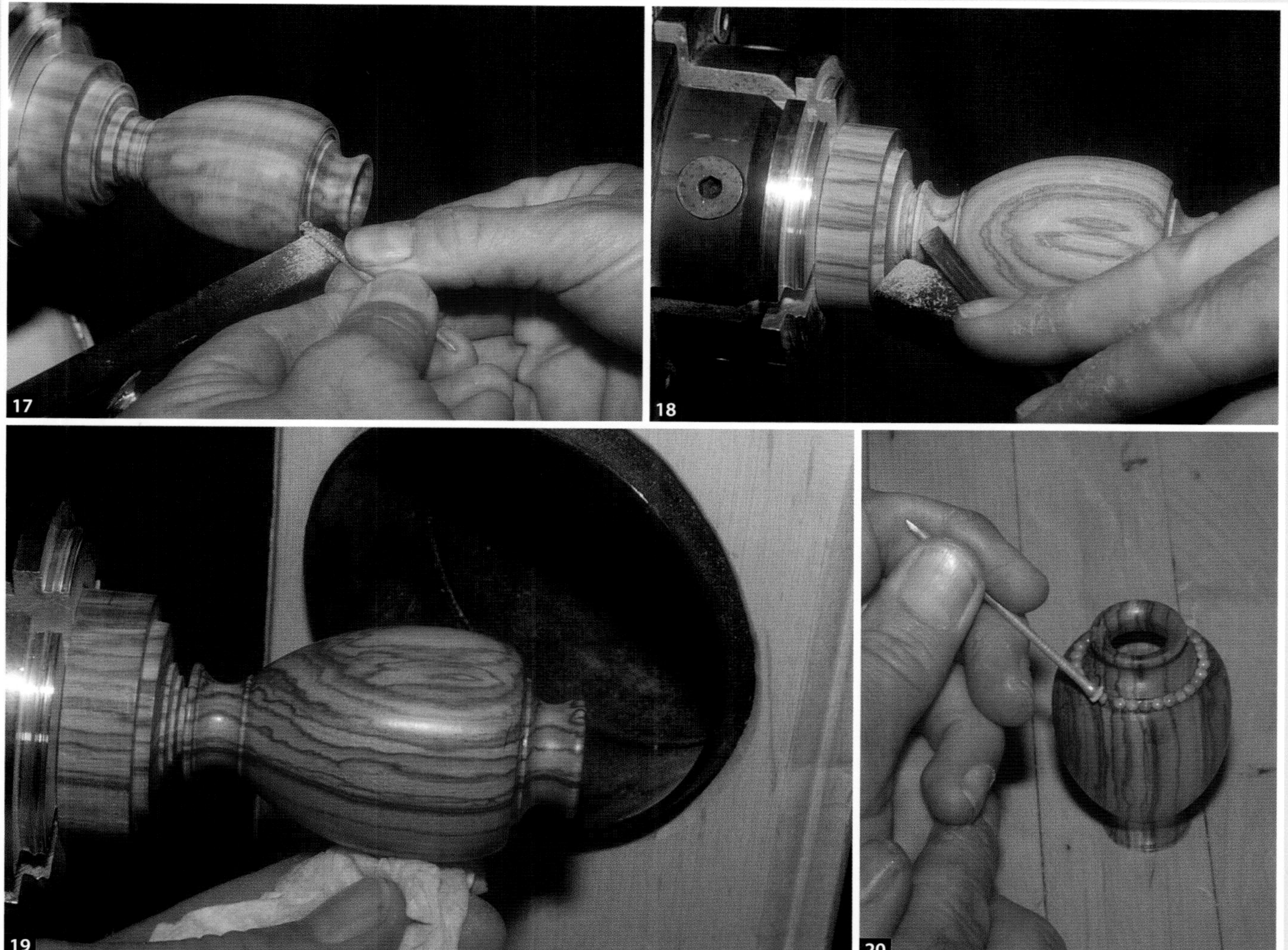
17
18
19
20

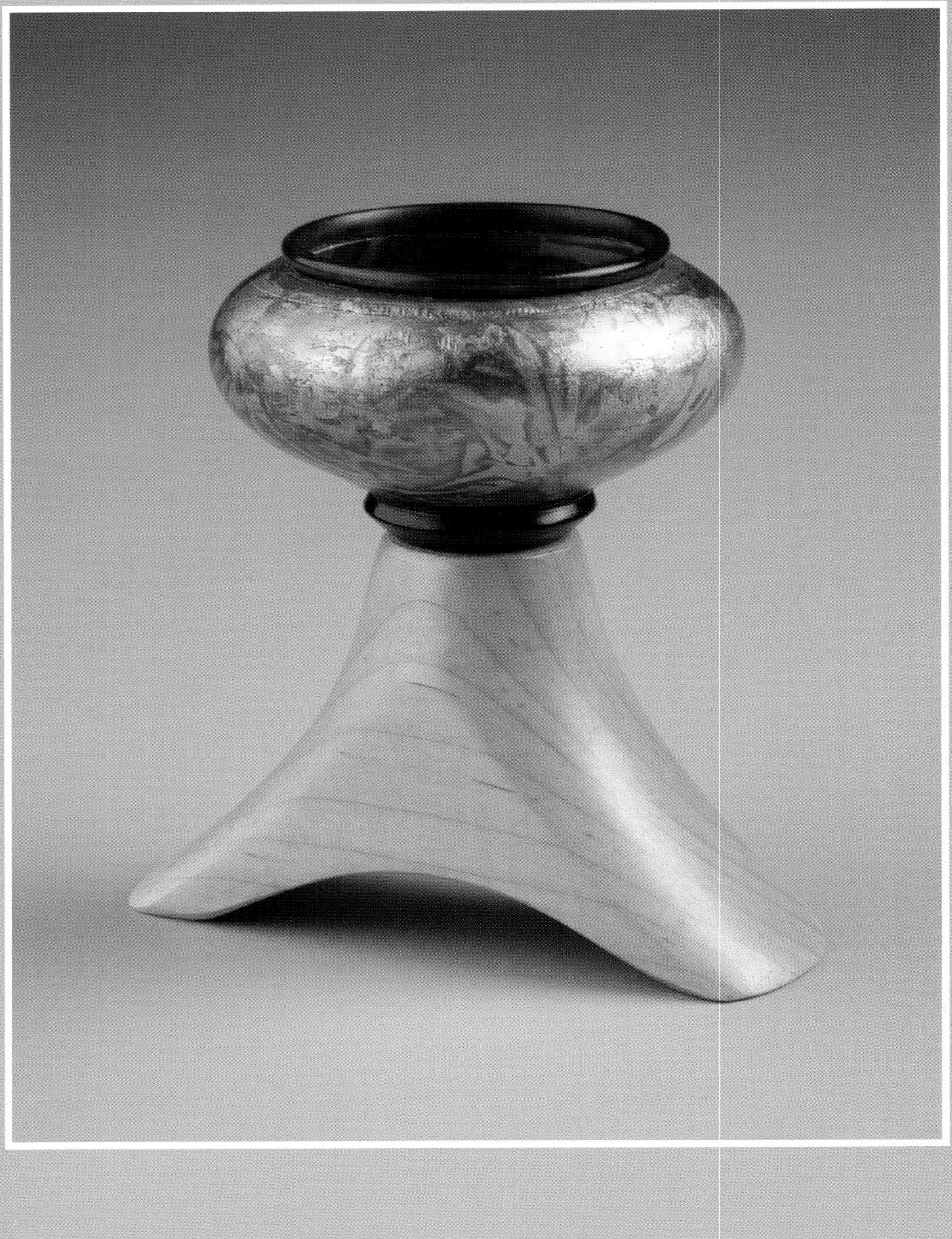

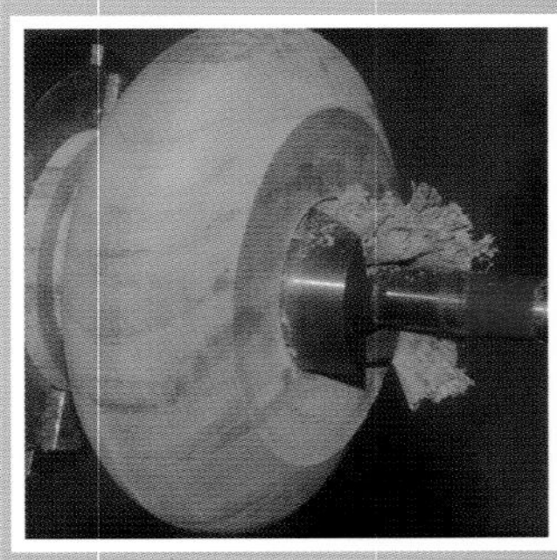

6 Metal Foil Bowl with Stand

Woodturning artists are always looking for new, different and better ways to create beautiful turnings. A nice technique is to take ordinary wood and make it look extraordinary by applying metal foil to it.

J. Paul Fennell of Scottsdale, Arizona was one of the first turners to apply the metal-foil technique to woodturnings, and his turned art is some of the best in its field. One of his pieces inspired this project.

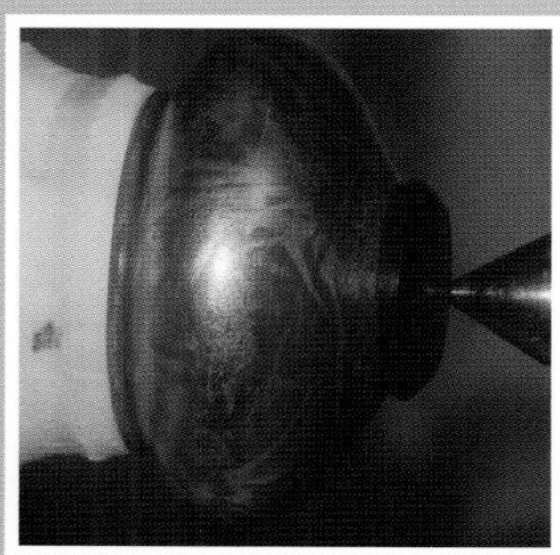

A small turning that can be held in your hands allows a special type of interaction that you don't get with larger work. To turn it, to inspect it from different angles, to feel the textures of the surfaces and the fairness of the curves, to test its weight and balance – these are encouraged with small turnings.

Art Liestman

Bill of goods

- Plain, unseasoned wood approximately 5 x 5 x 5in (125 x 125 x 125mm)
- Two pieces of contrasting wood:
  Rim: approximately 4in (100mm) diameter, 1/2in (13mm) thick
  Foot: 2in (50mm) diameter, 1/2in (13mm) thick
- Stand: maple, 5 x 3 1/2 x 2in (125 x 89 x 50mm)
- PVA and cyanoacrylate glues
- Metal foil
- Adhesive (size) or spray lacquer to attach the metal foil
- Masking tape or latex masking liquid
- Small piece of felt cloth to rub the foil

Roughing out

Start by mounting a piece of good wet wood between centres. Unseasoned wood will provide you with useful practice in the technique of drying and remounting wood. A plain-looking wood should be used for the body of the bowl, since it is going to be covered by the metal foil.

Orientate the wood so that you are cutting long grain, not cross grain. One disadvantage to cutting long grain is that the centre of the bottom is liable to crack once dried – especially if it includes the pith of the log – but this is not a problem for us because we will be gluing a contrasting bottom of dried wood onto the bowl before we are finished. Fig 1 shows the details of the construction.

Use your bowl gouge to rough out the turning, making it round (Fig 2).

Initial shaping

Most of the initial shaping of the bowl will be done with your regular bowl gouge. You can use a small 3/8in (10mm) spindle gouge to reach into the bottom curve of the bowl (Fig 3).

Drilling out the inside

Use a Forstner bit to make the initial hole into the turning blank. Attach a piece of electrical tape to serve as a depth gauge (Fig 4). Leave the bottom about 3/4in (19mm) thick at this stage; once the bowl has dried it will be finish-turned to 3/16–1/4in (5–6mm) thickness.

Hollowing the inside

Hollow the inside of the bowl using your bowl gouge, round-nose scraper, or a specialist hollowing device if you have one. Cut to an even thickness of 1/2in (13mm) from top to bottom. Regularly check the thickness of the bowl using callipers (Fig 5).

Notice the two pencil circles on the top of the bowl. Once the bowl has been dried and finish-turned, a contrasting insert will be placed on the outside line. By keeping 1/4–5/16in (6–8mm) inside this line at this stage, you will have room to finish-turn the opening to the correct diameter once the bowl has dried.

Make a small dent in the centre of the bowl with a live centre before taking it off the lathe. This will allow you to re-centre the spigot once the bowl has been dried.

1 Cross-section of the bowl and stand

2 A sharp bowl gouge is very useful for rough-turning the bowl blank

3 A spindle gouge is very good for cutting the cove shape at the bottom

4 Forstner bits make hollowing the inside much easier. Use electrical tape as a depth gauge

5 Using callipers to check the thickness

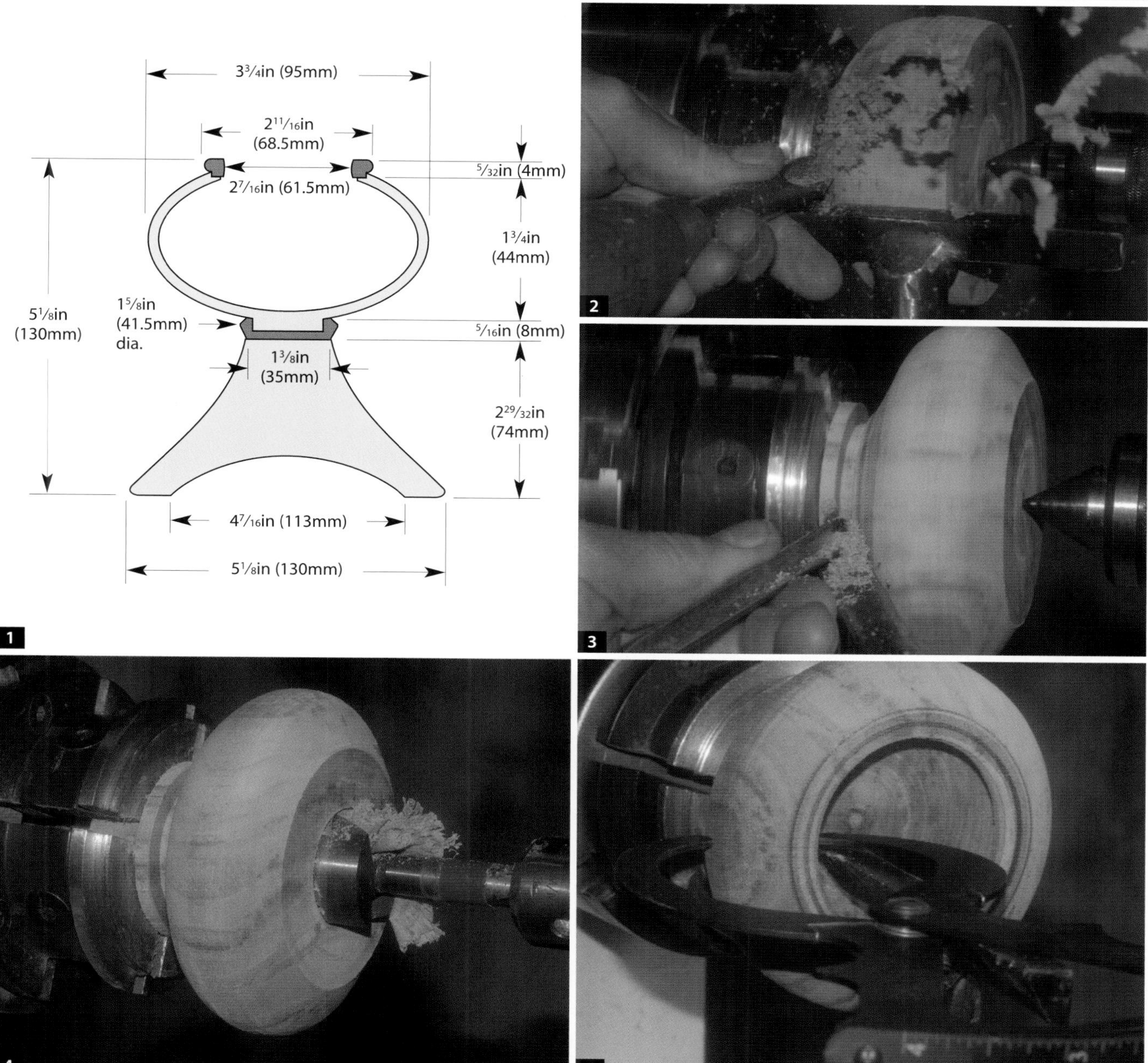
3¾in (95mm)
2 11/16in (68.5mm)
5/32in (4mm)
2 7/16in (61.5mm)
1¾in (44mm)
5⅛in (130mm)
1⅝in (41.5mm) dia.
5/16in (8mm)
1⅜in (35mm)
2 29/32in (74mm)
4 7/16in (113mm)
5⅛in (130mm)
1
2
3
4
5

Drying the bowl

Dry the bowl using one of the techniques described in Chapter 3. The drying will cause some warping and possibly some small cracks. Cracks can be filled with a mixture of cyanoacrylate glue and sawdust; reapply the mixture if cracks reappear during the re-turning process.

Re-turning the spigot

The drying process will cause both the bowl and the spigot to warp. The spigot must be re-trued before finish-turning the bowl. Place a small spur drive into the headstock and centre it in the small dent you made before taking the bowl off the lathe to dry. Place a live centre into the indent in the spigot end of the bowl. Turn the spigot round again (Fig 6).

Finish-turning

Place the re-turned spigot into the four-jaw chuck. Support the tailstock end with a live centre. Use a sharp bowl gouge to re-true the outside of the bowl. Remember that when the bowl gouge is cutting the bottom of the bowl, it is exerting a force toward the tailstock that would tend to push the bowl out of the four-jaw chuck. The live centre counteracts this force, helping to hold the bowl in place (Fig 7).

Turning the dried inside

Turning the inside of the bowl is challenging, because the wood is now very hard; and because it has shrunk to an oval shape you will find yourself cutting air half the time. Place the toolrest very close to the work area, and use very sharp bowl gouges and round-nose scrapers to make the inside cuts.

Cutting the rebate

Cut a 1/4 x 1/4in (6 x 6mm) rebate into the mouth of the bowl. A small skew or square-end scraper works well for this (Fig 8). Check carefully to make sure that your cut forms a 90° angle.

Sanding the inside

Use a hook-and-loop sanding disc in an electric drill to sand the inside of the bowl (Fig 9), which gives a far superior finish to hand-sanding. Sand to about 400 grit and then apply finish on the inside.

The stepped insert

Make a stepped insert from contrasting wood to fit into the rebate. Glue the wood to a waste block, mount it in the four-jaw chuck and use your callipers to mark the correct diameter. Use a small skew or beading tool to cut the rebate in the black wood. Make a plunging cut into the wood 1/4in (6mm) inside the rebate (Fig 10). Once a parting cut has been made from the side, about 1/4in (6mm) toward the headstock, the area left outside the plunging cut will become a loose ring. The step of the insert should overlap the top of the bowl by about 3/32–1/8in (2–3mm).

Gluing the insert

Remount the bowl in your four-jaw chuck. Apply a small amount of PVA glue to the rebate and spread evenly. Use a flat piece of scrap wood to apply even pressure to the ring from the tailstock.

Shaping the insert

Once the glue has set, cut a bead into the black insert. There needs to be a clear junction on the inside and outside of the bowl between the black trim and the rest of the bowl, so the metal foil can be trimmed neatly at this point. Sand the outside of the bowl (Fig 11).

Making a spigot on the bottom

Use a parting tool to cut a tenon or spigot on the bottom of the bowl (arrowed in Fig 11). A foot of contrasting wood will fit over this spigot to make the base of the bowl.

6 Truing the spigot after the bowl has dried

7 Use a live centre to help keep the bowl in the four-jaw chuck

8 Cutting the rebate for the contrasting insert

9 A hook-and-loop sanding disc, used with an electric drill, makes sanding much easier

10 Cutting the stepped insert to fit into the rebate in the bowl

11 Make a clear demarcation line between the bowl body and the black insert. The arrow indicates the spigot or tenon to which the foot will be attached

Applying the metal foil

Apply a mask to the outside of the bowl and to the black wood on the inside. A liquid latex mask, available from your local art supplier, can be painted on (Fig 12), and becomes transparent when dry.

Spray the inside of the bowl with size, following the manufacturer's instructions. Allow time for this to become tacky, and then start applying the metal foil. Break the foil into small sections – about 1–2in (25–50mm) square – and press these down carefully with cotton wool. Cover the entire inside of the bowl in this way (Fig13). The pieces of foil will overlap in places; afterwards the surplus can be removed by lightly brushing the foil with a soft felt cloth (Fig. 14).

Foil clean-up

Once the metal foil has been applied and the size has set, place the bowl back on the lathe. Set the lathe to a low speed and carefully trim the mask at the junction point. Make sure that the tool you are using is very sharp. Peel the mask away from the bowl. This should leave you with a very sharp boundary between the foil-covered surface and the contrasting black insert. Clean up the insert and lightly re-sand if necessary. Finish the interior by spraying on several coats of lacquer to protect the metal foil.

> *Every vessel gives me a way to express my feelings about the things I see around me and to share those visions with others.*
>
> *Ron Fleming*

Reverse-mounting

Make a jam-fit chuck to fit the inside of the bowl. The wood of the jam chuck must be very soft and the fit should be snug, without applying enough pressure to break the bowl.

Gently re-turn the bottom of the bowl, leaving a spigot ¼in (6mm) long. Turn a foot from contrasting wood, about ½in (13mm) larger in diameter than the spigot, and glue it on (Fig 15). Once set, round over the side of the foot while applying very light pressure with the tailstock.

Applying foil to the outside

Mask the black wood on the outside of the bowl, top and bottom. Masking tape works well; trim it with a sharp knife (Fig 16). Spray size onto the bowl while it is still on the lathe. Allow the size to become tacky and then apply the metal foil (Fig 17). Apply foil to all areas on the outside of the bowl, then gently brush with the felt cloth.

Spray on several coats of lacquer while the lathe revolves slowly at about 40–60rpm (Fig 18). If your lathe does not have such a low speed, you can revolve it by hand as the lacquer dries. This will help to prevent the lacquer pooling – but the sprayed coats must still be very light.

12 Apply a liquid latex mask to the black insert and the exterior of the bowl before applying foil to the inside

13 Apply overlapping, torn pieces of metal foil to the sticky size

14 Gently brush away the overlapping pieces of metal foil with a felt cloth

15 The bowl mounted on the jam-chuck, with the contrasting base attached

16 Masking tape is used to mask off the outside of the bowl

17 Apply overlapping pieces of foil once the size has become tacky

18 Apply several coats of lacquer while the bowl is still on the lathe

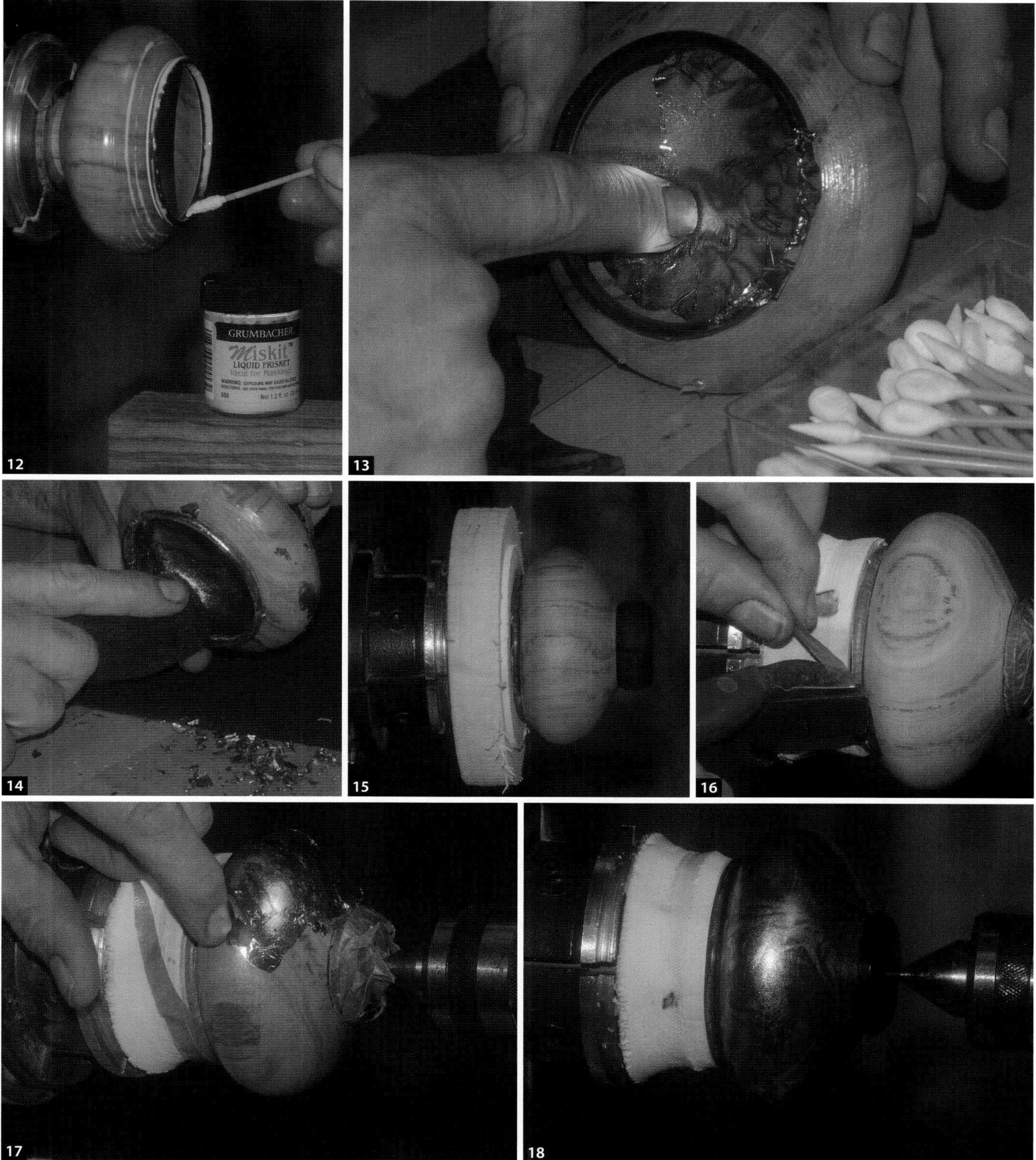
12
GRUMBACHER
Miskit™
LIQUID FRISKET
Ideal for Masking
13
14
15
16
17
18

Making the stand

You can turn very attractive stands on your lathe. A full circular stand is easy to turn, and looks nice. The stand shown here, one of my own designs, has the advantage of supporting the bowl with either the narrow or the wide end up. The disadvantage is that it is difficult and, if you're not careful, dangerous to turn, since the wood will be rotating in the lathe like a propeller. Be sure to keep your finger from getting on the wrong side of the toolrest (refer back to Fig 1 on page 17).

● Tip

If you are apprehensive about turning a stand from a flat bar of wood, an alternative method is to turn it circular and cut the sides flat afterwards. This would obviously be less economical than the method shown here.

Start with a piece of stock 5 x 3½ x 2in (125 x 90 x 50mm). Glue some type of backing onto both sides, which will help prevent tear-out during turning. Mount the piece between centres (Fig 19).

Use your bowl gouge to turn the stand (Fig 20). Develop a pleasing concave curve to the turning. Cut slowly and carefully. Use a skew or a beading tool to cut a spigot at the top of the stand (arrowed in Fig 20).

When you have finished turning the outside of the stand, take it off the lathe. Draw a partial circle on the bottom of the stand where you want to cut away wood. Use a bandsaw to cut away the bulk of the waste material.

Mount the spigot of the stand into your four-jaw chuck and position your toolrest with care, rotating the work by hand to make sure that it will not foul the rest. Turn the inside of the stand carefully (Fig. 21), keeping your fingers in the safety zone behind the toolrest at all times. Use a belt sander to sand away the backing board that was glued onto each side (Fig. 22), then use your tablesaw to remove the spigot which was held in the four-jaw chuck. Do the final sculpting of the stand using a drum sander fitted with 120–150-grit abrasive (Fig 23), and then apply your chosen finish.

Fig 24 shows an alternative stand in a similar style.

Design is always a challenge: the slight firming or slackening of a curve; an incised line in the right place; the combination of convex and concave curves. All can lift an object from the ordinary to the exceptional if the maker has the eye needed.

Ray Key

19 Glue a backing material to both sides of the base to prevent tear-out

20 Turn a gentle concave curve using a bowl gouge. Cut a spigot on top (arrowed) for your four-jaw chuck

21 Keep your fingers out of the way when turning the inside of the stand

22 Sand away the backing board on both sides

23 Do the final shaping of the stand with a drum sander

24 An alternative design for the stand

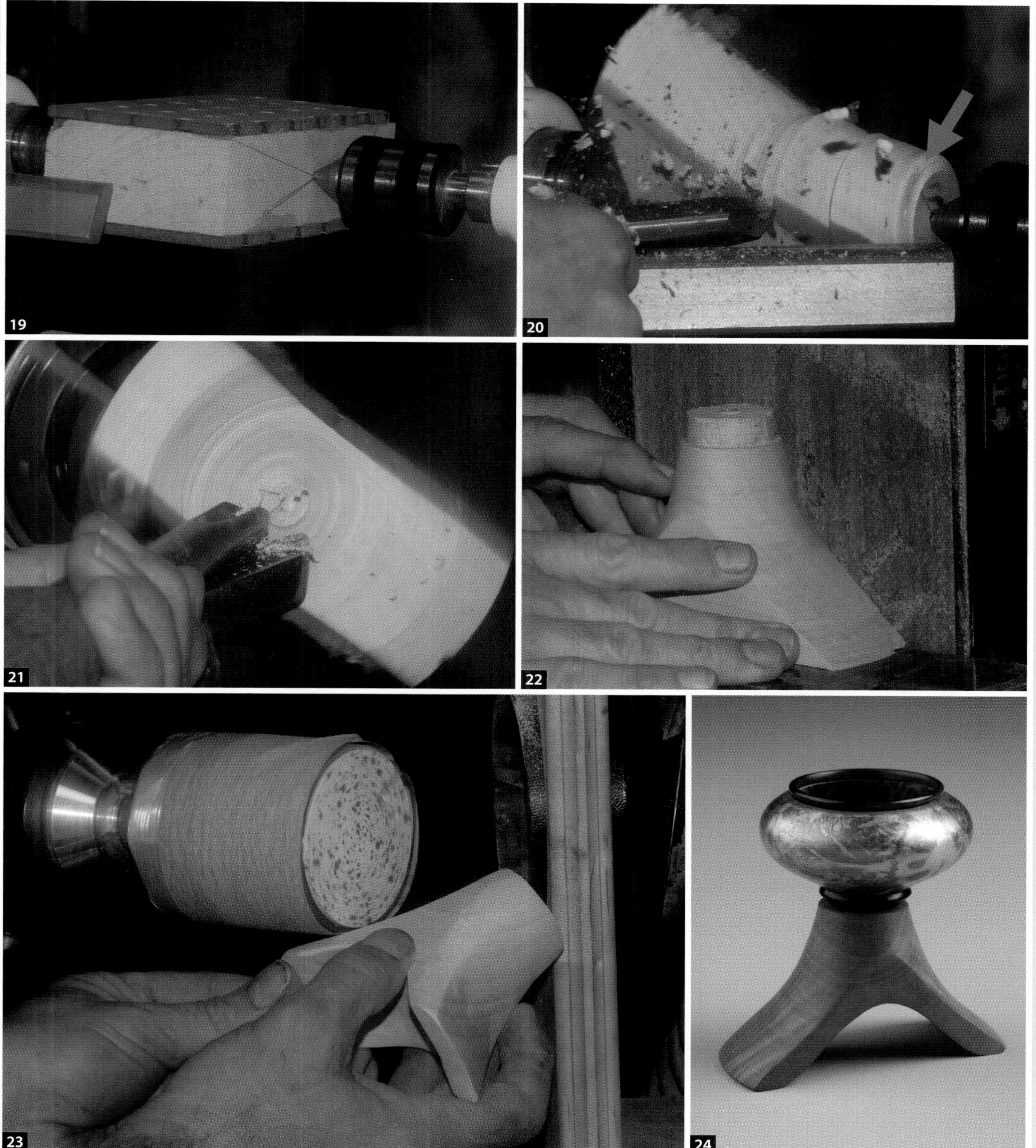
19
20
21
22
23
24

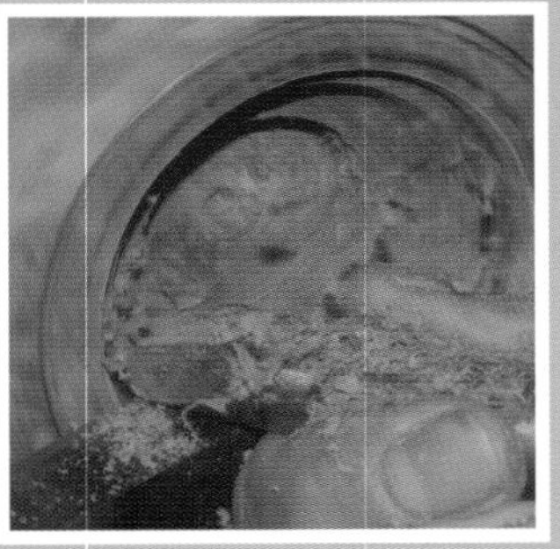

7 Lidded Box with Finial

Small lidded boxes are some of the most popular items that a turner can produce, and they are enjoyable and easy to make. When tastefully designed and skilfully made, the lidded box can become a very fine artform. Cindy Drozda of Boulder, Colorado has elevated the finial box to a very high level of art – her boxes are among the best in the world of turning. The box that we will make in this chapter is similar in appearance to those made by Cindy.

When creating a turned container, I like to decorate the inside of the piece. When the lid is opened a hidden treasure is revealed, and a secret is shared with the person who opens it.

Cindy Drozda

Bill of goods

- Attractive, unseasoned wood, about 4–6in long by 4–6in diameter (100–150 x 100–150mm)
- Contrasting wood:
  Foot: 3 x 3 x 1in (75 x 75 x 25mm)
  Rim inserts: two pieces 4 x 4 x 1in (100 x 100 x 25mm)
  Finial: 4 x 1 x 1in (100 x 25 x 25mm)
- Gold leaf, or substitute
- Gold-leaf adhesive (size)
- Masking tape or latex masking liquid
- Small piece of felt cloth to rub the foil
- Non-stretch packing tape
- PVA and cyanoacrylate glues
- Scrap softwood to make a jam-fit chuck
- Scrap hardwood for a glue block

Getting started

For this project we will be using wet or 'green' wood. I used the double-baked technique as described in Chapter 3 to dry the wood after rough-turning. For the trim, I used Australian red mallee burl and black Texas ironwood. Fig 1 shows the construction, which involves six separate pieces.

Start by rough-turning the green wood between centres, using a spur drive and a live centre, to the approximate dimensions given in the bill of goods. At this stage the lid and body of the box are turned as one piece, leaving a little spare height so they can be separated later.

Spigots must be turned at both ends. I did not have enough available wood to form a spigot on the bottom of the box, so I glued a maple block to the underside of the red mallee, using pressure from the tailstock to hold it while the glue set (Fig 2).

Mounting on a four-jaw chuck

Place the turning blank in the four-jaw chuck and support it at the tailstock end with a live centre. Use your bowl gouge to develop the initial shape of the box. Leave a large enough area between the box and lid sections so that your parting tool can cut without interfering with the shape of the bowl (Fig 3).

Shaping the bottom

Use your bowl gouge to shape the bottom. Leave the turning oversize at this stage, to allow for finish-turning after it has been dried.

Parting off the lid

The lid – roughly shaped but still oversize – is now parted off from the body of the box, to allow the body to be hollowed.

Initial hollowing

Use a sharp Forstner bit to make the initial cut on the inside. Attach a piece of electrical tape to the shank of the bit as a depth gauge (Fig 4). Leave the bottom thick – about 7⁄8in (22mm) at this stage.

Use a 3⁄8–1⁄2in (10–13mm) bowl gouge to do the bulk of the hollowing. Notice the two pencil circles drawn on the bowl (Fig 5). The inner circle is about 3⁄8in (10mm) inside where the final dry cut should be. Cutting to this inside line will leave you room to re-turn the bowl once it has dried and warped a little.

1 Cross-section of the Lidded Box with Finial

2 To make your expensive mallee burl go further, glue a waste block of maple or other scrap wood on the bottom. Turn a spigot for your four-jaw chuck on the maple waste block

3 Turning the box and lid in one piece. The groove between lid and body must be wide enough to give clearance to the parting tool

4 Boring out the centre of the box with a Forstner bit

5 Beginning to hollow the inside with a bowl gouge

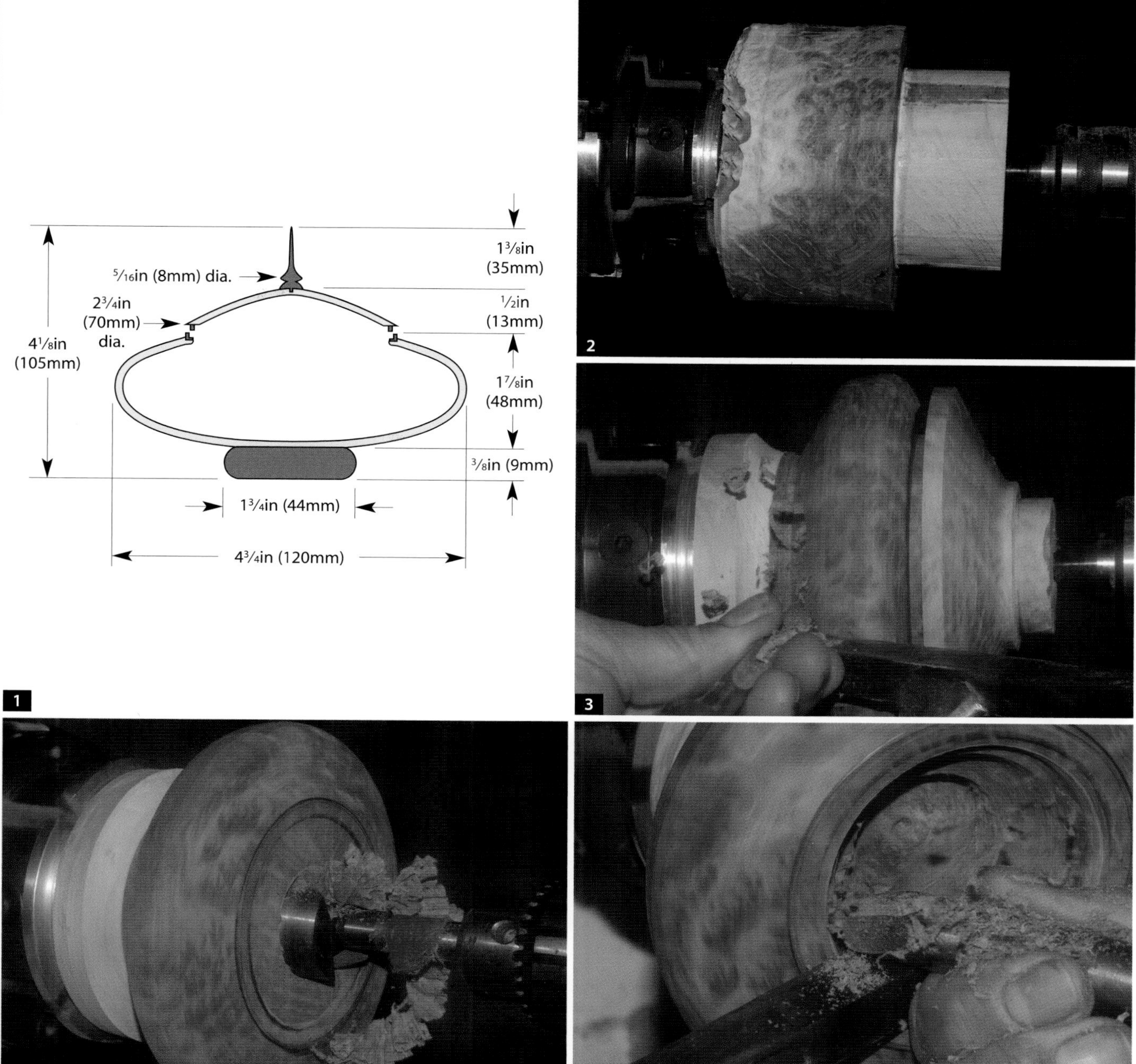
5/16in (8mm) dia.
2 3/4in
(70mm)
dia.
4 1/8in
(105mm)
1 3/8in
(35mm)
1/2in
(13mm)
1 7/8in
(48mm)
3/8in (9mm)
1 3/4in (44mm)
4 3/4in (120mm)

1

2

3

4

5

You can make the initial undercuts in the bottom using either a round-nose scraper or a specialized hollowing tool such as the Kelton undercutter (Fig 6). Leave the wall of the bowl about 1in (25mm) thick at this stage.

Make an indent with the live centre in the middle of the bowl; the spur drive will be located here when the bowl is remounted.

Rough-turn the lid, then dry both parts by your preferred method. Also dry the three pieces of black trim wood for the foot and the two rim inserts.

Re-turning the box

Remount the body of the box in the four-jaw chuck after it has dried. First mount the bowl between centres so that you can re-true the spigot on the base. Next, place the spigot back into the four-jaw chuck and re-true the outside of the bowl. Place your tailstock into position so that the live centre can support the bowl while you are making the external cuts.

Truing the opening

The drying and remounting process will have caused the opening to become out of round. With the lathe turning at a slow speed (100–300rpm), make a pencil mark to show the largest hole that can be cut in continuous wood. Using a sharp, pointed tool, cut straight into the bowl at the pencil mark.

Cutting the first rebate

Cut a 3/8 x 3/8in (10 x 10mm) rebate into the opening. Be sure that the two walls of the rebate are square and flat. A square-nose scraper is very useful for making sure that the final cut is square; it should be sharp, both on the front of the scraper and on the left-hand side.

Re-turning the inside

Be very careful when re-turning the inside of the bowl: the work is now unsupported at the tailstock end, and the wood is very hard and out of true. A bowl gouge and round-nose scraper are both used to re-cut the inside. Sand the inside using hook-and-loop sanding pads.

Making the rim insert

Glue the dried blank to a waste block, which can be mounted either on a faceplate or in a four-jaw chuck. Use callipers to measure the diameter of the rebate in the mouth of the box, and transfer this measurement to your dried black wood blank with a pencil mark. Use a small, sharp tool to cut a stepped rebate to the pencil line. Stop often to check the fit by offering the box up to the black wood – it should be snug without being tight. The outside of the black wood should overhang the rebate in the bowl mouth by about 1/8in (3mm). Once you have a nice fit, set the black insert aside.

Applying gold leaf to the inside

Gold leaf, or a suitable substitute, can be purchased from your local art suppliers. The process, illustrated in the previous chapter, requires a bit of patience. Apply a latex mask to the rebate area and the outside of the bowl; it will make cleaning up much easier.

Carefully spray a gold-leaf adhesive (size) to the inside of the bowl – don't overdo it! Allow the adhesive time to dry until it is tacky.

Tear the gold leaf into small sections of about 1–2in (25–50mm) square and apply these to the inside of the box, pressing down gently with your finger or a cotton swab. There will be some overlap, which is OK. Continue adding the pieces of leaf and pressing them down until the entire inside is covered.

Using a small piece of clean felt, gently brush the gold leaf. This removes the overlapping layer of foil so that you have only one thickness.

6 Using the Kelton undercutting tool to enlarge the cavity; a round-nose scraper could be used instead

7 Using the square-ended scraper to refine the rebate in the rim insert

8 As you shape the base you will need to cut away part of the glue block to improve access

Gold foil clean-up

Use your finger, a cotton swab, or a rubber eraser to roll up the latex mask. Use a cotton swab to clean up the rebate. Protect the foil by spraying on several coats of lacquer.

Gluing the insert

Apply glue to the rebate area, being careful that the glue does not run into the gold foil area. Seat the insert carefully. Use a square piece of plywood and your tailstock to apply gentle pressure while the glue sets overnight.

Shaping the black insert

Thin the insert to slightly less than 1⁄16in (1.5mm) thickness, making very light cuts with a sharp tool. Use a small skew chisel to cut a small bead into the black insert. Blend the bowl into the insert and make a nice clean junction.

Cut a small rebate, about 1⁄16in (1.5mm) square, into the upper surface of the black wood. Use a square scraper to make the final clean-up cut. This scraper should be sharp, both on the leading edge and the left side (Fig 7). Sand and apply finish to the edge of the box.

Parting off the box

Shape as much of the bottom of the box as you can reach at this stage, using a small bowl or spindle gouge to open up the base area by cutting away part of the glue block (Fig 8). Sand and apply finish to the accessible part of the bottom.

6
7
8

Reverse-turning the underside

The bottom of the box will be turned using a jam-fit chuck. Mount a piece of soft, wet wood on your four-jaw chuck and cut a small spigot to fit the inside of the box. Stop and check often that the box fits securely onto the spigot.

Wet wood is the best option for a jam-fit chuck, because it is softer than dry wood and therefore less likely to crack the bowl by applying too much pressure. If you have only dry wood available, pine is very good for a jam-chuck.

Attaching to the jam-chuck

Locate the mouth of the box on the spigot of the jam-fit chuck, using non-stretch packing tape (visible in Fig 9) for added security. Use very light pressure from the tailstock to give additional support to the bottom of the box.

Turning the bottom

Use a sharp bowl gouge with a light touch to do the final shaping of the bottom of the box, turning away the remains of the glue block in the process. Create a 1in (25mm) diameter flat spot on the bottom of the bowl – the black base will be attached here. Use a straightedge to make sure that this central circle is truly flat.

Making the base

Turn a spigot in a piece of scrap hardwood to fit your four-jaw chuck, then glue a 1in (25mm) diameter piece of black wood to this. Once the glue is set, turn the tailstock end of the black wood perfectly flat. This is the side that will be glued to the bottom of the box.

Gluing the base

Apply a small amount of glue to both the bottom of the box and the base. Centre the base into position by bringing the live centre up to the indent in the bottom of the wood. Apply light pressure with the tailstock and allow the glue to set overnight.

Shaping the base

A skew or beading tool works well to shape the base (Fig 9). Use a thin parting tool to part the base off, making the underside slightly concave for stability.

When the bottom is finished, remove the tape and protect the bottom from tailstock pressure with a soft foam pad while you apply your chosen finish (Fig 10).

Shaping the lid

The lid has already been rough-turned and dried. Now remount it between centres and true the spigot. Turn the entire tailstock side of the lid flat; the black insert will be glued to this. Check to make sure it is absolutely flat, using a straightedge. Centre the black wood onto the lid and hold in place with the live centre on your tailstock as before (Fig 11). Allow the PVA to set overnight. The underside of the lid can now be turned as if it were one solid piece of wood.

Shaping the inside of the lid

Make a very shallow depression on the inside of the lid. Cut a short rebate in the black insert to fit into the rebate in the body of the box, and stop often to check that it fits – it should be snug but not tight. Fig 12 demonstrates a bit of showing off on my part, because the rebate of the lid is only 1⁄16in (1.5mm) deep.

9 Shaping the black wood base. Note the strong tape securing the body in the jam-fit chuck

10 Using foam to protect the bottom as the finish is applied

11 Gluing the black insert to the underside of the lid

12 Checking the fit between the box and the rebate of the lid

9
10
11
12

Applying gold leaf to the lid

Use the same technique on the inside of the lid as for the inside of the bowl. Apply a latex mask to the areas where gold foil is not required, and use your finger or a cotton swab to gently rub away the latex mask afterwards (Fig 13). Protect the inside of the lid with a spray lacquer after cleaning up.

Secondary shaping of the lid

Use your bowl gouge or scraper to shape the top of the lid as far as you can reach (Fig. 14). Check for any imperfections in the profile. Place a pencil mark on any high spots, rotating the lid by hand to make a mark, and remove any high spots with a sharp scraper. Shape as much of the top as you can at this stage.

Part off the lid using a thin parting tool (Fig 15) and set it aside in a safe place.

Reverse-turning the lid

The lid must now be remounted so that the top of it can be finished. The body of the box is too delicate to use as a jam-chuck, so start by turning some soft, wet wood round. Use a skew, a beading tool or a square-end scraper to cut a rebate of the correct size to hold the lid.

Secure the lid to the rebate of the jam-chuck with non-stretch packing tape. Very lightly bring up the live centre to give just a whisper of support to the top of the lid. Make the final cuts on the top surface and sand to 400 grit.

Drilling the hole for the finial

Drill a 5⁄32in (4mm) hole in the top of the lid, using a drill bit in a Jacobs chuck. Stick a piece of tape on the bit as a depth gauge at about 1⁄4–3⁄8in (6–10mm) deep (Fig 16).

Making the finial

Mount your fourth piece of black accent wood in a four-jaw chuck. Very gently and slowly cut it away at the tailstock end so as to produce a long, thin point. A 1⁄4in (6mm) skew works well for this procedure. As the turning becomes long and thin, support the point from behind with a finger (Fig 17) or a small piece of kitchen paper.

● Caution

I believe I can safely support a small finial with my finger; a beginner might be better advised to use a small piece of kitchen paper as a support. If the paper is grabbed by the lathe it will tear harmlessly. Avoid using leather gloves, which have the potential to become entangled in the lathe, causing catastrophic damage.

Use your skew to cut a small bead about 1in (25mm) from the end of the finial (Fig 18); the general shape you are aiming for is a long, stretched-out 'genie' bottle. Flare the base of the finial to about 5⁄16in (8mm) diameter, to cover the small hole drilled into the lid for the spigot of the finial. Sand and apply your chosen finish while the finial is still on the lathe.

Use a small skew to cut a spigot at the base of the finial, which must be an accurate match for the hole drilled in the top of the lid. Use your callipers to ensure it fits exactly (Fig 19).

Gluing the finial

Apply a small amount of cyanoacrylate glue to the finial. If the glue you are using comes with an accelerator, spray a small amount of this into the rebate and quickly press the finial into position.

13 Removing the latex mask after gilding the inside of the lid

14 Shaping the top of the lid

15 Parting off the lid

16 Drilling the hole for the finial. If you accidentally drill all the way through, cover your mistake by gluing an artificial pearl on the inside.

17 Use a small, sharp skew to cut a long, thin finial

18 A 1⁄4in (6mm) round skew is nice to use for cutting the bead on the finial

19 Checking the size of the spigot at the base of the finial

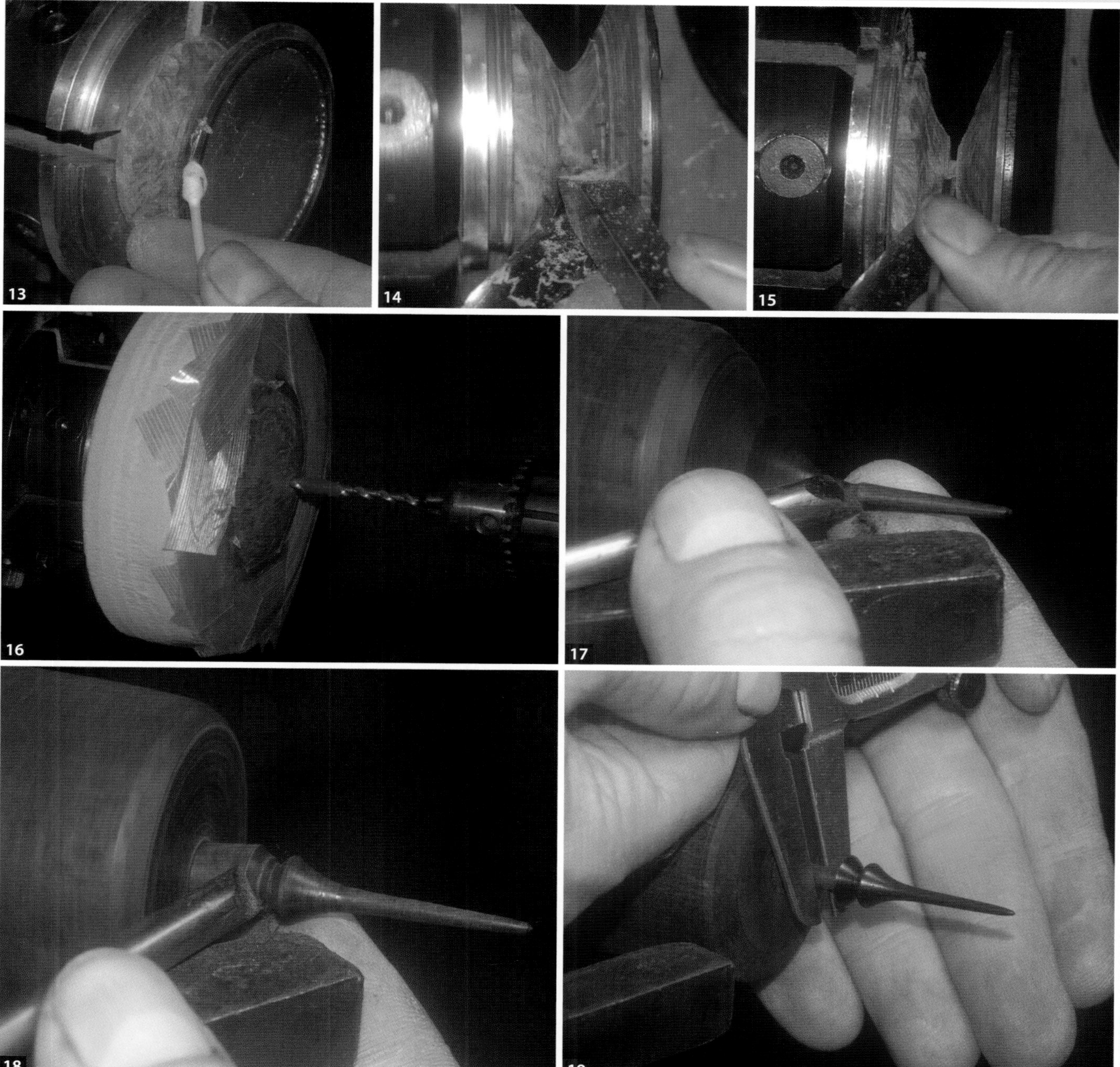
13
14
15
16
17
18
19

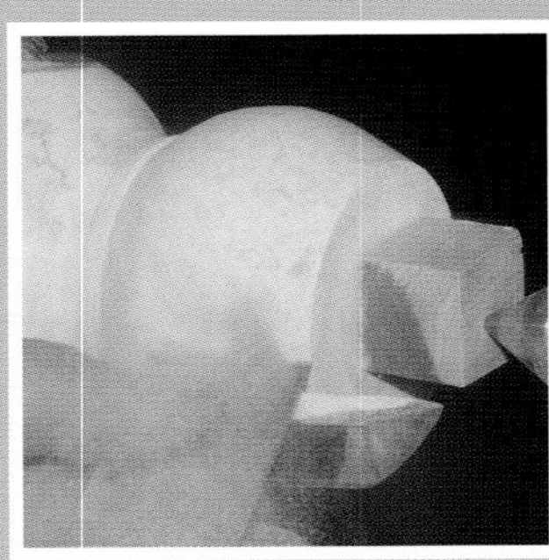

❽ Alabaster Angel

'There is joy in the presence of angels' (Luke 15: 10). Bring joy into your life by crafting and displaying this beautiful alabaster angel, which is elegant enough to suit any art gallery or private home.

This artform was developed by David MacFarlane of Roseburg, Oregon, a world-class turner excelling in both alabaster and wood. David calls these pieces 'winged vessels'.

This is a multipart project made from alabaster and wood. A number of separate turnings are needed, as well as some flat sawn work. Three pieces of alabaster make up the body of the angel. The top part of the angel is a lid, composed of seven pieces of wood. Although it looks rather complicated, it is not particularly difficult to make. The alabaster can be worked with ordinary woodturning tools.

Fabergé never
let size confine his vision. Rather,
he let his vision dictate size.

Ron Layport

Bill of goods

- Alabaster, 3 x 3 x 7in (75 x 75 x 180mm)
- Contrasting piece of alabaster, 1 x 3 x 3in (25 x 75 x 75mm)
- Scrap hardwood (not plywood) for glue blocks
- Dried burl wood, 4 x 4 x 6in (100 x 100 x 150mm)
- Ebony for finial, ½ x ½ x 3⅛in (13 x 13 x 80mm)
- Five-minute epoxy cement
- Cyanoacrylate glue (superglue) and hot-melt glue
- Components for lid:
  wings: burl maple or mallee, 4 x 4 x ⅛in (100 x 100 x 3mm)
  central hub: mallee or maple burl, 2 x 2 x 5in (50 x 50 x 125mm)
  halo: mallee or maple burl, 2 x 2 x 1in (50 x 50 x 25mm)
  halo support: mallee or maple burl, ¾ x ¾ x 3in (20 x 20 x 75mm)
  finial: ebony, ⅜ x ⅜ x 2¾in (10 x 10 x 70mm)

Turning materials

For this project the working materials are very important: you need beautiful alabaster and beautiful wood. The Internet is probably the easiest way to locate alabaster. Fig 1 shows all the components.

Getting started

Start by sawing your alabaster to size; I used my bandsaw (Fig 2). You can use a belt sander to square the ends (Fig 3); notice the vacuum hose attached to the sander.

Glue blocks

Attach glue blocks to both ends of the alabaster turning blank (Fig 4); I prefer five-minute epoxy because of its high strength.

● Caution

Do not use plywood for glue blocks – it can disintegrate during turning. Maple makes the best glue blocks.

Roughing out

Mount the alabaster blank between centres (Fig 5) and ensure that the live centre and tailstock are securely locked in position. Turn a spigot on each of the glue blocks (Fig 6). Form a square shoulder that will fit closely against the four-jaw chuck, using a skew chisel or a square-ended tool such as a beading tool.

Round the alabaster turning blank using a sharp bowl gouge.

● Caution

Always use a low speed when turning alabaster – in the range of 80–150rpm, and never more than 300rpm. Dust control is particularly important with this material.

Filling cracks

Fill any cracks in the alabaster immediately, using cyanoacrylate glue mixed with alabaster dust of the same colour (Fig 7).

1 Cross-sections of the body and lid of the Alabaster Angel vase

2 Good alabaster can be cut with a bandsaw

3 Using the belt sander to flatten the ends of the alabaster

4 Glue maple waste blocks to the alabaster with epoxy glue. Do not use plywood

5 The alabaster blank mounted between centres

6 Turn a square-shouldered spigot on the waste block to fit a four-jaw chuck. A square beading tool is a good choice for this job

7 Filling a gap with superglue and alabaster dust

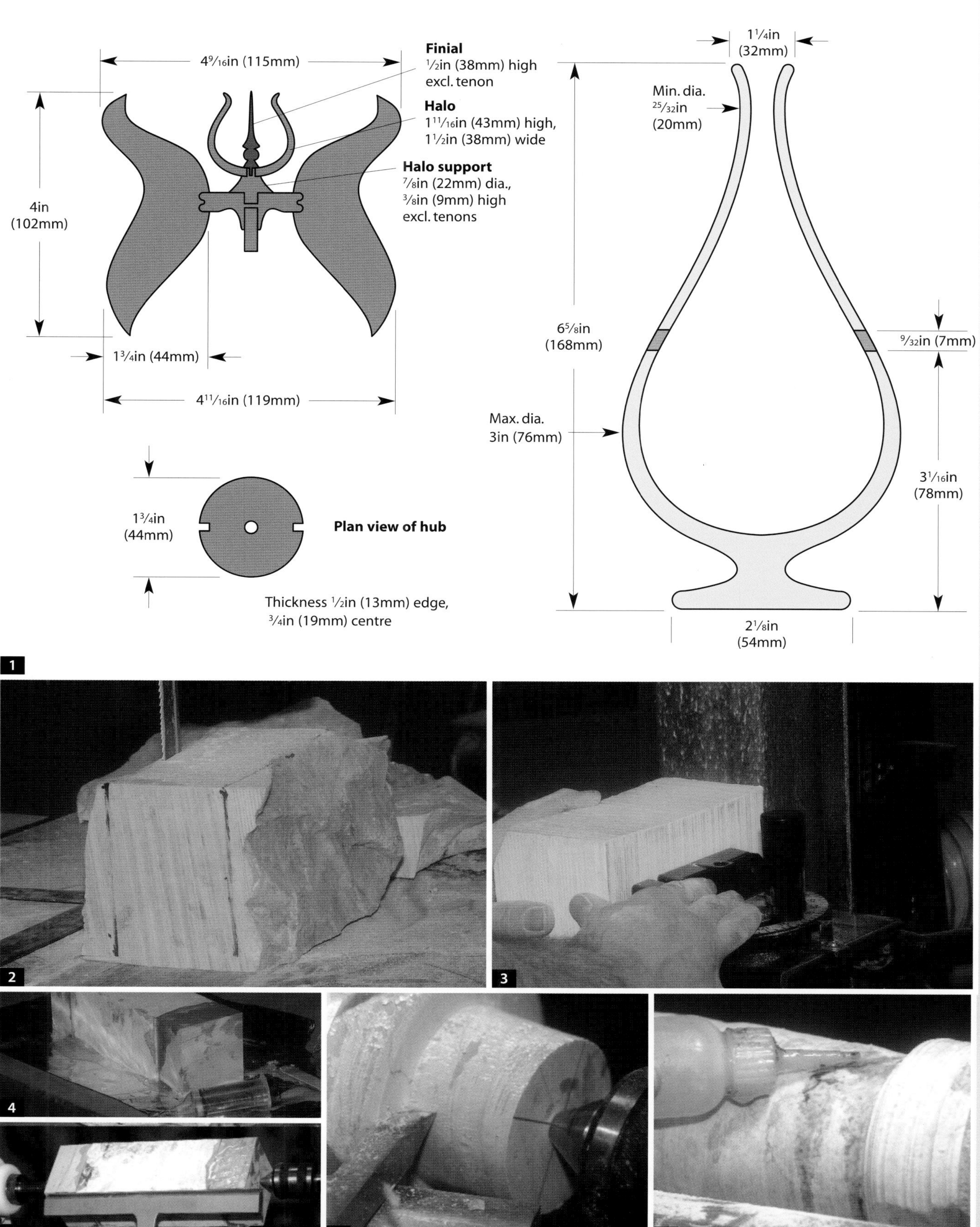

4 9/16in (115mm)
Finial
1/2in (38mm) high
excl. tenon
Halo
1 11/16in (43mm) high,
1 1/2in (38mm) wide
Halo support
7/8in (22mm) dia.,
3/8in (9mm) high
excl. tenons
4in
(102mm)
1 3/4in (44mm)
4 11/16in (119mm)
1 3/4in
(44mm)
Plan view of hub
Thickness 1/2in (13mm) edge,
3/4in (19mm) centre
1 1/4in
(32mm)
Min. dia.
25/32in
(20mm)
6 5/8in
(168mm)
9/32in (7mm)
Max. dia.
3in (76mm)
3 1/16in
(78mm)
2 1/8in
(54mm)
1
2
3
4
5
6
7

Initial shaping of the vase

Develop the initial shape of the whole vase using any of your regular woodturning tools, which will work fine on good alabaster (Fig 8). My preference is to do most of the shaping using a bowl gouge, and for cutting coves I like to use a 3/8–1/2in (10–13mm) round-nose scraper slowly and gently. The vase will later be parted in half to allow the contrasting ring to be inserted, so be sure to allow some room in this area for the width of the parting tool.

Part off the top section at this stage (Fig 9), and attach new glue blocks to the cut ends of both parts.

Turning the lower section

Now shape the bottom section of the vase (Fig 10), leaving the lower part oversize until the vase is almost completed; this is necessary to give it sufficient strength during the turning process. Once the top has been completed and joined to the base, the bottom can then be refined to a smaller, more delicate shape.

Drill out the inside with a drill bit, just as you would do with a woodturning (Fig 11), then use a small, sharp 1/4–1/2in (6–13mm) skew tool to complete the hollowing of the inside (Fig 12). The pencil line visible in this photo indicates the final position of the inside surface. Finish cuts are made with a 1/2in (13mm) round-nose scraper.

Sand to about 320 grit (Fig 13) and apply your chosen finish to the inside.

Making the central belt

The top and bottom will be joined together with a central belt made of alabaster in a contrasting colour. Mount the new piece using glue blocks as before. Cut the outside diameter of the belt, and be sure to cut the bottom perfectly flat. Using callipers, mark the inside diameter of the belt. Use a thin parting tool to make a straight plunge cut on the inside; then, using the same tool from the side, cut the belt free (Fig 14).

Gluing the belt to the base

Remount the bottom section on your lathe. Glue on the belt with cyanoacrylate (superglue) or PVA, and hold it in place using a piece of softwood and gentle pressure from the tailstock. Once the glue has cured, blend the belt into the bottom of the vase. Turn the top of the belt flat so that it can mate with the top section of the vase.

Turning the top half of the vase body

Mount the blank for the top section using glue blocks as before, and with its top end towards the headstock. Mark the desired diameter on the lower end of the blank, to match the central belt (Fig 15). Drill out the inside using a drill bit, and hollow it out as you did the lower part. Cut the upper section to a uniform thickness of 1/4–3/8in (6–10mm) (Fig 16). You will not be able to hollow all the way through to the mouth of the vase at this stage.

8 Shape the alabaster with ordinary turning tools

9 Make a parting cut in the middle of the alabaster vase with a thin parting tool

10 Shape the lower half of the vase, leaving plenty of spare material at the bottom for now

11 Drill out the inside of the lower section with a Forstner bit. Pencil marks indicate where the bottom will be

12 Cut the inside very slowly, keeping inside the pencil mark that indicates the inside diameter

13 Sand the inside to 320 grit and apply finish

14 Making the central belt from a contrasting colour of alabaster

15 Cut the top section of the vase to the correct diameter to fit the alabaster belt

16 Hollow the inside of the top before it is glued to the belt and bottom

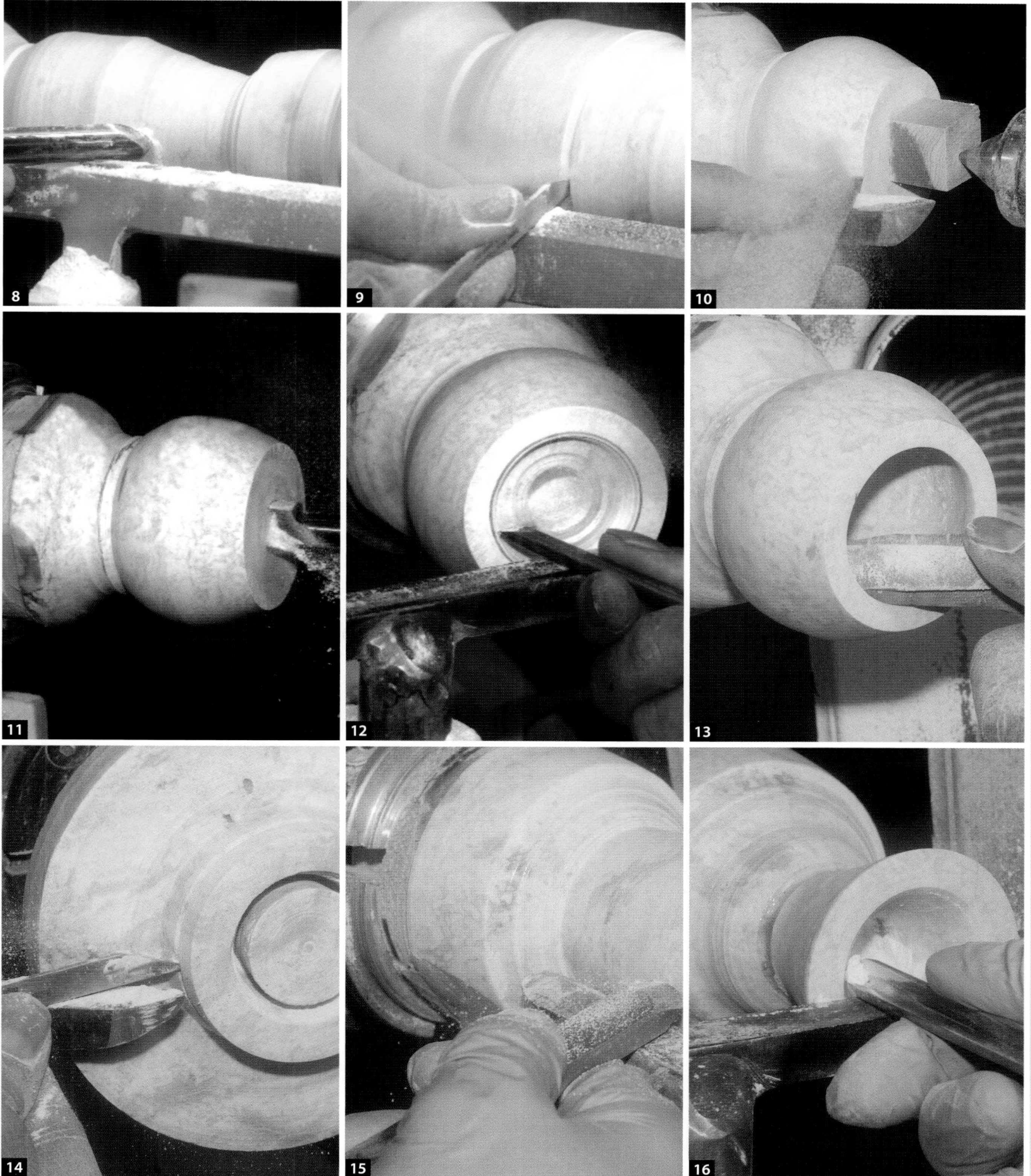
8
9
10
11
12
13
14
15
16

Turning the outside of the vase

Remount the bottom section, which now includes the central belt, onto the lathe. Glue the top to the belt and apply light pressure with the live centre in the tailstock. Allow this glue to set fully before turning.

Turn the final outside shape of the vase, except for the bottom end, which must still be left oversize. Use a bowl gouge or a round-nose scraper to develop the shape of the top of the vase (Fig 17). Sand and apply your choice of finish to the outside of the vase (Fig 18). The top can then be parted off.

Final turning of the inside

Final turning of the inside requires the use of a steady rest, since the vase will no longer be supported by the tailstock. Place some tape around the neck of the vase where the rubber wheels of the steady rest will be rubbing.

● Tip

A steady rest is a device which supports a fragile turning and helps to prevent it flexing or vibrating unduly. It usually consists of a metal or plywood ring bolted to the lathe bed, with three or four soft rubber wheels (like those of a rollerblade) which can be adjusted to apply even pressure to the work from different directions.

Drill out the centre, using a 3/16in (5mm) drill bit. Enlarge the opening to about 5/16in (8mm) if the neck is large enough to accommodate this inside diameter. My final wall thickness was 5/16in (8mm), with a 5/16in (8mm) hole in the smallest part of the neck.

Use the drill bit for support while you hollow out the inside of the mouth of the vase (Fig 19). If you cut very slowly and gently you should not make a lot of dust. Sand and apply finish to the mouth of the vase.

Making the lid

The lid is composed of seven pieces of wood, as shown in Fig 1 on page 73:

- the central hub
- an internal spigot, which holds the lid in position
- two wings
- the halo
- the halo support
- the finial.

The wings

Use the drawing to make a pattern (you could photocopy it to the required size), or design your own wing pattern using a French curve. Prepare a piece of stock approximately 4in (100mm) square. Use a tablesaw to slice off two bookmatched squares slightly thicker than the thickness of the saw blade. Once you have finished sanding it, the wood should be the same thickness as the saw blade that will be used to cut the slots in the central hub (Fig 20).

Place the wing pattern on the wood to take best advantage of the wood's figure (Fig 21). Use a scrollsaw to cut out the wings, then hand-sand them to round over the edges.

17 Gently blend all the curves of the vase together

18 Sand and apply finish to the outside of the vase before parting the top free

19 Support the vase with a steady rest while you drill through the top and then enlarge the opening with a small gouge or skew

20 The wings, once sanded, should be the thickness of your tablesaw blade

21 Use a scrollsaw to cut out the two wings

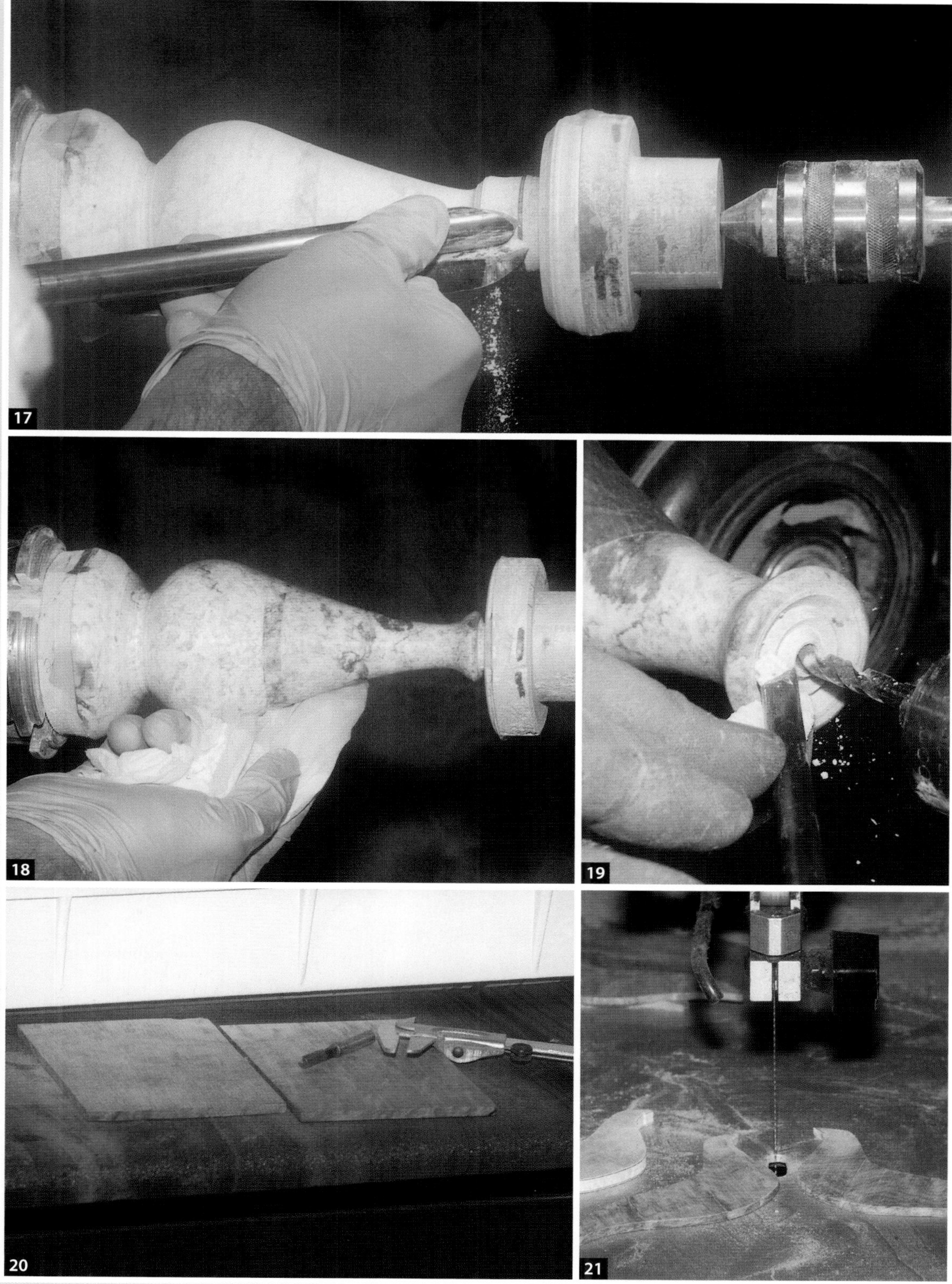
17
18
19
20
21

The central hub

Prepare a piece of wood approximately 2 x 2 x 5in (50 x 50 x 125mm) for the central hub. The wood must be square. The central hub has two slots cut into it for the wings to fit into. Mark the centre of the block and set the tablesaw fence so that the blade will cut down the centre line. Adjust the depth of cut so that there is a central part of the wood – 1in (25mm) diameter – not cut by the saw blade. Make two saw cuts on opposite sides of the block, using a suitable push block to keep your fingers well away from the blade (Fig. 22). The wings will fit into these slots after the block has been turned.

The slots must be filled in for turning, to avoid tear-out on the edges. Cut two pieces of scrap wood to fit accurately into the two slots. Glue these filler strips into the slots using hot-melt glue (Fig 23).

Turn the central hub to approximately 1³⁄₈in (35mm) diameter. There must be enough of the slot left to give adequate support to the wings. Slope the bottom surface of the hub (arrowed in Fig 24) so that it fits accurately to the inside of your vase. Drill a hole for the internal spigot in the bottom of the hub, the same size as the hole drilled in the vase. Sand and apply your chosen finish to the hub. Part the hub off, hand-sand the top and apply finish.

Drill a ³⁄₁₆in (5mm) hole in the top of the hub to take the halo support.

The internal spigot

An internal spigot holds the lid in position. Turn the spigot ⁵⁄₁₆in diameter by 1¹⁄₂in long (8 x 38mm). The spigot should fit well in the mouth of the vase without being tight. Insert the spigot into the bottom of the central hub. Glue it in position with cyanoacrylate (superglue).

> *Perfection is like the end of a rainbow – always just out of reach.*
>
> *Richard Raffan*

Gluing the wings

It is important to get the best possible height and spread of the wings – test for the best fit before gluing in place using cyanoacrylate (Fig 25).

Making the halo

Trace a pattern to make the angel's halo, and transfer the pattern to a piece of attractive wood ³⁄₈in (10mm) thick. Drill a ³⁄₁₆in (5mm) hole through the centre so that the tenon of the halo support can fit flush on the inside of the halo. Cut the pattern out using a scrollsaw. Use a belt sander to thin the halo at the top. Hand-sand the edges to round them over, or use a hand-held power tool, such as a Dremel, with a drum sander. Apply your chosen finish.

The halo support

Turn a small support for the halo. It must have a ³⁄₁₆in (5mm) diameter spigot on each end, to fit the halo and the central hub (Fig 26). The top of the support should be narrow to make it look graceful (Fig 27); the base of it must be small enough to fit between the wings on top of the central hub. Sand and apply finish to the halo support, then glue it to the central hub. Drill a ³⁄₃₂in (2.5mm) hole in the top of the halo and halo support for the finial to fit into.

Turning the finial

Select a contrasting piece of wood for the finial and mount it between centres. Use a small skew chisel to shape it to a long, narrow point, then cut a ball and a half-bead, making sure that the half-bead will fit within the halo. Cut a ³⁄₃₂in (2.5mm) diameter spigot at the lower end of the finial. Support the slender finial with a finger or a small piece of kitchen paper (Fig 28; see note on page 68). Part the finial off and glue it into the top of the halo support to complete the vase.

22 Using a push block on the tablesaw to cut the slots in the hub

23 Fill the slots temporarily with a scrap-wood shim, using hot-melt glue

24 The underside of the central hub has the same slope as the mouth of the vase

25 Glue the wings to the central hub. The internal spigot is also shown here

26 The halo support fits onto the central hub

27 The halo mounted on its support

28 Turning the finial

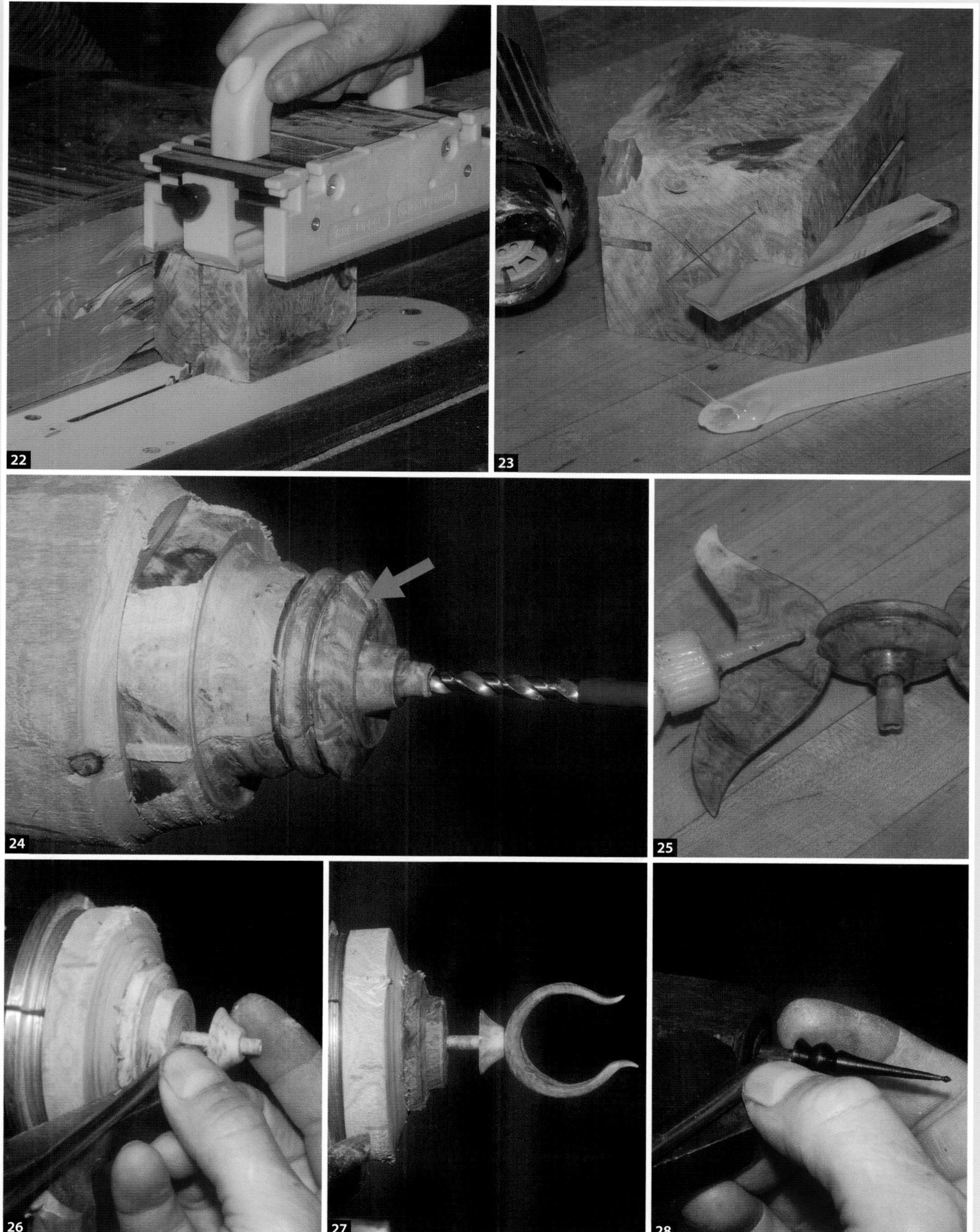
22
23
24
25
26
27
28

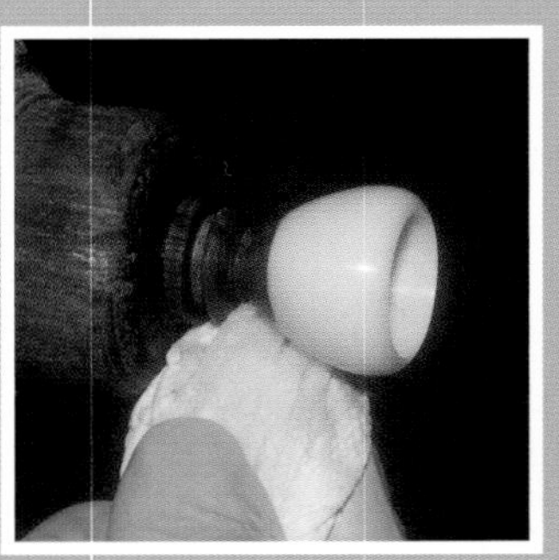

9 Ultra-Small Turnings

Ultra-small turnings – under 1in (25mm) in height or width – are a lot of fun to do, for several reasons. They are quick and easy to make. Your children will love them; they may want some for their dolls' houses. The added challenge of making something beautiful that is so small also contributes to the pleasure, and one of the biggest advantages of ultra-small turning is that you can use the smallest pieces of scrap wood that would otherwise be thrown away.

In this chapter we will turn three very small vessels. After completing them you should feel comfortable tackling almost any small turning project.

Form is paramount as all wood darkens or fades with time.

Richard Raffan

Bill of goods

- One tagua nut
- Any offcuts of attractive wood, such as tulipwood, walnut, maple or padauk
- Hardwood offcuts for glue blocks
- Cyanoacrylate (superglue) and hot-melt glue

Equipment

A set of miniature turning tools is useful for ultra-small turning. Crown and Henry Taylor, among others, make nice sets. I used a ¼in (6mm) round skew, which I made myself, for the vast majority of my initial roughing and shaping. High-speed steel can easily be purchased in ¼in (6mm) round stock and can be used to make excellent small skews; or you can improvise quite satisfactorily using 7⁄64in (2.8mm) and 11⁄64in (4.5mm) diameter nails (Fig 1).

Ring-cutting tool

You can easily make a ring-cutting tool from a piece of scrap metal about ⅛ x ½ x 6in (3 x 13 x 152mm).

I enjoy the intimacy of making small-scale work; there is something about cradling a piece in my hands that speaks volumes to me.

Mike Lee

Start by drilling a 5⁄16in (8mm) diameter hole ¼in (6mm) from each end (Fig 2a). Then use your bench grinder to remove the excess metal (Fig 2b). Grind the cutting edge to a 45° angle. Touch-up sharpening can be done with a small, conical diamond sharpening tool in a hand-held grinder.

Preparing stock

Turn some spigot glue blocks using scrap maple or other hardwood, and glue an assortment of attractive wood offcuts to them (Fig 3). This method allows you to use up every last bit of expensive wood left over from other projects.

1a and **b** Home-made round skews are very useful for ultra-small turning

2 Making the ring-cutting tool
(a) Drill two holes near the ends of the steel bar
(b) Grind away the shaded parts
Grind both cutting tips to a 45° angle on the underside

3 Glue blocks save you cutting spigots in your exotic material

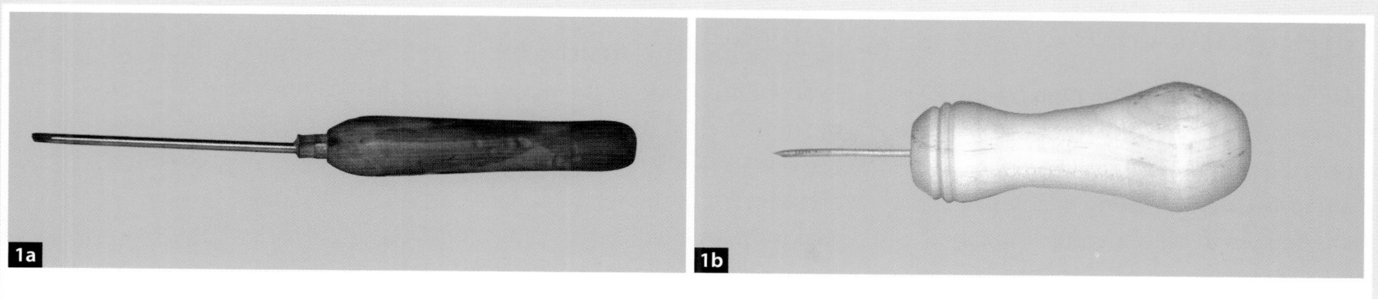

1a

1b

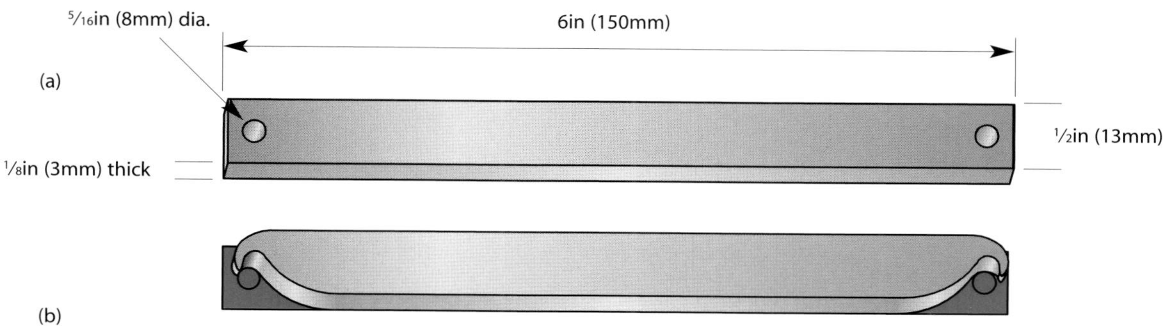
5⁄16in (8mm) dia.
6in (150mm)
(a)
½in (13mm)
⅛in (3mm) thick
(b)
Grind away the parts shaded red

2

3

Tagua-nut vase

This piece measures 1⅛in high by 1in diameter (28 x 25mm). Use hot-melt glue to attach the round nut to the end of a piece of scrap wood. Then, using a tablesaw and a mitre gauge, cut off the end of the tagua nut so that you have a flat spot for gluing. For the vase shown here I also glued on, with PVA, a piece of contrasting walnut to form a base.

● Tagua nut

The tagua nut is the dried seed pod of the tagua palm tree, which grows in the rainforests of Ecuador. Often called 'vegetable ivory', it can be used as a sustainable and legal substitute for elephant ivory. Nuts are usually 1–2in (25–50mm) long, with a small void in the centre.

Turning

Start by turning a spigot on a piece of scrap wood. Centre and glue a 1 x 1 x ½in (25 x 25 x 13mm) square of walnut onto this. When dry, glue the flat part of the tagua nut to the walnut with PVA. Mount this whole assembly, when dry, in your four-jaw chuck (Fig 4). In this photograph, the live centre is holding the tagua nut in place while the glue sets.

Use a small, sharp tool to make your workpiece round (Fig 5). Tagua nuts turn nicely, but only if you are gentle with them – aggressive or rough turning will cause the surface to tear out during the cut. Now you can turn the nut to a pleasing shape on the outside.

Hollowing the inside

Drill out the inside of the nut using a 21/64in (8.5mm) drill bit (Fig 6). Hollow the inside of the nut – in Fig 7 I am using a bent-end scraper, part of the set made by Henry Taylor. Cut to a uniform thickness of about 1/32–1/16in (0.8–1.5mm), which is not that difficult to achieve, but requires that you stop often to measure the thickness using callipers. Sand the inside as required.

Finish-shaping the outside

Do the final shaping of the outside of the turning after the inside has been turned and sanded. Carefully cut a small bead at the foot of the turning (Fig 8).

Finishing

Sanding on such very small turnings is considerably different from sanding on large vessels. On small turnings you can usually start with 220-grit sandpaper, but regard 220 grit as coarse when working on ultra-small turnings. Sand to at least 320 grit before applying your finish (Fig 9).

Part off using a thin parting tool, angling it slightly towards the tailstock so as to cut a slight depression in the base – this will ensure that the vase sits flat. Sand the bottom and apply finish.

One thing about creating shapes on the lathe – good or bad – they happen in a hurry.

Kip Christensen

4 Attaching the turning blank to its glue block

5 Tagua nuts cut cleanly if you work slowly and gently

6 Start the hollowing process by drilling out the inside. Electrical tape on the drill bit makes a good depth gauge

7 Hollow the inside with a round-nose scraper

8 Cut a small bead on the bottom of the vase and sand carefully

9 Apply finish while the turning is still on the lathe

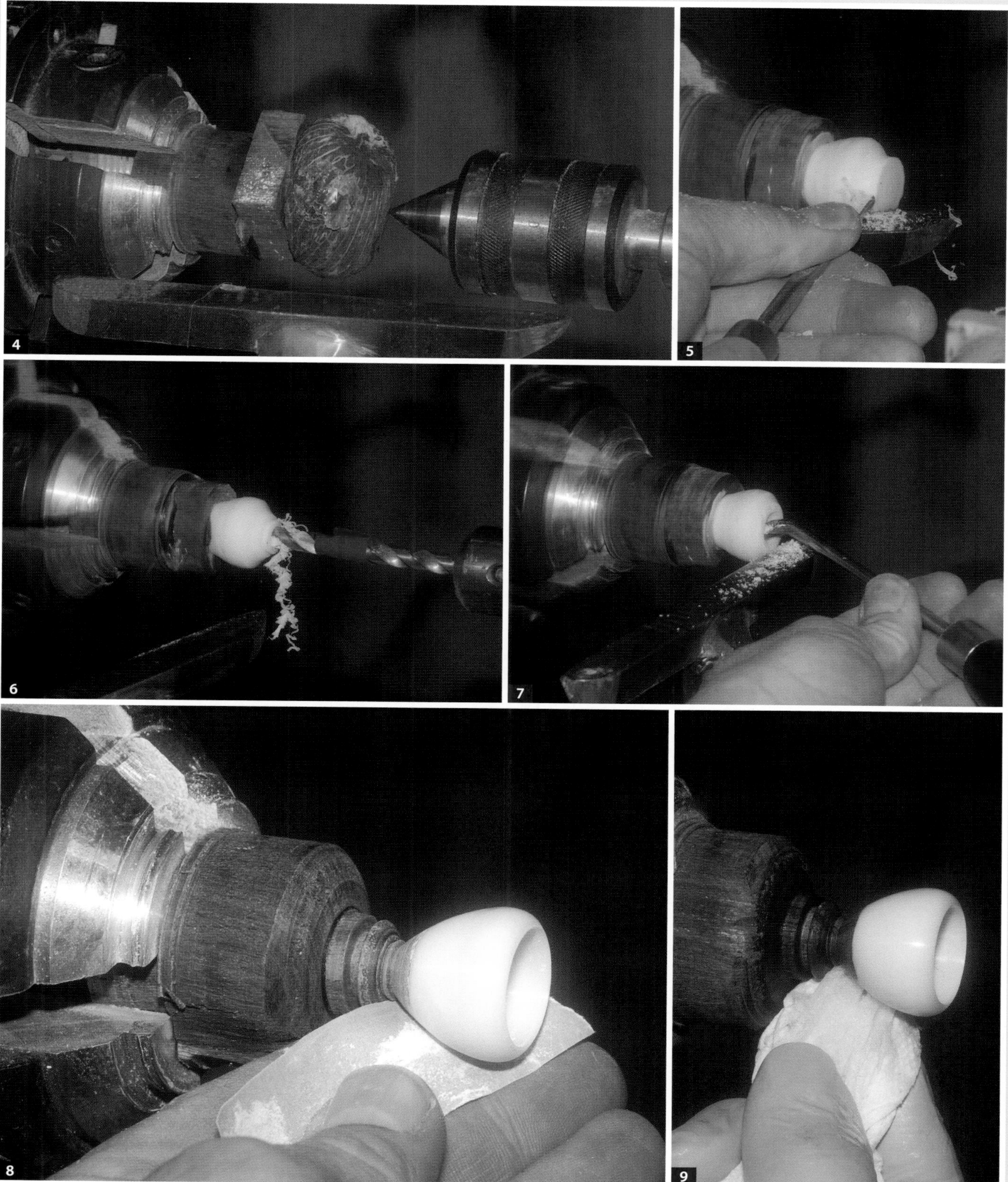
4
5
6
7
8
9

Tulipwood lidded vase

This little lidded vase is 1⁹⁄₁₆in high by ⁷⁄₈in diameter (40 x 22mm) (Fig 10). This is a pretty project that will give you practice in reverse-turning with a jam-fit chuck. The body of the vase is attractively figured tulipwood, and the black trim is ebony.

Preparation

Glue a 1 x 1 x ½in (25 x 25 x 13mm) piece of ebony to a piece of scrap wood that has a spigot turned on it. Once the PVA has set, attach a ¾in (19mm) cube of tulipwood with the grain running lengthwise, again using PVA. Once this has set, add a second piece of ebony the same size as the first.

Mount the spigot in the four-jaw chuck and turn the blank round (Fig 11). Here I am using a ⅜in (10mm) diameter bowl gouge. Use a gouge or skew to shape the outside of the main body of the vase (Fig 12). Be sure to leave the base oversize until the inside has been turned and sanded. Notice that my toolrest is always very close to the turning.

Hollowing the inside

Drill ⁷⁄₁₆in (11mm) deep. Hollow the inside with a gouge or round-nose scraper – in Fig 13 I am using a ⁷⁄₁₆in (11mm) spindle gouge. Use a small round-nose scraper for your finish cuts. Finish to a wall thickness of ¹⁄₃₂–¹⁄₁₆in (0.8–1.5mm), leaving a straight-sided wall for the top ⅛in (3mm) so that the lid can fit inside snugly. Sand and apply finish to the inside (Fig 14).

Finishing the outside

Use a small skew chisel to make a small bead at the foot of the vase (Fig 15). You will need good magnification (see below) if you are having any difficulty seeing the small detail. Sand the outside (Fig 16) and apply finish. Finally, part off the vase body using a thin parting tool; cut slowly, with the tool angled slightly towards the tailstock.

● Tip

Unless you have exceptionally good eyesight, magnification headgear is essential for really small work. Typical units have interchangeable lenses of 2x, 4x and 6x magnification. I suggest you buy all three, but be aware that with 6x magnification you will be working very close to the object. The units available from hobby stores are just as good for our purposes as the much more expensive ones that are designed for medical use; see Fig 14 on page 25 for an example.

10 Cross-section of the lidded vase

11 A small spindle gouge is nice for roughing out and doing detail work on a small vase

12 A small spindle gouge shaping the outside of the vase. Leave the bottom large until the inside has been cut

13 A small spindle gouge is used for roughing out the inside of the vase. A round-nose scraper is used for the finish cut

14 Sand the inside and apply finish

15 A small round skew can be used to cut a nice bead near the bottom

16 Sanding the outside

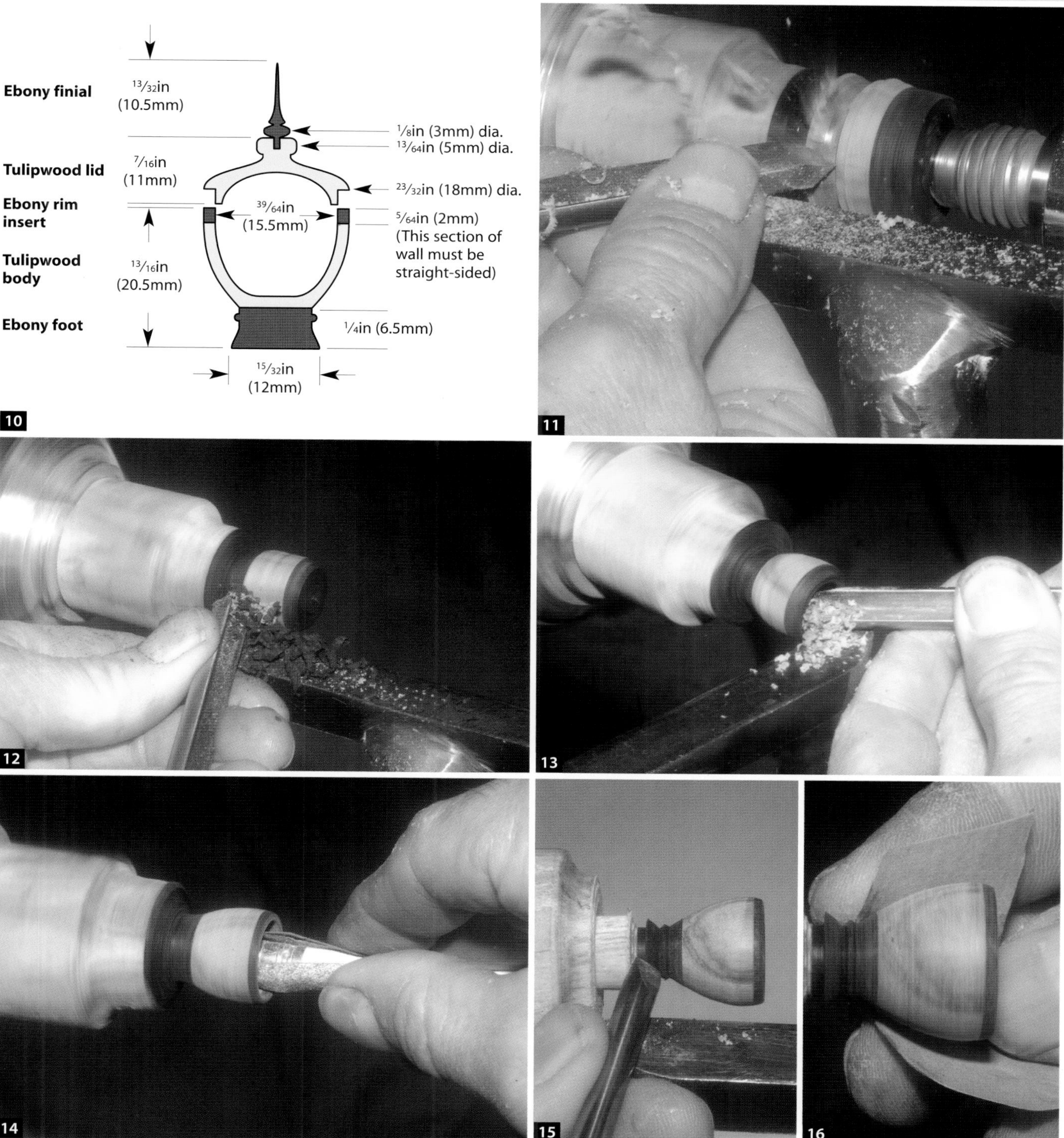

Ebony finial
13/32in (10.5mm)
1/8in (3mm) dia.
13/64in (5mm) dia.
Tulipwood lid
7/16in (11mm)
23/32in (18mm) dia.
Ebony rim insert
39/64in (15.5mm)
5/64in (2mm) (This section of wall must be straight-sided)
Tulipwood body
13/16in (20.5mm)
Ebony foot
1/4in (6.5mm)
15/32in (12mm)
10
11
12
13
14
15
16

Making the lid

The lid is made from a separate piece of tulipwood mounted on its own glue block. Turn a small spigot that will accurately fit into the ⅛in (3mm) straight rebate on the inside of the base. This should be a snug fit without being tight. Run the lathe slowly so that you can sand and apply finish to the bottom while it is still on the spigot (Fig 17). Shape the top of the vase with a ¼–½in (6–13mm) skew or small spindle gouge. Do as much shaping of the top as you can while it is still on the original glue block. Sand and apply finish to the inside of the lid, then part the lid off.

Reverse-mounting the lid

Use a piece of soft, wet wood to make a jam-fit chuck. Use a small skew, or a scraper with a straight edge on the left side, to cut a small rebate for the lid to fit into. This should be a snug fit, without being tight. Finish cutting the top (Fig 18). Note the live centre holding light pressure on the top. The indent caused by the live centre is not a problem, because a finial will be put here. Use a 1⁄16in (1.5mm) drill bit to form a shallow recess in the top of the lid for the finial. Sand and apply finish to the lid.

Making the finial

Mount a piece of ebony in the four-jaw chuck, orientated long grain. You will need to leave about 1–1½in (25–38mm) of ebony exposed. Reduce 1in (25mm) of the end of the ebony to approximately ¼in (6mm) diameter using a skew. This will get you used to working with the skew before you move on to the more difficult parts.

Set the lathe speed to 1000–2000rpm. Make sure that your lathe does not vibrate and that you are wearing a face shield. Using the small skew, slowly cut a gentle taper from the headstock toward the tailstock. When the ebony begins to get very narrow you might want to support it from the back with a finger, or with kitchen paper (Fig 19). About ½in (13mm) from the tip of the ebony, cut a small bead with the skew. Use the skew to cut a ⅛in (3mm) spigot. Measure carefully to make sure it will fit into the rebate cut in the top of the lid. Sand and apply finish, then part the finial off and glue it into the lid using a small amount of cyanoacrylate glue.

● Tip

A very safe way to support the finial is with a piece of kitchen paper about 1in (25mm) square, folded to ¼in (6mm) wide. If it catches in the work it will just tear away and do no damage to you or to the work.

17 Use the lid as a jam-chuck to sand and apply finish to the bottom of the vase

18 Finishing the top surface of the lid in a jam-fit chuck

19 Turning the finial, with finger support from behind

Woodturning offers an excellent outlet for anyone interested in creating work of utility or beauty. It is fast, fluid, therapeutic and allows a person to design on the fly.

Kip Christensen

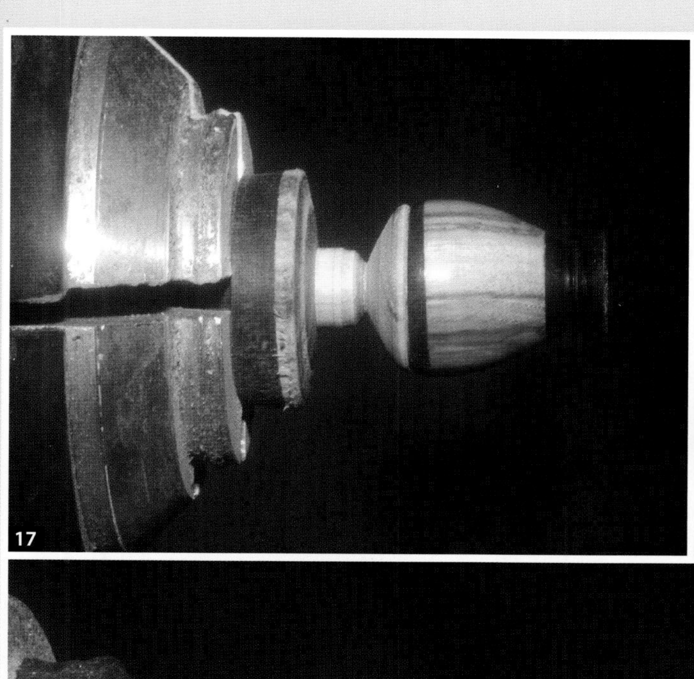
17

18

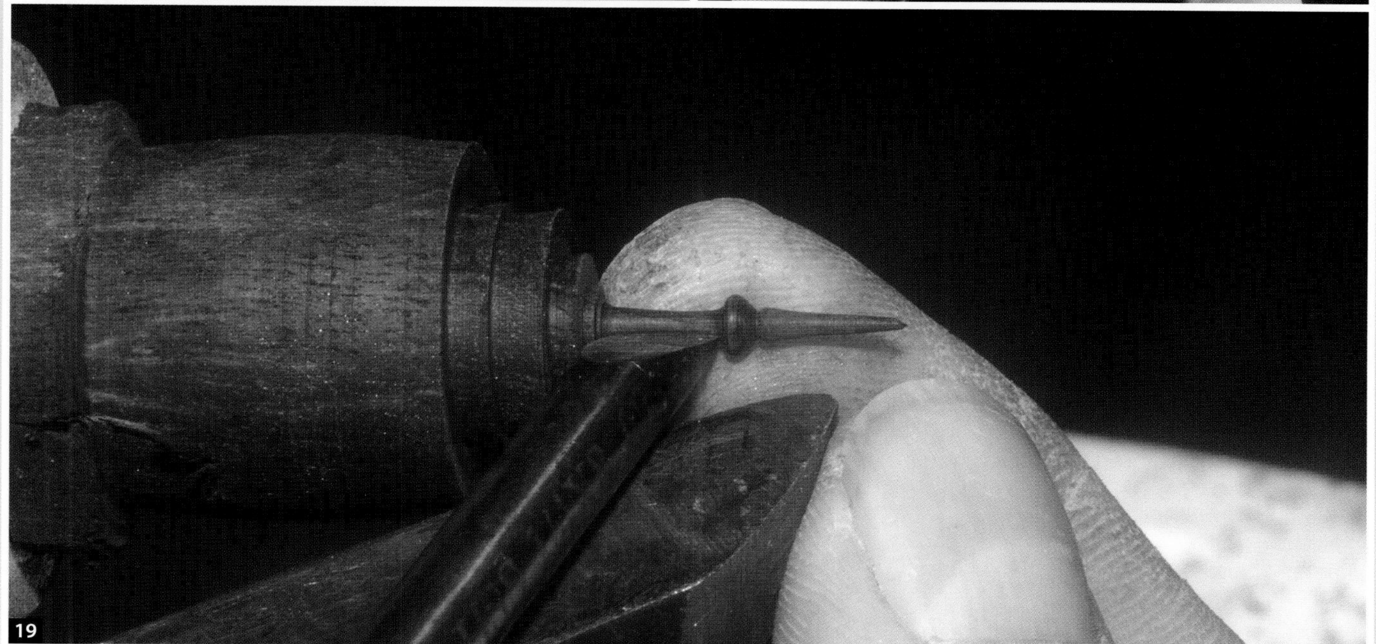
19

Ringed goblet

The goal of this project is to see how small you can make a ringed goblet – so good magnification is a key requirement here! You will need to use very good, tight-grained wood, possibly a bit oily. Ebony would be perfect for this project, but as it does not photograph well for me (everything just looks black), I have used tulipwood for the example illustrated here, which works just as well.

This goblet is 9⁄16in (14mm) tall. One of the goblets I made is 5⁄32in (4mm) tall, but you can probably make one much smaller. The longer the stem, the easier it is to make a ringed goblet. The difficult thing is making a short-stemmed ringed goblet.

Getting started

Mount a small piece of good-quality wood on the lathe. Turn a small spigot to 3⁄8in (10mm) diameter and 3⁄8in (10mm) long, and mount this in the four-jaw chuck. Use a very sharp, small skew chisel to shape the outside of the cup section. Do not make the base of the cup too narrow at this stage (Fig 20). Use the long-pointed tip of your home-made round skew to cut the inside of the cup, making sure the bottom is smooth. Reduce the cup part of the goblet to about 1⁄32in (1mm) thick. Sand and apply finish to the inside of the cup.

Shaping the outside of the cup

Finish shaping the outside base of the cup. Cut a small bead where it meets the stem (Fig 21). Here I am using an 11⁄64in (4.5mm) diameter skew made from a medium-sized nail. (The bend in the skew is not necessary – it was designed for another project.)

Making the ring

Use the ring-cutting tool described on page 82 to form the ring. Start by making a little working room at the base of the cup, using a small skew, then use the ring-cutting tool slowly and gently to cut the top side of the ring. Cut a little less than halfway through (Fig 22). Sand the top half of the ring inside and out – once the ring is cut free you will not be able to sand it.

Now use your small skew to clear some space on the bottom side of the ring. Do not cut the stem of the goblet to size at this stage – this should only be done after the ring has been completed. Use the other end of the ring-cutting tool to cut the bottom side of the ring. Cut slowly and gently to slightly less than halfway through (Fig 23). Stop and sand the underside of the ring inside and out. Cut a little further on the top of the ring and then sand again (Fig 24). Notice how the folded sandpaper is being used to sand the inside of the ring. Now finish cutting the very short distance to break the ring through. Almost all of the ring will have been sanded before being cut free.

Shaping the stem

Use your 7⁄64in (2.8mm) home-made skew to shape the stem. Although this skew is unprepossessing to look at, it is very sharp. Support the goblet from behind while you are cutting (Fig 25). If you are careful, and cut gently on good wood, you can make the stem very thin; in this case it is approximately 3⁄32in (2.5mm) diameter. However, it is possible to go considerably thinner than this with good wood and a sharp skew.

Finishing the goblet

Sand and apply finish while the goblet is still on the lathe. Use a small piece of kitchen paper to apply finish with the lathe turning fairly slowly. Be careful not to allow the paper to be taken in by the turning. Part the goblet free from the stock (Fig 26), angling the parting tool slightly towards the top of the goblet so that the base will be slightly concave.

See how small you can make your turnings (Fig 27) – after a little practice my examples will seem huge!

20 Use a small skew to cut both the inside and outside of the cup

21 Use a small skew or a thin spindle gouge to shape the bottom of the cup

22 Using the home-made ring-cutter to shape the top half of the ring

23 Use the other end of the ring-cutter to cut the bottom half of the ring

24 Sand the inside and outside of the ring before parting it free

25 Use a small home-made skew to shape the stem of the goblet

26 Parting off the finished goblet. This one is 9⁄16in (14mm) tall

27 A ringed goblet only 5⁄32in (4mm) tall – why not try one smaller still?

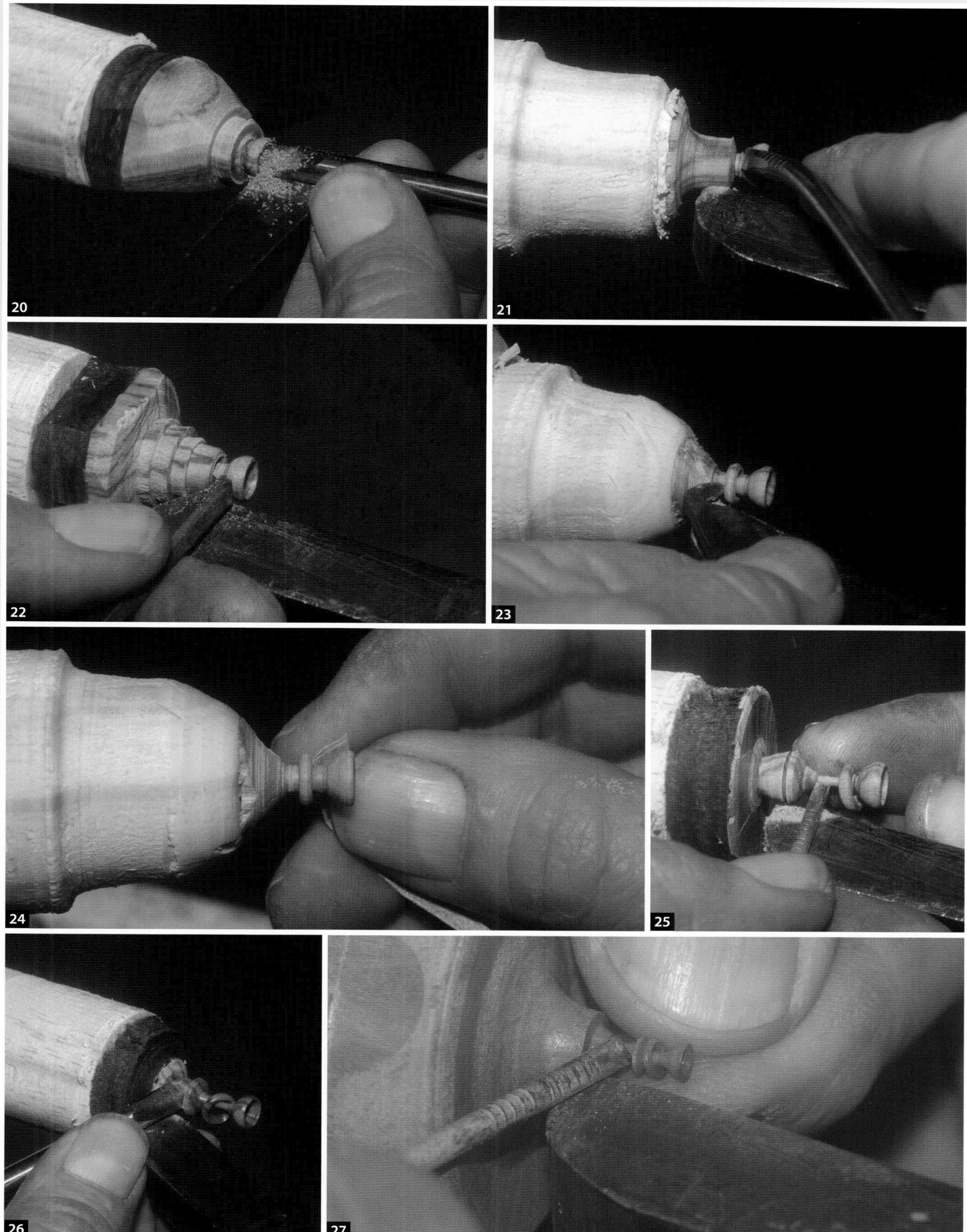
20
21
22
23
24
25
26
27

10 Pedestal Table

In this chapter we will turn a beautiful three-legged circular jardinière table that stands 4¾in (120mm) high and has a segmented top. This project was inspired by Tom Pockley, from Kent, England. Tom teaches woodturning and is on the Register of Professional Turners. His table is a quarter-scale reproduction, 10in (254mm) high.

This project introduces two advanced procedures which we have not met before: making segmented rings, and creating mortise and tenon joints for the legs. The segmented rings can be made using a home-made cutting board on the tablesaw. The mortise and tenon joints involve a couple of straightforward, step-by-step procedures.

We owe it to the trees we use to show the beauty of the wood that is within them.

Tom Pockley

Bill of goods

- Walnut, 3 x 2 x 24in (75 x 50 x 610mm)
- Maple burl, 1 x 1½ x 24in (25 x 38 x 610mm)
- Maple dowel, ½ x ½ x 4in (13 x 13 x 100mm)
- For the pedestal: walnut, ½ x ½ x 8in (13 x 13 x 200mm); note extra length to keep fingers away from saw blade
- For the legs: walnut, 9 x 2½ x 1in (228 x 63.5 x 25mm)
- Hot-melt glue and scrap wood for temporary hole-filling
- Spray adhesive
- Cyanoacrylate glue (superglue)

Getting started

Refer to Fig 1 to see how the various parts of the table relate to one another. The centre and edge of the table top are made separately by the segmented method; the central pedestal is a delicate but straightforward piece of spindle turning; while the legs involve no turning at all.

Making the table top

The 12-segment ring

The most challenging part of this project, for those unused to segmented turning, will be the two rings that make up the table top. The 12-segment ring that makes up the outside edge of the table top is made using a cutting board (Fig 2), which is described in detail in my previous book (see the box, below right). The key feature of the cutting board is the stock guide, a sliding fence which can be adjusted by two screws to feed the wood into the tablesaw at the correct angle.

The 15° angle required at each end of each segment is found by making a few test cuts on the tablesaw. First cut three test segments and arrange them between the blade and stock of a try-square to make a 90° angle. At the first attempt there will probably be a gap between the segments, either on the inside or the outside of the ring. If the gap is on the outside of the ring, move the head of the stock guide on the cutting board inwards. You should do the opposite if the gap is on the inside. The memory device for this is '*in* for *out*side gap and *out* for *in*side gap'. Make the adjustment and do another test cut. When you have no gap, and the three segments make an accurate 90° angle, cut 12 new test segments, pull them together with a hose clamp, and inspect for the smallest gap. Adjust again and make another test cut.

Once you are cutting perfect rings on scrap wood, you are ready to cut 12 segments from your chosen piece of maple. Start with a piece 1 x ¾ x 18in (25 x 19 x 460mm). You will use approximately 12in (300mm) of the stock; the additional length is to keep your fingers away from the saw blade. Set the stop block of the cutting board so that the segment length is 1¼in (32mm). Cut 12 segments, flipping the stock over each time before making the next cut.

● Tip

Further segmented turning projects, and more detailed information on the techniques involved, can be found in my previous book, *Segmented Turning: A Complete Guide* (Guild of Master Craftsman Publications, 2003).

1 Details of the miniature pedestal table

2 A fully adjustable cutting board allows easy cutting of segments of any size or angle

(a) Side elevation

2 29/32in (74mm) dia.

1/4in (6mm)

1/2in (13mm)

43/64in (17mm) dia.

19/64in (7.5mm) dia.

7/32in (5.5mm) dia.

3 7/16in (87.5mm)

4 3/4in (120mm)

13/32in (10.5mm) dia.

1 1/32in (26mm)

1 1/32in (26mm)

(b) Plan of top

2 29/32in (74mm) dia.

1/4in (6mm)

3/8in (10mm)

5/64in (2mm)

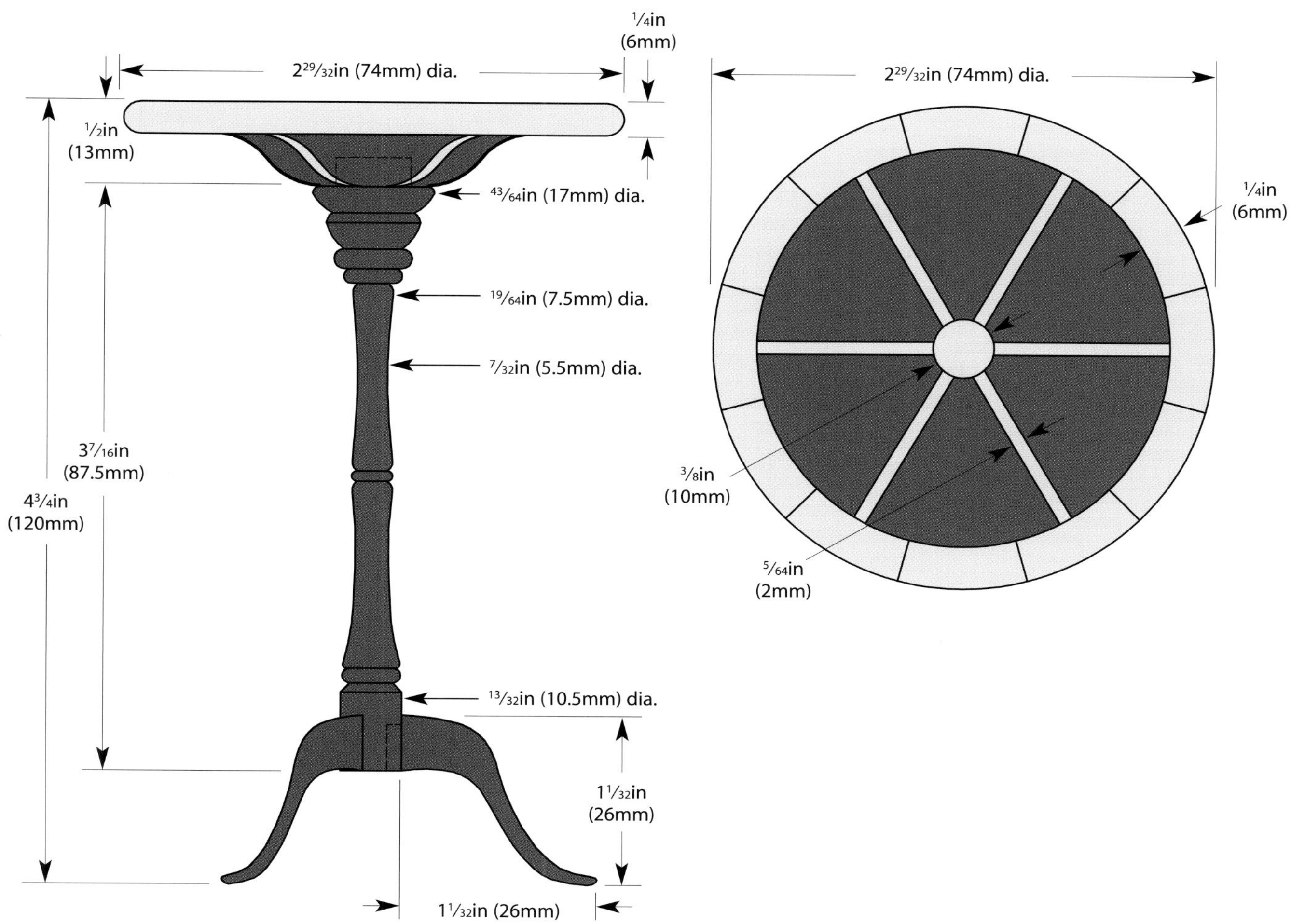

1

2

The six-segment ring

The six-segment ring, which forms the main part of the table top, is made from walnut. Cut six segments of walnut 1½ x ¾ x 6¼in (38 x 19 x 158mm). The ring is made this long so that it will be easy to grip with a four-jaw chuck. Tilt your tablesaw blade to 30° and set the saw fence so that it cuts the bottom edge of the wood closest to the saw blade. Make a cut in some spare stock to begin with, then turn the stock end for end and make a second cut on the other side. This will give you a 6¼in (158mm) length of wood that has a 30° angle cut on each side of it. Adjust the saw tilt by trial and error until you make a perfect ring, then cut six pieces of your chosen walnut with a 30° cut on each side. Cut 1⁄16in (1.5mm) thick maple spacers to go between the six walnut pieces.

Assembling the rings

Use two hose clamps on the tall ring and one on the maple ring. Assemble the glued segments into a ring and pull them together with the hose clamp (Fig 3).

The maple ring needs to be made flat after the glue has cured; either sand it to thickness – about 7⁄16–½in (11–13mm) at this stage – or turn both sides flat and parallel to each other. The six-segment ring will be turned flat on the lathe.

Turning the six-segment ring

Mount the six-segment ring between centres on your lathe, and cut a spigot that will fit into your four-jaw chuck (this can be seen in Fig 7). Mount it in the four-jaw chuck and use a parting tool to cut the tailstock end flat (Fig 4).

Drill a ⅜in (10mm) hole through the centre of the six-segment ring (Fig 5). This will later be filled with a maple plug or spigot for the sake of neatness.

Filling the centre

Turn an accurate ⅜in (10mm) diameter maple spigot that is as long as the six-segment ring (Fig 6), making sure that the spigot is the same diameter throughout its length. Take the spigot off the lathe and test that it fits into the hole of the six-segment ring; it should fit snugly without being tight. Apply glue to the spigot and insert it into the ring (Fig 7). Remount the six-segment ring and part off the excess maple spigot. Re-true the tailstock end of the six-segment ring.

3 The two rings assembled with the aid of hose clamps

4 Trimming the end of the blank with the parting tool

5 Using a Jacobs chuck in the tailstock to drill the spigot hole through the centre of the six-segment ring

6 Turning the spigot to plug the hole in the table top

7 The spigot glued in and ready for trimming to length

> *Forms and textures that can be held in the palm of one's hand evoke a tactile response that even the most hardened 'big bowl' turner can relate to.*
>
> *Mike Lee*

PREFERRED BY
3 TO 1
PROFESSIONALS
3
4
5
6
7

Joining the two rings

Mount the 12-segment maple ring in the four-jaw chuck. Very accurately cut a rebate in the maple ring the exact diameter of the six-segment ring. Apply PVA glue to the inside of the rebate. Press the six-segment ring into the rebate. Allow this glue to set for 24 hours (Fig 8).

Turning the table top

Mount the whole ring assembly on the four-jaw chuck and turn the table top round (Fig 9). Cut or sand the tailstock end of the table flat; this area will become the underside of the table top. Use a Forstner bit to drill a ½in (13mm) hole 3⁄16in (4.5mm) deep into the underside (Fig 10). This rebate is for the pedestal to fit into. Be careful not to drill too deep.

Using a thin parting tool, cut in where the top surface of the table will be, around ½in (13mm) from the tailstock end (arrowed in Fig 11). Make sure that the thickness of the table top is enough for the hole in the bottom not to come through.

Use a bowl gouge to reduce the thickness of the table from the underside, except for a ¼in (6mm) margin around the rebate in the centre. When finished, the table top should be about 3⁄16in (5mm) thick at the edge, and ¼–5⁄16in (6–8mm) further in. Use a round-nose scraper to cut the gentle cove where the flat part of the table curves up to the much thicker central boss which houses the rebate for the pedestal.

Use your thin parting tool to cut approximately 1in (25mm) deep on the upper side of the table top (Fig 12). The purpose of this is to give you a clear working area so that you can then round the edge of the table top, using a skew chisel laid flat on the toolrest. Sand the bottom and the edge. Apply finish to the underside of the table (Fig 13), then part off the table top from the lathe.

Finishing the table top

Make a temporary spigot from scrap hardwood, ¼in (6mm) in diameter, to fit into the rebate for the pedestal in the underside of the table top. This must be a good snug fit, without being so tight that there is a risk of breaking the table top. Fit the table top onto the spigot, and with the lathe rotating slowly, apply your chosen finish (Fig 14).

The more you understand about design principles the more likely you are to be able to break the rules and still be successful.

Ray Key

8 The two rings glued together ready for turning

9 Rounding the blank for the table top

10 Drilling the recess for the pedestal

11 Trimming the underside of the table top. The arrow shows the position of the top surface which has been cut in with a parting tool

12 Creating clearance around the table top prior to rounding the edge

13 Using kitchen paper to apply finish to the underside of the table top

14 Power-sanding the top surface with the lathe set to a low speed

3 TO 1
PROFESSIONAL
8
9
10
11
12
13
14

Making the pedestal

The pedestal will have three mortises cut in it, which can be done by a very simple procedure. The secret to simplicity is to cut the mortises with a router while the stock still has flat sides.

Start by cutting a triangular prism with 60° angles. You will only have to cut two of the angles, and the third will automatically be correct. Cut some scrap wood about 1¼in (32mm) square and 12in (305mm) long, and cut the walnut blank for the pedestal to the same dimensions.

Set the angle of the tablesaw blade to 60°. Adjust the fence of the tablesaw so that the saw blade just barely touches the bottom corner of the wood. Use a push stick to feed the test stock when making the first cut. Now turn the test stock end for end and make another 60° cut, but this time there is no need to cut through the last few inches of the stock. Cut the triangle free at the red mark (Fig 15), thus leaving a triangle with three 60° angles. Use callipers to measure the width of each side of the triangle. If one side is wider or narrower than the other two you will need to adjust the tilt of the saw blade and make further test cuts until it is right. Once the angle is correct, cut the blank for the pedestal to the same shape.

● Caution

Always use a push stick when cutting stock on the tablesaw – your fingers need never go near the blade.

Cutting the mortises

Draw bisecting lines from each 60° angle; these will give you the centre of the wood. Use a compass to draw a ⅜in (10mm) circle from the centre of the triangle; this will be the final diameter of the foot of the pedestal, to which the legs will be attached. Make a mark 5/32in (4mm) inside the drawn circle, indicating the depth of the mortise cut.

Fit a ⅛in (3mm) diameter spiral-cutting straight bit in your router. Set the router so that it cuts to the correct depth – 5/32in (4mm) inside the circumference of the circle drawn on the end of the stock. Set your fence so that the router bit will cut into the centre of each face of the triangle, and set a stop block so that you can make a cut that is ¼in (6mm) long. Hold the triangle firmly against the fence while you slowly advance the wood towards the stop block. Making sure that you keep your fingers well away from the router, make the three cuts on one end (Fig 16).

Temporary mortise fillers

The mortises must be filled until the turning is completed; if they were left open, the trailing edge would be bound to split out during the turning process. Use hot-melt glue to fix the temporary spacers into the mortise (Fig 17).

15 Cutting the 60° angle on the tablesaw. There is no need to cut further than the arrow marked on the stock

16 Cutting the leg mortises on the router table

17 The mortises filled with temporary shims

Turning the pedestal

Turn the triangular blank to a cylinder (Fig 18), turning it end for end so that you do not have to bring the tool too close to the spur drive. Carefully cut a $\frac{1}{4}$in (6mm) diameter spigot on the top end of the pedestal; this should fit snugly into the rebate on the bottom of the table top.

Make some small beads and coves near the top (Fig 19). The miniature gouges from Henry Taylor and Crown are very good for making small coves. Use a small skew to cut a bead at the midpoint of the pedestal (Fig 20). Make a pencil mark $\frac{3}{32}$in (2.5mm) above the top of the mortise (visible in Fig 21); this is where the top of the leg will come. Use a beading tool or skew to cut the bottom of the pedestal to the correct diameter (Fig 21). Stop and check often that you are not cutting away too much of the mortise. Using a round-nose scraper, make a long cove on either side of the central bead.

Finishing the pedestal

Sand and apply finish while the pedestal is still on the lathe (Fig 22). Remove the temporary mortise spacers by using a hairdryer to warm the spacers for a couple of seconds. Lift the spacers out and clean all the glue out of the mortise.

Making the legs

Prepare some walnut stock slightly thicker than $\frac{1}{4}$in (6mm). Note that the legs on this table have shoulders that extend about $\frac{1}{32}$in (1mm) past the mortise. Cut at least six pieces of stock $2\frac{1}{2}$in (65mm) long and about $\frac{3}{4}$in (20mm) wide – the extra pieces are for making test cuts. Cut one end of each piece to a 45° angle (Fig 23) so that the grain of the wood runs in the long direction of the leg; this is essential for the sake of strength.

Cutting the tenons

Set the height of the saw blade to just slightly less than the depth of the mortise in your pedestal. Set the tablesaw fence against the leg stock, then move the fence toward the blade a very small amount to create the shoulder of the tenon. Roughly $\frac{1}{32}$in (0.8mm) must be removed from each side, but trial and error is the only way to get an accurate fit. For safety's sake you must always use a push stick to move the work past the saw blade. Make a cut on both sides of one of your spare pieces, then test the fit of the tenon in the mortise. Adjust the blade in and out until you have a perfect fit, then cut three pieces for the three legs.

18 Rounding the blank for the pedestal

19 Detailing the top of the pedestal. The spigot that fits into the table top can be seen on the right

20 Forming the bead halfway up the pedestal

21 Turning the bottom end of the pedestal. The pencil mark indicates the position of the top of the leg

22 Applying finish to the pedestal

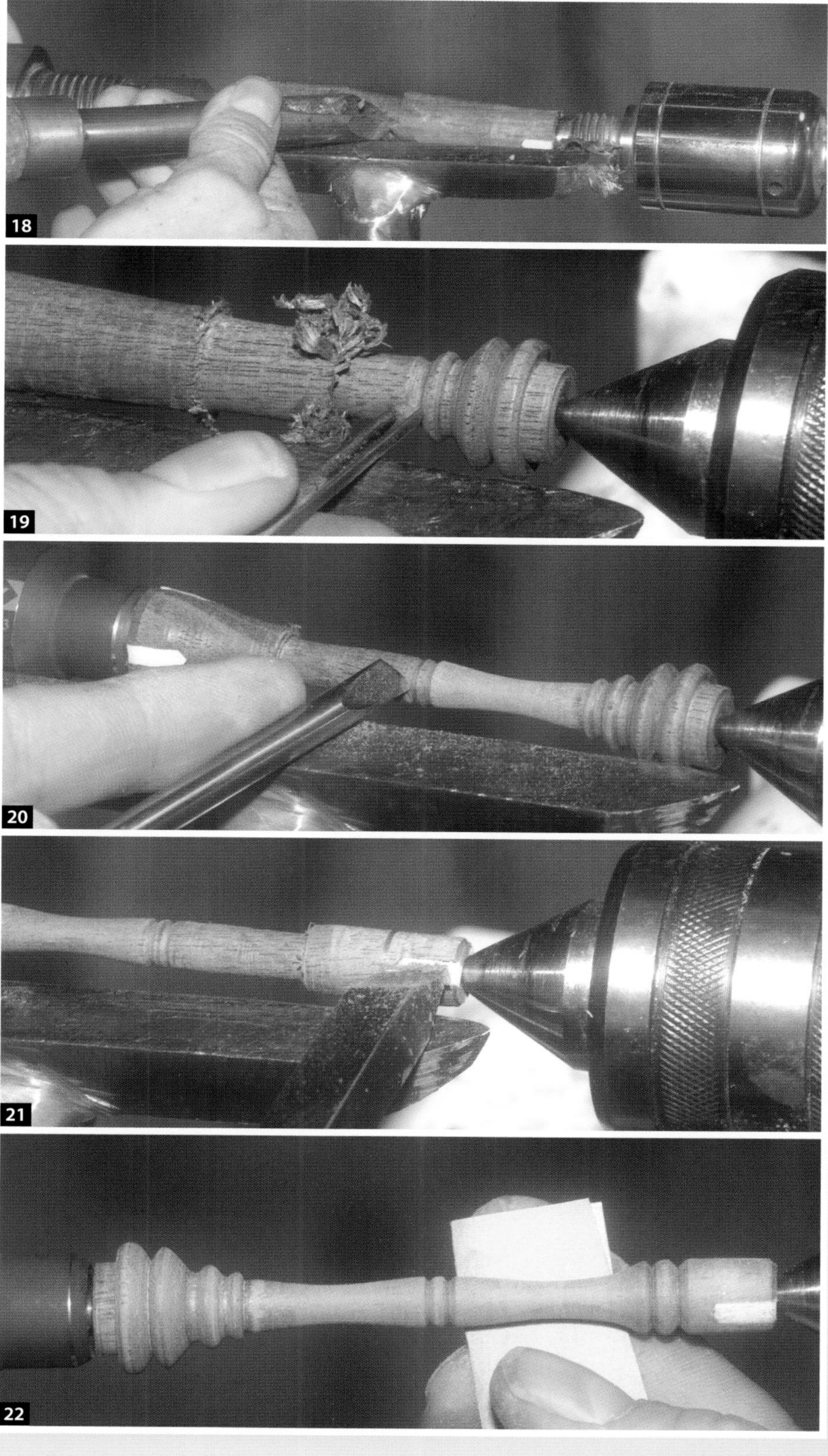
18
19
20
21
22

Preparing to shape the legs

In order to make all three legs identical, it is best to cut them at the same time. Join them temporarily with spots of hot-melt glue (Fig 24). Make sure the glue is very hot and that you use only a very small amount. All three tenon edges must be flat to the table.

Applying the pattern

Make a photocopy of the leg drawing, and attach this to the wood stack using spray adhesive, making sure that the edge of the drawing is flush with the tenon shoulder on the edge of the stock (Fig 25).

Cutting the legs

Use a scrollsaw to cut the outline of the legs, keeping just outside the line the entire way (Fig 26).

Cut out a 5/64in (2mm) notch from the top of the tenon (Fig 27), which will allow the leg to overlap the top of the mortise.

Shaping the legs

For this stage you will need effective magnification and a comfortable chair to work in. Use a sanding drum on a rotary tool to round the edges so that the leg looks delicate (Fig 28).

Do the final sanding by hand (Fig 29). Notice that the grain of the wood runs in exactly the same direction as the leg.

Final assembly

If the cyanoacrylate you are using comes with a separate accelerator, spray a small amount of accelerator onto the spigot at the top of the pedestal, and place a drop of glue in the rebate on the bottom of the table top. Insert the pedestal into the rebate and hold in position until the glue sets. Spray a small amount of accelerator into one of the mortises at the bottom of the pedestal. Apply a small amount of glue to the tenon of the leg, insert the leg and hold in place until the glue sets; repeat for each leg (Fig 30).

● Caution

When using cyanoacrylate (superglue), always wear latex gloves so there is no risk of sticking your fingers to the assembly.

Final finish

Apply the final finish to the top and bottom of the table top, the pedestal and the legs. I prefer to use a high-gloss lacquer, sprayed on in a thin coat and allowed to set for about an hour before applying the next coat (Fig 31).

Fig 32 shows the completed table.

Having a focused body of work is important to me. Converging efforts in one direction with gradual change, shows me the greater path. I may have the ability to make many things which are all good, yet I need only to do one of them well.

Jacques Vesery

23 Cutting the ends of the leg blanks at 45°

24 Use hot-melt glue to join the three leg blanks together for cutting out

25 The leg pattern glued to the leg blanks

26 Sawing the legs to shape

27 Notching the top of the tenon

28 A small drum sander rounds the edges of the legs

29 Hand-sanding the leg to its final finish

30 Gluing the legs into their mortises

31 Three thin coats of sprayed-on lacquer complete the table

32 The finished pedestal table.

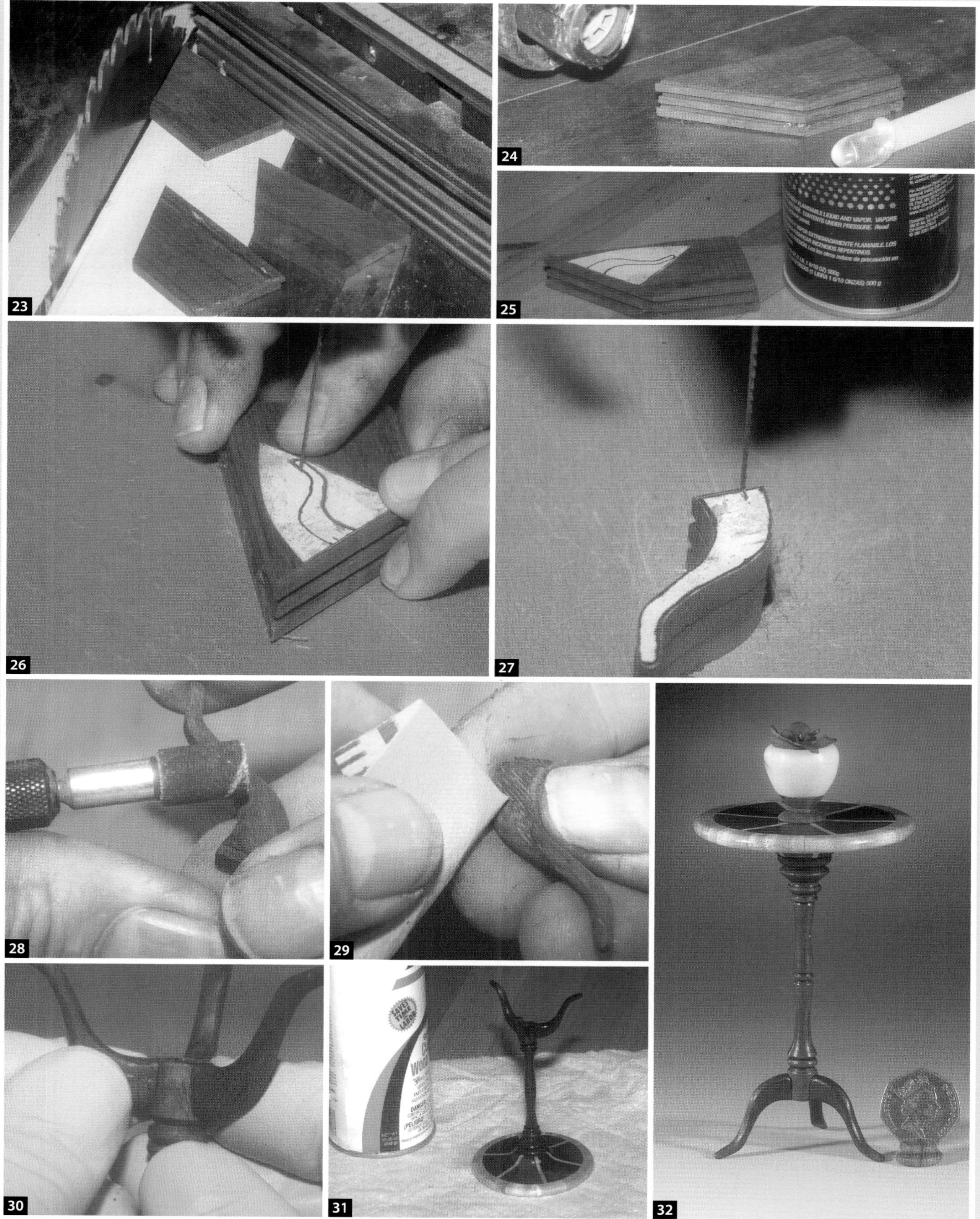

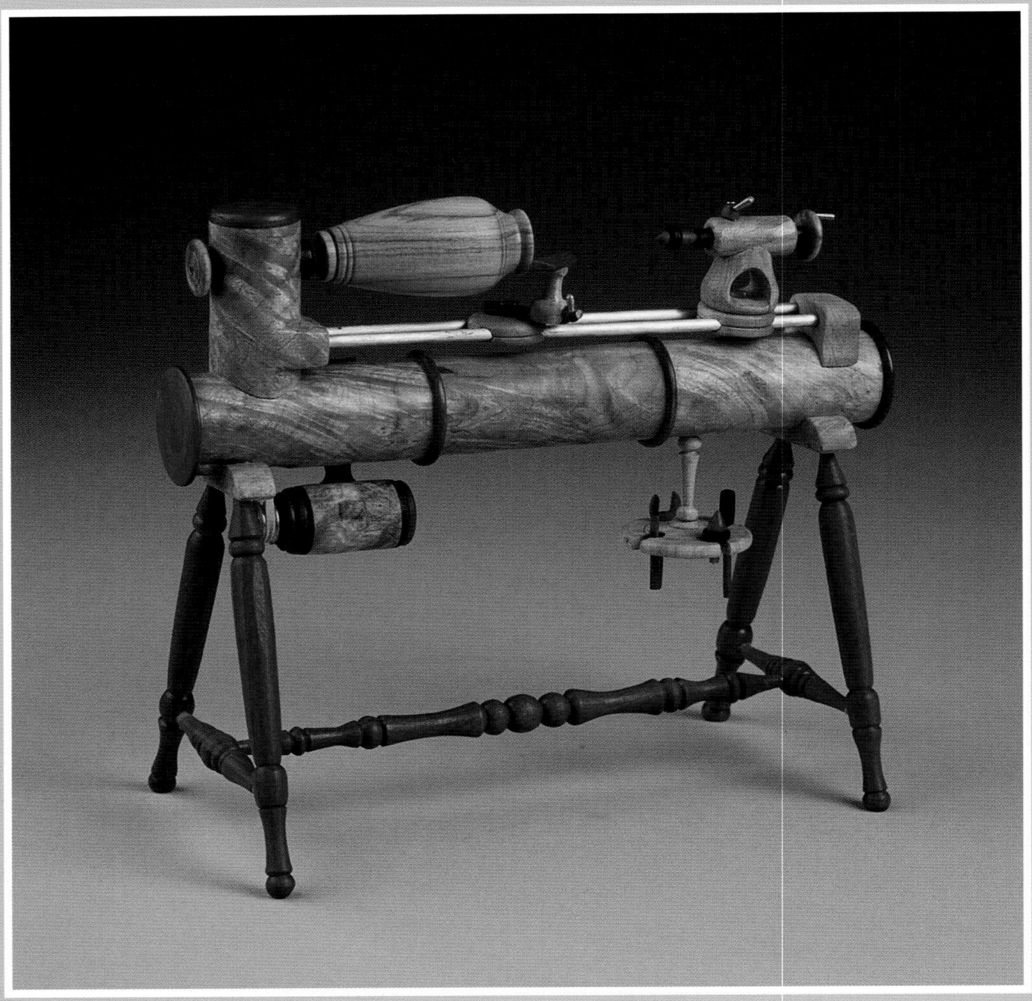

11 Miniature Lathe

In this chapter we will make a lovely little lathe. This project is derived from a full-size model of a lathe in the Smithsonian Institution, Washington, DC, which was a collaborative project by the Glendale Woodturners Guild of Glendale, California, made for the American Association of Woodturners' 1999 Symposium in Tacoma, Washington. Their lathe is 34in (864mm) tall; ours will be 8in (203mm).

Although I do make larger pieces,
I am drawn to small work. I like to think
of small turnings as 'shelf jewellery'.

Art Liestman

Bill of goods

- Maple burl, 2 x 2 x 14in (50 x 50 x 355mm)
- Padauk, 2 x 2 x 6in (50 x 50 x 152mm)
- Padauk, 1/2 x 1/2 x 24in (13 x 13 x 609mm)
- Tulipwood, 1/2 x 1/2 x 4in (13 x 13 x 100mm)
- Ebony, 1/2 x 1/2 x 4in (13 x 13 x 100mm)
- For the vase, tulipwood or other attractive wood, 1/2 x 1/2 x 3in (13 x 13 x 75mm)
- Hardwood offcuts to make glue blocks
- 1/8in (3mm) brass rod, 2in (50mm) long
- Two 1/8in (3mm) brass nails, around 3/16in (5mm) long
- Rubber band for drive belt
- Two brass tubes, 1/16in (1.5mm) diameter by 10in (255mm) long
- PVA glue

Getting started

Although this project looks daunting, it breaks down into a number of separate subassemblies which are not particularly complicated in themselves. Fig 1 shows the general layout of the whole piece; some of the individual sections will be illustrated in more detail as we come to them.

This project requires many of the turnings to have pre-drilled holes, which must be drilled while the stock is still square. These should be temporarily filled with wooden dowels and hot-melt glue so that the wood around the holes will not tear out during turning. Once the turning is completed, the hot-melt glue can be heated in a microwave oven for 6–12 seconds and then easily removed.

Initial glue-up

Glue up the stock for the lathe bed and headstock. The stock material for the lathe bed should be 2in (50mm) square. You will need three maple blocks, 3in (75mm) long, plus four squares of contrasting red padauk, 1/16in (1.5mm) thick. The red squares will be placed between the three maple sections and at both ends. A waste block is then added after the red square at each end.

The headstock is made from 1 1/2in (38mm) square stock. The padauk is 1/16in (1.5mm) thick and the maple body should be at least 2in (50mm) longer than the finished height of the headstock – long enough for a 1 1/4in (32mm) Forstner bit to be fully engaged in the wood in order to form the curved surface which fits over the lathe bed. Add 1/2in (13mm)-thick glue blocks at both ends.

The main part of the motor is maple, 1 3/8in (35mm) square by 2 3/8in (60mm) long, with thin veneers of ebony and padauk added at the ends for contrast. A non-functioning pulley could also be made as part of the glue-up, but I chose to make a freely rotating brass pulley instead.

Hold the pieces in a straight line while gluing by clamping them in a V-shaped trough (Fig 2). Line the trough with foil or plastic so the blank does not stick to it.

1 General arrangement of the miniature lathe

2 Gluing up the blank for the lathe bed, using a 'hog trough' to hold the pieces in line

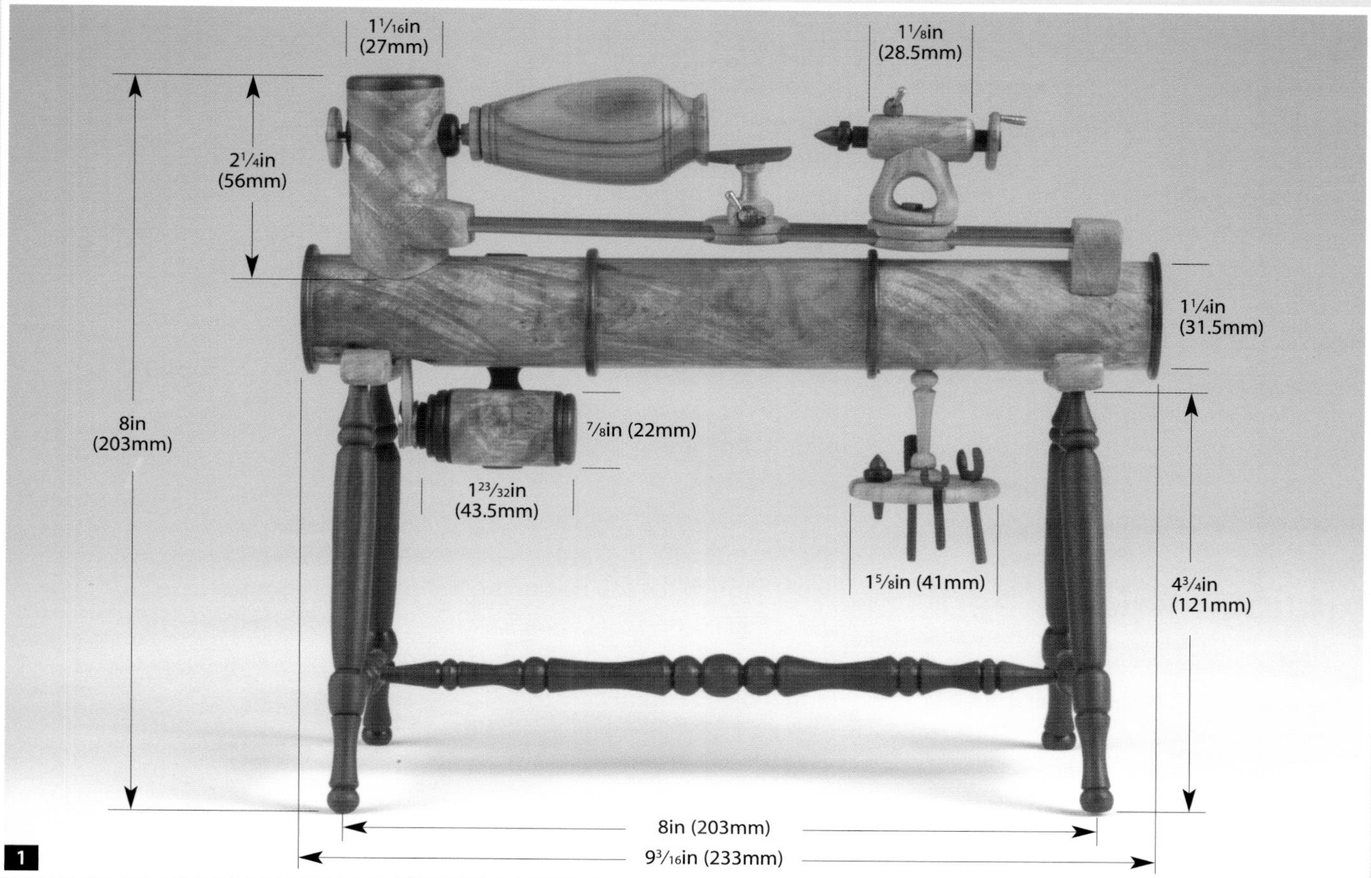

1 1/16in (27mm)

1 1/8in (28.5mm)

2 1/4in (56mm)

8in (203mm)

1 1/4in (31.5mm)

7/8in (22mm)

1 23/32in (43.5mm)

1 5/8in (41mm)

4 3/4in (121mm)

8in (203mm)

9 3/16in (233mm)

1

2

Drilling the initial holes

The lathe bed must have two holes drilled into it while the stock is still square. Drill a 1/2in (12.5mm) hole, 1in (25mm) from the headstock end of the lathe. The drive belt will go through this hole from the motor to the headstock pulley. Drill a hole 1/8in diameter by 1/4in deep (3 x 6mm) on the underside of the lathe bed, 1in (25mm) from the tailstock end, for the suspended toolholder. Temporarily fill these two holes with plugs made from scrap wood. These are glued in with hot-melt glue, so they can be removed once the turning is complete.

Turning the lathe bed

Mount the lathe bed turning blank between centres and turn it to a cylinder. Turn a spigot on one end to fit your four-jaw chuck (Fig 3). Remount the blank in the four-jaw chuck by means of the spigot. Turn the entire blank to 1 5/16in (33mm) diameter using a flat-edged tool such as a skew or a beading tool. Then, leaving the red inserts at this diameter, reduce the burl maple to 1 1/4in (31.5mm) diameter. Part off the tailstock end, sand and apply your chosen finish. Then part off the headstock end.

Making the headstock

The headstock is shown in Fig 4. Drill four holes into the headstock turning blank while it is still square. The two 5/32in (4mm) diameter holes are drilled 3/8in (10mm) deep (Fig 5); the larger hole for the headstock spindle goes all the way through. The fourth hole is the large one, 1 1/4in (32mm) diameter, which forms the curve at the base of the headstock where it fits over the cylindrical lathe bed. The centre of this hole lies 2 5/8in (67mm) from the top edge of the headstock.

Place the headstock blank between centres and turn it to a cylinder (Fig 6). Turn a spigot on the top of the headstock and mount the turning in your four-jaw chuck. Turn the headstock to 1in (25mm) diameter, except for an area 1/8in (3mm) either side of the two holes for the bed bars. Sand and apply finish to the top part of the headstock. Use a thin parting tool to part off the bottom, 21/64in (8.5mm) from the top edge of the 1 1/4in (32mm) hole (Fig 7).

Drill a 1/2in (13mm) diameter hole into the bottom of the headstock so that it goes 1/8in (3mm) past the hole for the drive shaft (Fig 8). This will accommodate the drive belt that passes from the headstock spindle, through the lathe bed to the motor slung underneath.

Remove the temporary filler from the 1 1/4in (31.5mm) diameter hole in the headstock by heating the hot-melt glue.

Use a coarse sandpaper wheel in a rotary grinding tool to carefully remove the excess wood from the sides and back of the area where the bed bars will be attached. Carefully hand-sand the headstock to 320 grit – it should be so smooth that it looks as if it has been turned (Fig 9). Sand and apply finish to the completed headstock.

3 Turning the lathe bed between centres; note the spigot for the four-jaw chuck on the right. The red inserts will be left standing proud of the maple

4 Details of the headstock

5 Drilling the holes in the unturned headstock blank

6 Beginning to turn the headstock blank

7 Parting off the headstock after turning to its final diameter; the area around the holes for the bed bars is left intact

8 Drilling out the centre of the headstock

9 A rotary grinding tool and a coarse sandpaper wheel are used to remove the excess wood from around the attachment for the bed bars, followed by hand-sanding

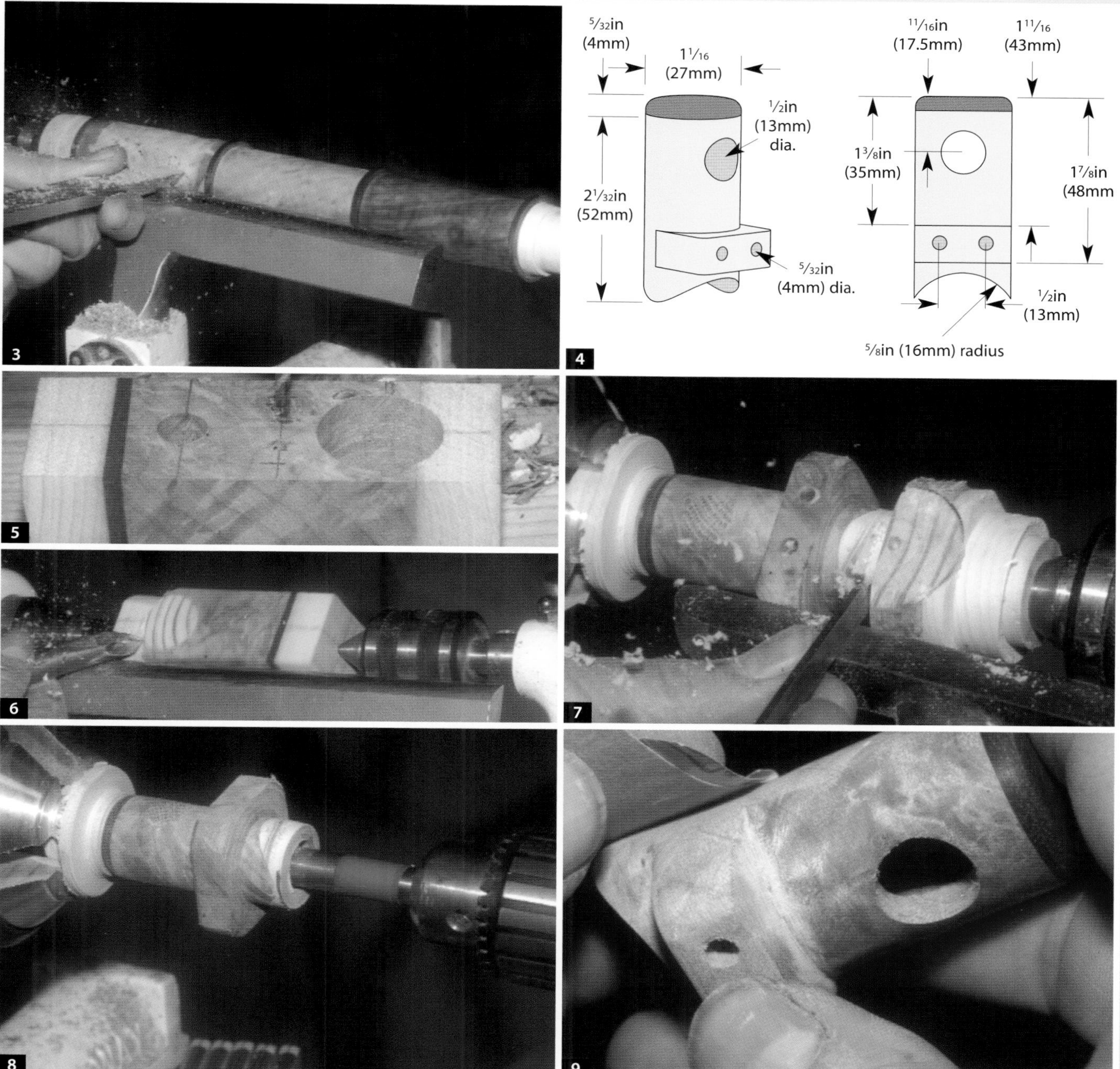

3
5⁄32in
(4mm)
1 1⁄16
(27mm)
1⁄2in
(13mm)
dia.
2 1⁄32in
(52mm)
5⁄32in
(4mm) dia.
11⁄16in
(17.5mm)
1 11⁄16
(43mm)
1 3⁄8in
(35mm)
1 7⁄8in
(48mm
1⁄2in
(13mm)
5⁄8in (16mm) radius
4
5
6
7
8
9

Making the underframe

The underframe is composed of four legs, two short stretchers, one long stretcher and two bed rests, which are the supports for the lathe bed. The stock for the legs and stretchers is ½in (13mm) square.

Fig 10 gives the measurements for the components of the lathe underframe. Be sure to leave at least ½in (13mm) waste at each end of each piece.

Use your drill press to drill the mortise holes $^3/_{16}$in diameter by ¼in deep (5 x 6mm) at a 20° angle into the short stretchers and the legs. This is easy to do using a wedge-shaped jig that has been cut to 20° and has nails placed to serve as stops (Fig 11). Temporarily fill the holes with hot-melt glue and sawdust.

Turning the short stretchers

It is easiest to mount the leg and stretcher stock by using your four-jaw chuck and a live centre. My live centre has a removable point, and when this is taken out it leaves a conical recess that is large enough to accept the end of the stock (Fig 12). If you use a pointed live centre, make a pilot hole so that the point does not split the stock.

Use a skew chisel or a sharp-pointed spindle gouge to turn the legs and stretchers. Taper the ends of the stretchers so that they will fit into the mortise holes in the legs. Sand and apply finish before parting off. The arrows in Fig 13 show where the stretchers will be parted off.

Turning the legs

Start by developing a shape around the mortise – I chose to make a sphere at this point. Taper the top of the leg (the right end in Fig 14) to $^3/_{16}$in (5mm) so that it will fit into the underside of the bed rest.

Using a sharp skew or a spindle gouge, cut the fine details into the legs. The hot-melt glue and sawdust will keep the mortise holes from chipping out (Fig 15). Sand to 320 grit before applying finish to the legs.

Leave the unturned ends at the top and bottom until it is time to cut the foot to length. Cut off the foot using your tablesaw and a mitre gauge set to 20°. Be sure to have the mitre hole in the leg facing to the inside of the 20° angle when making this cut!

10 Details of the underframe

11 Using a wedge to drill the mortise holes in the legs at a 20° angle

12 Turning one of the short stretchers

13 Applying finish to the stretcher. The arrows show where the work will be parted off

14 Beginning to turn the legs by forming a sphere around the stretcher mortise

15 Further detailing of the leg; use a sharp skew or spindle gouge

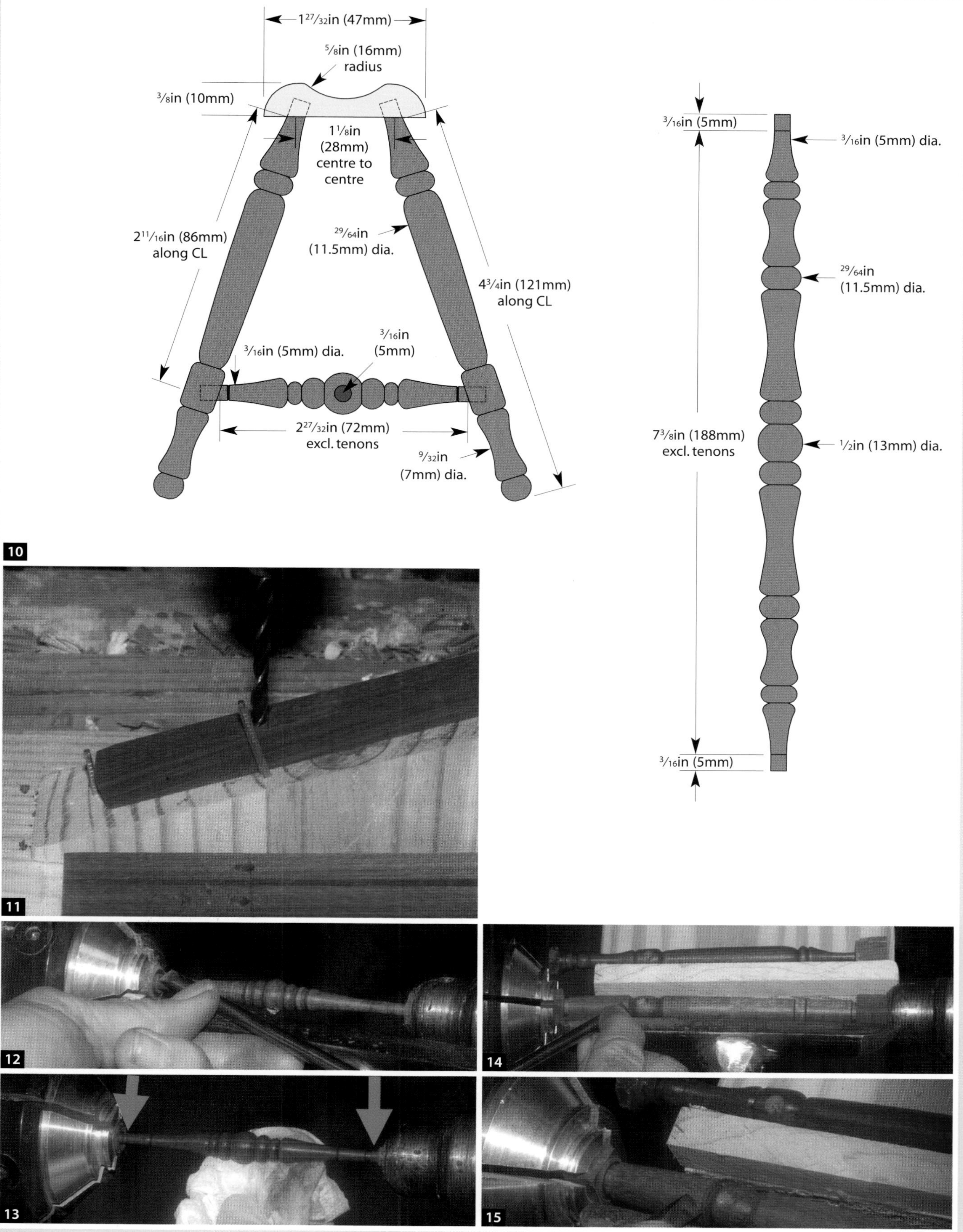
1 27/32in (47mm)
5/8in (16mm) radius
3/8in (10mm)
1 1/8in (28mm) centre to centre
2 11/16in (86mm) along CL
29/64in (11.5mm) dia.
4 3/4in (121mm) along CL
3/16in (5mm) dia.
3/16in (5mm)
2 27/32in (72mm) excl. tenons
9/32in (7mm) dia.
3/16in (5mm)
3/16in (5mm) dia.
29/64in (11.5mm) dia.
7 3/8in (188mm) excl. tenons
1/2in (13mm) dia.
3/16in (5mm)
10
11
12
13
14
15

Turning the long stretcher

The long stretcher must be supported from behind with your fingers (or with kitchen paper; see the tip below) once the turning becomes small in diameter. Use a skew chisel or small spindle gouge to develop the shape, working from the centre outwards (Fig 16). Make the ends come to a graceful 3/16in (5mm) diameter taper at the end so that they will fit into the mortises in the short stretchers (Fig 17).

Making the bed rests

Drill a 1¼in (32mm) hole – the same diameter as the bed of the lathe – through the middle of a block of maple burl 2½in square by ½in thick (64 x 64 x 13mm) (Fig 18). Use the tablesaw to cut through the stock so that two thirds of the hole is left in one piece and one third in the other. Both the bed rests will be made from the smaller part; save the larger part for the bed-bar support, described in the next paragraph. Using the tablesaw, cut two sections ½in (13mm) thick (Fig 19).
Drill the 3/16in (5mm) holes on the underside of the bed rest using the 20° incline as before (Fig 20). Use a belt sander to round the corners of the bed rest.

Making the support for the bed bars

This support goes at the tailstock end of the lathe bed; at the other end the bars are supported by the holes already drilled in the headstock. Use the piece of wood left over from making the bed rest. Cut it down using the tablesaw so that a third of a circle remains on the inside, and make it ½in (13mm) wide. Carefully mark the locations for the two ⅛in (3mm) holes for the bed bars (Fig 21). These must be exactly the same distance apart and the same height from the bed as the corresponding holes in the headstock. Use a sanding drum and a Dremel tool or similar to refine the shape of the support.

● Tip

A very safe alternative to supporting the stretcher with your finger while turning is to use a piece of kitchen paper about 1in (25mm) square, folded to ¼in (6mm) wide. If it catches in the work it will just tear away and do no damage to you or the work.

16 The long stretcher must be supported from behind once the diameter becomes small

17 Finishing the long stretcher; the ends are elegantly tapered to fit the mortises in the short stretchers

18 Boring out the centre of the maple burl block which will make the bed rests and the bed-bar support

19 Cutting the block apart on the tablesaw

20 Using the 20° wedge to drill the holes on the underside of the bed rest

21 Drilling the holes for the bed bars in the bed-bar support

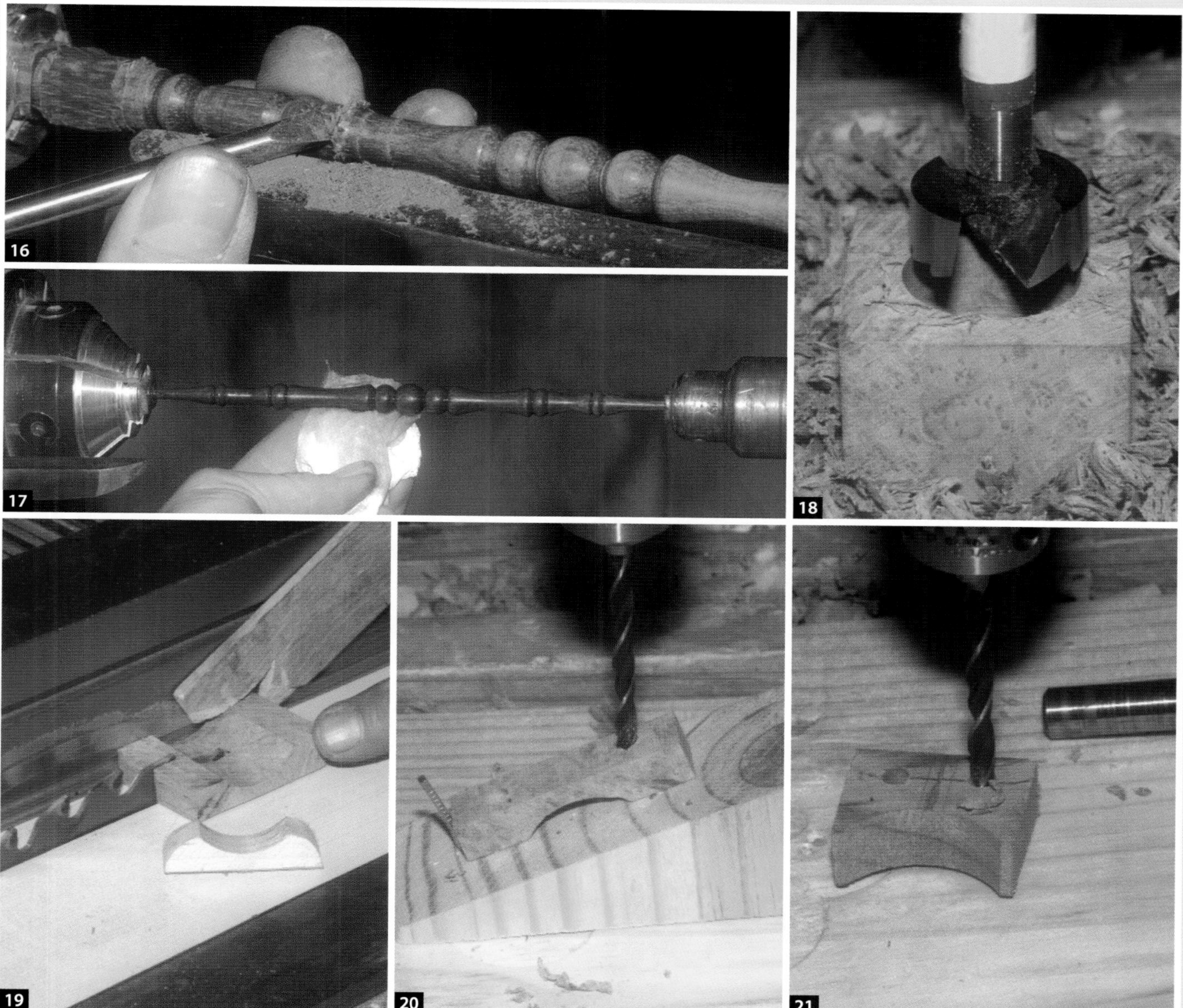
16
17
18
19
20
21

Headstock fittings

Pulley

Turn a cylinder 1/2in diameter by 1 3/16in long (13 x 30mm) for the headstock pulley. Cut a V in the middle of the cylinder to take the drive belt. Drill a 1/8in (3mm) diameter hole through the cylinder for the brass headstock spindle to go through (Fig 22).

Handwheel

Turn an 11/16in (17.5mm) diameter disc and drill a 1/8in (3mm) hole through it (Fig 23). Cut a 2in (50mm) length of brass tube of 1/8in (3mm) outside diameter. Fit this into the headstock pulley and press the handwheel onto it, then insert the whole assembly into the headstock.

Faceplate

Using the same wood as you used to make the handwheel, turn a disk 5/8in diameter by 7/32in thick (16 x 5.5mm). Cut away half the thickness of the wheel to a diameter of 1/4in (6mm) (Fig 24). With the lathe stationary, use a wood file to cut this reduced section into a square nut for the back of the faceplate. Push it onto the brass spindle as in Fig 25.

The motor

Turn the glued-up motor blank to 1 1/8in (28mm) diameter to begin with, then reduce the diameter to 7/8in (22mm) except for a 5/16in (8mm) wide band in the middle (Fig 26). All of this band is then sanded away, except for a portion just 3/16in (5mm) long which is shaped to represent the capacitor of the motor (Fig 27).

For visual contrast I turned a brass pulley, which is attached to the motor with a small brass nail.

● Tip

Brass is soft enough to be turned with thin, sharp high-speed-steel tools. The toolrest must be positioned close to the work, and the tool is advanced very slowly, with its cutting edge exactly at lathe-centre height. You will not get a perfect finish cut from the tool, so 180- and 220-grit sandpaper will be needed to improve the surface. 1200-grit automotive paper will give a mirror finish.

Carving on my pieces has taught me how to slow down, understand and, most importantly, enjoy the design process.

Mike Lee

22 Drilling the hole through the pulley cylinder for the headstock spindle to go through

23 Drilling the hole in the headstock handwheel

24 Turning the faceplate

25 The pulley, handwheel and faceplate installed on the brass spindle in the headstock

26 Turning the motor blank. The protruding band will be sanded away except for a small section which represents the capacitor

27 Sanding away the unwanted part of the protruding band

22
23
24
25
26
27

Toolrest and tailstock saddles

These are the supports for the tailstock and the toolrest. They surround the two tubular bed bars and slide along the bed of the lathe. Prepare a piece of stock 1¼in square by 3in long (32 x 32 x 75mm). Accurately mark the locations for the holes to be drilled, matching the spacing of the bed bars (Fig 28). Drill two pairs of holes, 5⁄32in (4mm) diameter and ½in (13mm) apart, and fill them temporarily with hot-melt glue and sawdust. (Only two pairs of holes are actually needed; the others shown in the photograph are spares in case of mishap.)

Turn the stock to 1in (25mm) diameter. Trim it so that the holes are centred and the final thickness is just shy of 5⁄16in (8mm). A shallow groove made with the skew gives the impression that the saddle is made in two parts. Drill a hole in the middle to accept the brass screw that attaches the toolrest or tailstock to the saddle (Fig 29).

The toolrest assembly

A toolrest assembly (Fig 30) will fit onto one of the two saddles. It has three main parts. For the slide, prepare a piece of padauk a good ¼in wide by ⅛in thick (6.5 x 3mm) and long enough to handle comfortably. Rout a slot ⅛in wide x 7⁄16in long (1.5 x 11mm), ⅛in (3mm) from one end, then cut the piece off to make it 1 3⁄16in (30mm) long.

For the upright toolpost, start by cutting a slot ¼in (6mm) wide all the way across the end of a piece of maple burl a little more than ½in (13mm) square. The slot should be just slightly deeper than the ⅛in (3mm) thick padauk; sanding will make the two flush. Turn the toolpost to the shape shown, making a ⅛in (3mm) diameter tenon at the top end. Glue the padauk into the slot of the maple piece and sand the bottom flush (Fig 31).

Cut a piece of padauk 1 x ¼ x ⅛in (25 x 6 x 3mm) to make the toolrest. Drill a ⅛in (3mm) diameter hole into the centre of the underside, ¼in (6mm) deep. Shape the toolrest by hand-sanding.

Toolrest hub and handle

The small hub for the toolpost adjusting handle is made using padauk. Drill a 1⁄16in (1.5mm) hole through the centre so that it can be mounted to the toolpost with a brass nail (Fig 32). A 1⁄16in (1.5mm) diameter hole is drilled part-way into the hub, at a 45° angle, for the handle (Fig 33).

Turn a small handle for the toolrest hub; I turned a brass handle for visual contrast (Fig 34). Superglue a short piece of brass rod into an accurately sized hole in a waste block that can be held in your four-jaw chuck, and shape it by cutting gently with a thin parting tool. A very sharp skew can be used to cut decorative grooves. Form a 1⁄16in (1.5mm) spigot on one end, and use callipers to make sure that this fits into the hub. Sand from 180 to 1200 grit. Good magnification (see page 86) is essential for this operation.

The toolrest assembly will attach to its saddle with a small brass screw. Grind the top of the brass screw flat and square to resemble a coach screw.

28 Drilling the holes for the bed bars in the blank for the toolrest and tailstock saddles

29 Drilling and parting off the saddle stock; the bed-bar holes have been temporarily filled

30 Details of the toolrest assembly

31 Sanding the toolrest assembly so that the underside is flush

32 Drilling the hub of the toolrest handle

33 Drilling the 45° hole for the handle

34 Turning the brass handle for the toolrest

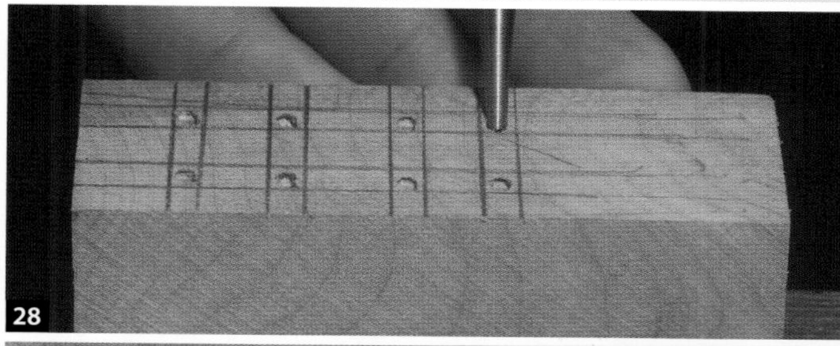
28

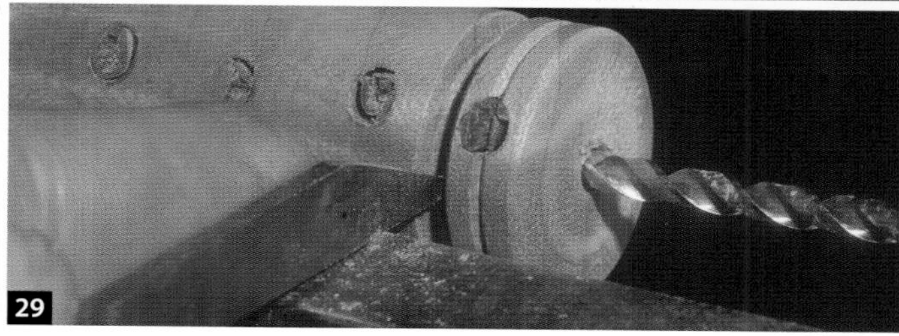
29

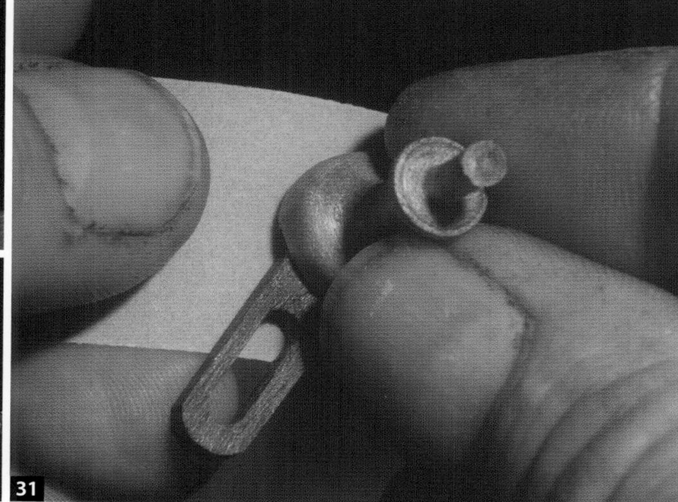
31

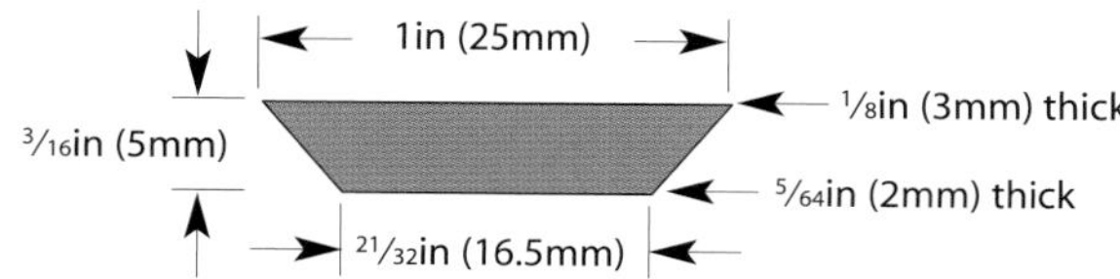

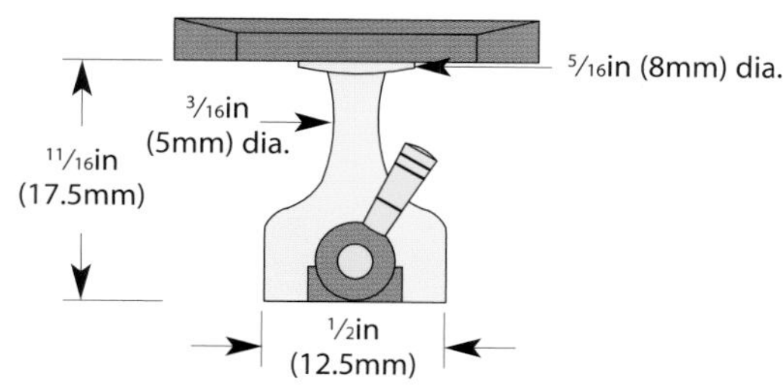

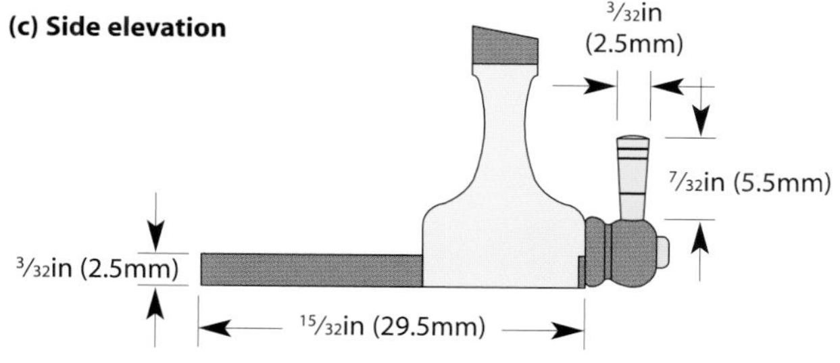

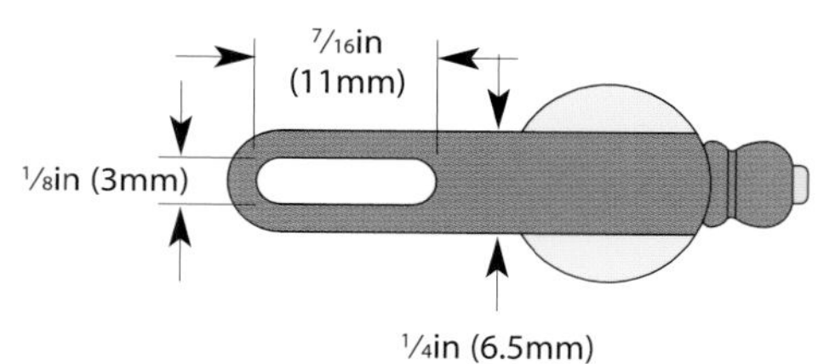

30

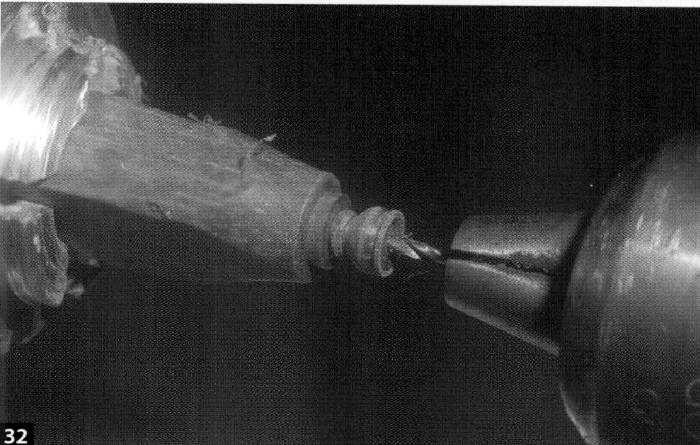
32

33

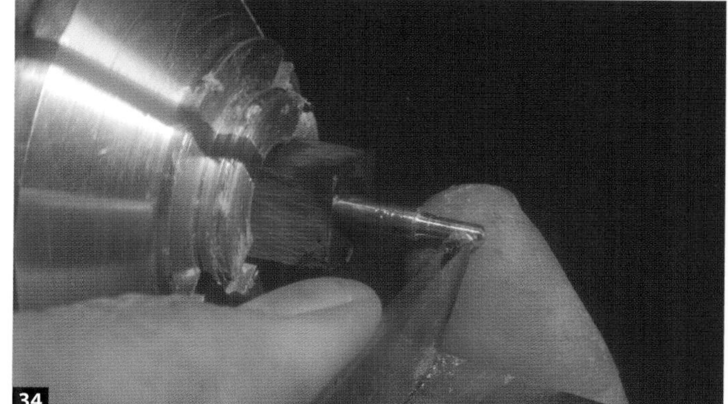
34

Partial assembly

Test-fit the two leg assemblies, each comprising two legs, a short stretcher and a bed rest. It is best to have an extra pair of hands available during assembly. Make sure that the mortise in the short stretcher which receives the long stretcher is pointing inwards. When satisfied, apply glue and assemble the two end frames, wiping off the excess glue straight away. Make sure that both assemblies are flat, and allow the glue to set.

Now place the lathe bed onto the leg assemblies and test-fit the long stretcher to make sure that everything is true. You should also test-fit the headstock, bed bars, bed-bar support and the toolrest and tailstock saddles, checking that the latter are free to slide on the bars. When satisfied, apply PVA glue and clamp (Fig 35).

The motor mount

The motor mount is made from ½in (13mm) stock. Use Forstner bits to drill one hole the same diameter as the lathe bed – 1¼in (32mm) – and another the same diameter as the motor – ⅞in (22mm). The distance between the adjoining circumferences – ¼in (6mm) – will be the amount the motor hangs below the lathe. Use a scrollsaw to cut a section 7/64in (2.75mm) wide from around the border of the two holes (Fig 36). The upper part of this will fit accurately around the lathe bed and the lower part around the motor. Refine the shape of the mount by sanding. Glue the motor to the mount and, once dry, glue the mount to the lathe bed, making sure that the motor is properly aligned (Fig 37). A rubber band around the motor and headstock pulleys makes a good drive belt.

35 Assembling the main components of the lathe; make sure that everything is square

36 Using a scrollsaw to cut out the motor mount

37 The motor installed on the lathe; a rubber band forms the drive belt

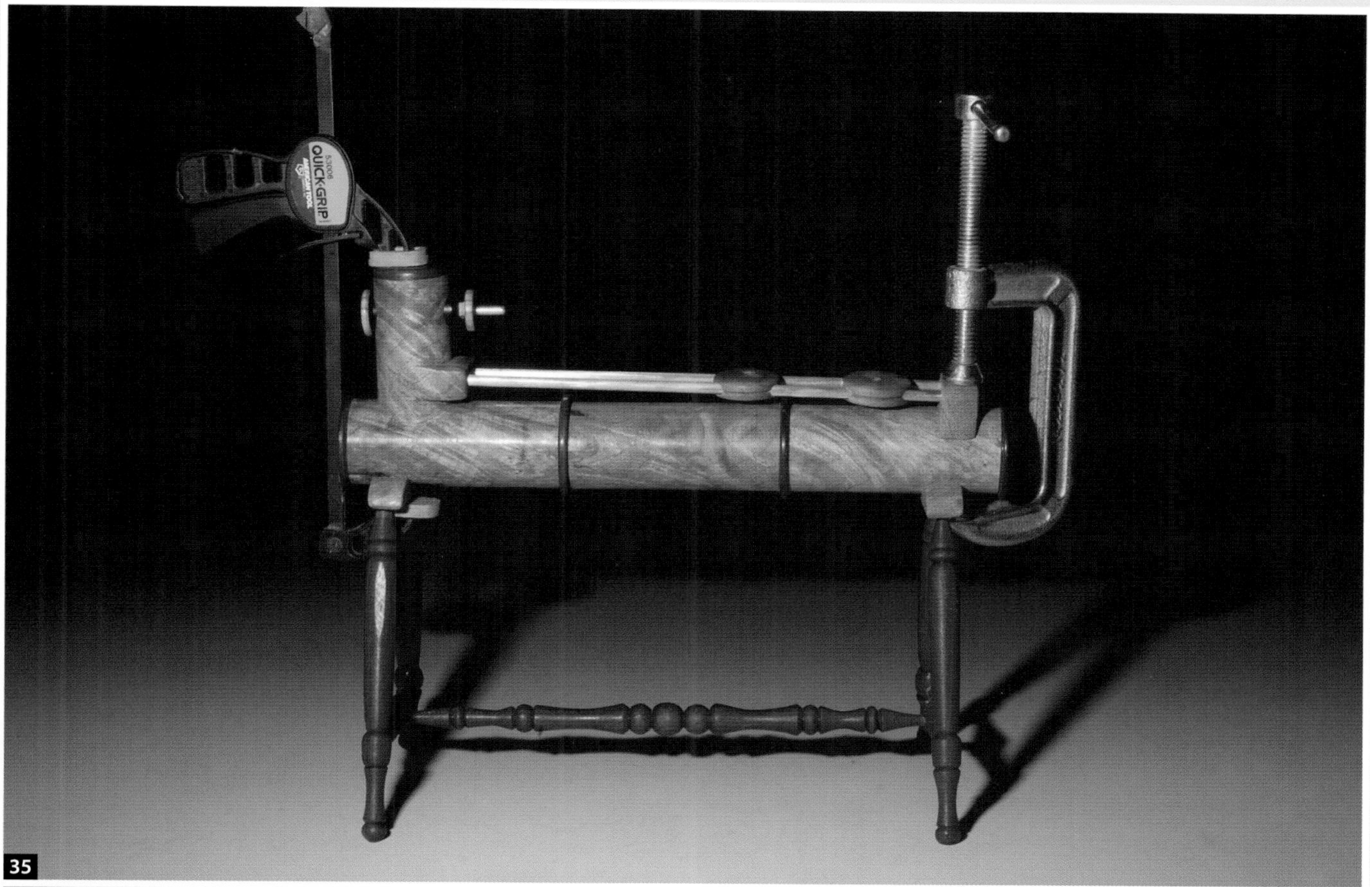

35

36

37

Making the tailstock

The details of the tailstock are shown in Fig 38. The upright part is the only tricky bit of the tailstock. You may need to adjust the height measurements to fit your headstock. Drill a ½in (13mm) hole ½in (13mm) from the tailstock end of a piece of maple stock 1in (25mm) square. Half of this hole will eventually be cut away to leave a channel in which the horizontal tailstock shaft will fit. Drill two holes ¼in (6mm) diameter, 1⅜in (35mm) from the same end, with their axis at 90° to that of the previous hole. These two holes will later be enlarged to make one large hole for a wrench to tighten the tailstock to the lathe bed. Fill all three holes temporarily with a tight-fitting dowel and hot-melt glue (Fig 39). Turn the upright to shape, turning away the upper half of the ½in (13mm) diameter hole in the process (Fig 40). Part the top off, leaving the bottom half of the dowel in the upright. Part off the bottom ⅛in (3mm) below the two bottom holes. Heat the work to soften the glue, and remove the three dowels. Use a Dremel tool, or similar, to cut out the centre of the upright where the bolt tightens the tailstock to the bed bars.

Turn a maple cylinder, 1 5/32in (29mm) long by ½in (13mm) diameter, for the horizontal housing of the tailstock. Drill a ¼in (6mm) hole through the centre. Sand and apply finish. Glue this piece to the tailstock upright. Turn an ebony shaft, ¼in (6mm) diameter by 1⅝in (41mm) long. Drill a ⅛in (3mm) diameter hole through the centre of this shaft for the live centre.

Tailstock accessories

The live centre is a fairly straightforward piece of spindle turning. Shape the pointed tip and collar first, then reduce the spindle until it fits the hole drilled through the ebony shaft. I added interest to mine by turning the collar from a contrasting wood (Fig 41).

The locking handle and handwheel are made in the same way as those on the toolrest and headstock respectively.

I'd rather be good than different.

Richard Raffan

38 Details of the tailstock assembly

39 Starting to turn the upright of the tailstock; note the temporarily filled holes

40 Taper the tailstock upright until the upper part of the large hole is removed

41 Turning the live centre

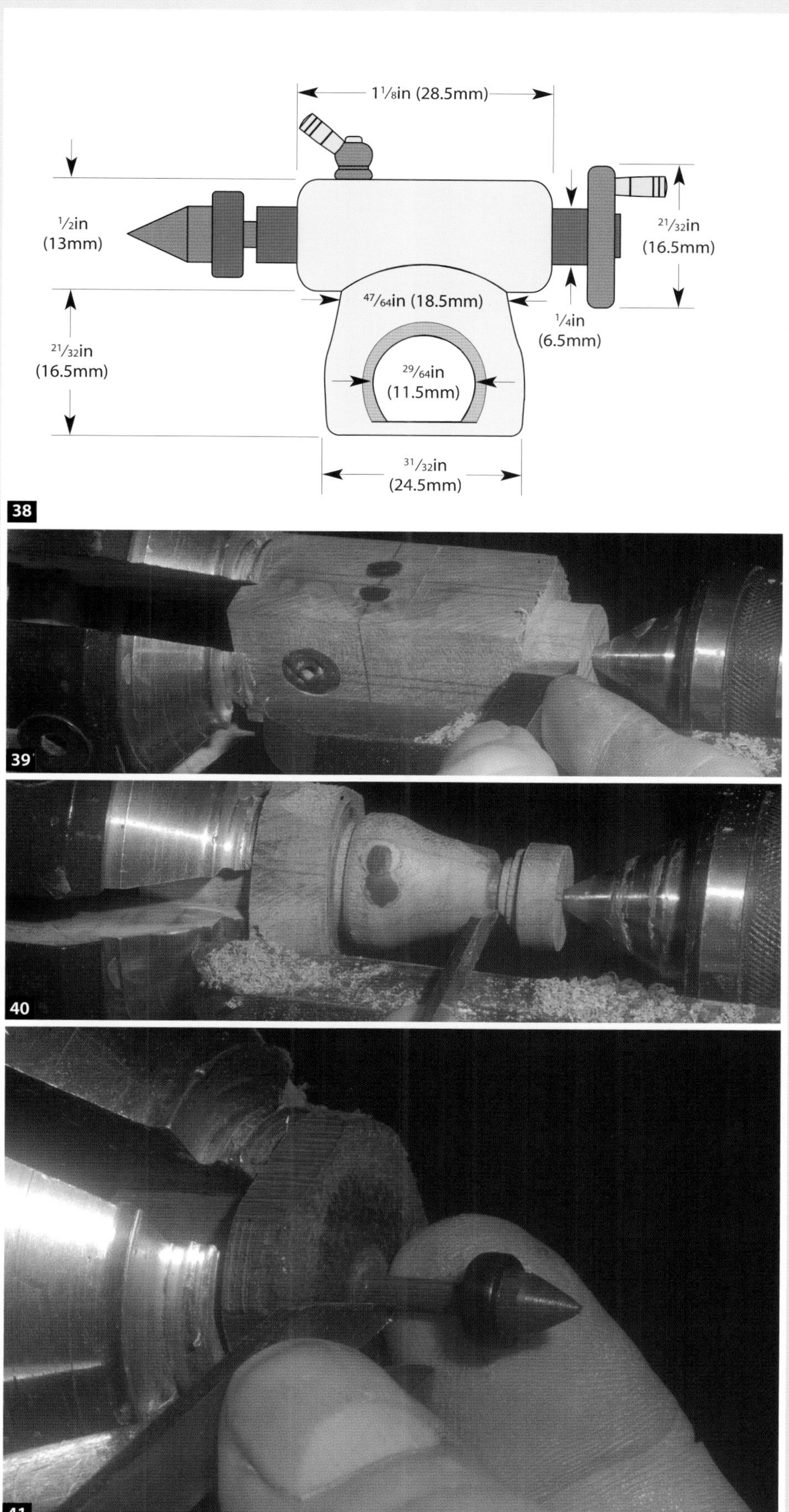

1⅛in (28.5mm)
½in
(13mm)
21/32in
(16.5mm)
47/64in (18.5mm)
¼in
(6.5mm)
21/32in
(16.5mm)
29/64in
(11.5mm)
31/32in
(24.5mm)
38
39
40
41

The toolholder

The lathe has a toolholder underneath, suspended by a 1$^3/_{16}$in (30mm) spindle with $^5/_{32}$in (4mm) spigots cut on each end (Fig 42). One spigot fits into the bottom of the lathe bed, while the other fits into the toolholder disc. This disc is 1$^5/_8$in (41mm) in diameter, with four $^7/_{32}$in (5.5mm) holes for the tools to fit into. Use a scrollsaw to cut a slot leading to each hole so that the tools may be slipped in easily from the side (Fig 43).

The tools can be quickly made from whatever hardwood scraps you have to hand. Full-size patterns for the two wrenches are given in Fig 44.

The vase

If you have made any of the ultra-small projects in Chapter 9, the vase will present no difficulties. It can be any shape you like, provided its diameter is within the capacity of the lathe and will not foul the toolrest assembly. The vase has a hole in the bottom the same diameter as the brass tube that goes through the headstock. Simply fit the brass tube into the bottom of the vase to hold it in place.

Fig 45 shows the completed lathe with all its accessories in position. The graceful curve of the motor mount can be seen clearly in this view.

A make-up artist does not only know the actor or actress's script in the play, they feel their character. Their goal is to express that feeling to the audience… What do I do? I put a soul into every piece I create. I don't make objects… I create characters. If the viewers can pick up on their soul, I've accomplished it.

Binh Pho

42 Details of the toolholder

43 The toolholder mounted beneath the bed of the lathe

44 Full-size patterns for the wrenches

45 Final assembly of the lathe. The vase fits over the brass spindle of the headstock

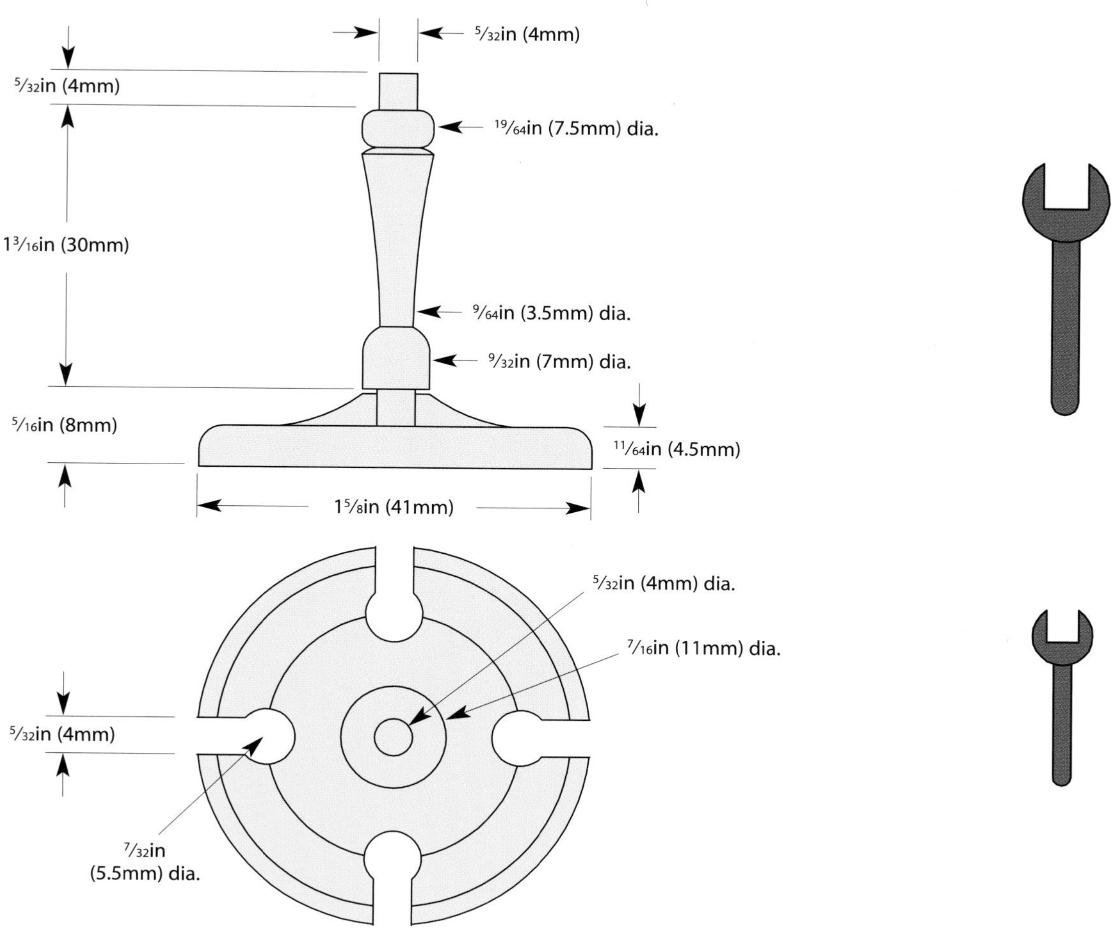
5/32in (4mm)
5/32in (4mm)
19/64in (7.5mm) dia.
1 3/16in (30mm)
9/64in (3.5mm) dia.
9/32in (7mm) dia.
5/16in (8mm)
11/64in (4.5mm)
1 5/8in (41mm)
5/32in (4mm) dia.
7/16in (11mm) dia.
5/32in (4mm)
7/32in (5.5mm) dia.

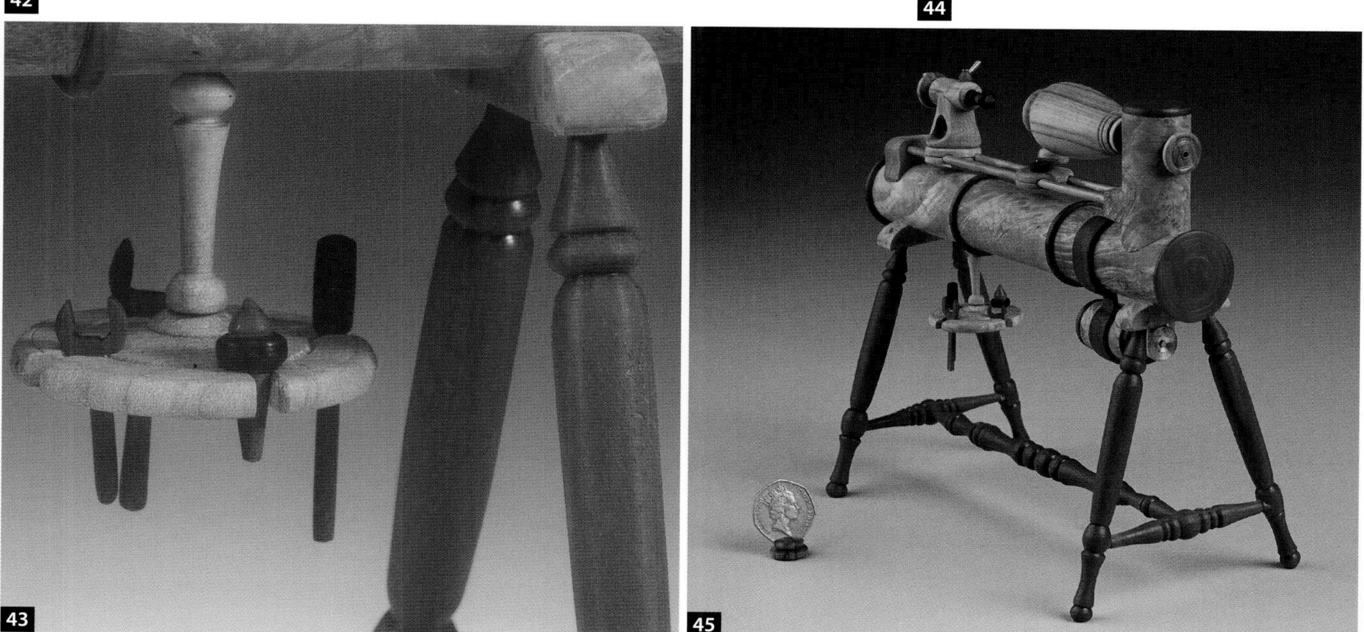
42
43
44
45

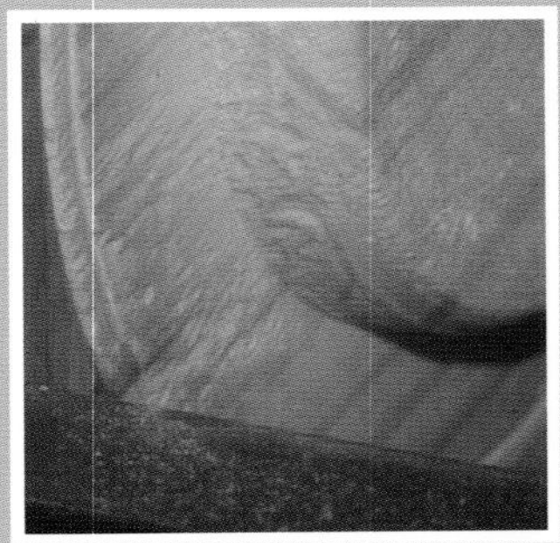

12 Spinning Wheel

The last project is an exquisite and ornate miniature spinning wheel – a fascinating project that should provide a great deal of enjoyment and a considerable challenge. Because it is an actual working spinning wheel, great attention to detail will be needed and all parts must fit accurately.

My design combines features from two different machines which are still in production today. Made by hand, these full-size wheels are exquisite pieces of equipment that show what a talented craftsman can achieve with just a few simple tools.

The craftsmanship is not so difficult if you have put the time in to learn the wide range of skills required to be a successful maker.

Ray Key

Bill of goods

- Padauk, 2 x 1 x 48in (50 x 25 x 1220mm)
- Maple burl, 1½ x 1 x 48in (38 x 25 x 1220mm)
- For jigs: pine, 2 x 4 x 12in (50 x 102 x 305mm)
- For the jam-fit chuck: pine, 10 x 10 x 2in (254 x 254 x 50mm)
- For spools: pink ivorywood, ½ x ½ x 4in (13 x 13 x 100mm)
- Padauk veneer for accent spacers, hand-cut to about 1/16in (1.5mm) thick
- Brass screw, 1/8–5/32in (3–4mm) diameter by 1in (25mm) long, for adjusting tension on drive belts
- Leather, approximately 2 x 2 x 3/16in (50 x 50 x 5mm)
- Brass tube, 1/8in dia. x 3¼in (3 x 82.5mm)
- For crankshaft/axle: brass rod, 1/16in dia. x 12in (1.5 x 305mm)
- White cotton thread for drive belts and to attach the foot pedals to the pitman rods
- PVA and cyanoacrylate glues

Stock preparation

Refer to Fig 1 for the overall layout of the spinning wheel. The uprights, finials and spokes must made from a hard, dense wood that turns well, such as padauk. The two tables, foot pedals and ring segments may be made from a less dense wood, such as burl maple.

My burl maple, purchased over the Internet, was wet wood with a moisture content above 22%. I used my kitchen oven, set at 180°F (80°C), to dry the wood. It was stacked with spacers between the stock and the door was left open at the top (Fig 2). The wood was dried for 24 hours and, according to my meter, the moisture content was reduced to 8.8%.

1 General layout of the spinning wheel

2 A kitchen oven may be used to dry stock slowly

6in (152mm)
Leather bearings
Flyer
Flyer harness
Traveller
Upper table
4 1/8in (104mm)
2 3/4in (70mm)
Floor support
Wheel posts
Lower table
Pitman rods
Foot pedals
8 7/8in (225mm)
5in (127mm)
8 1/2in (215mm)

1

2

Making the wheel rim

The big wheel will be made using 12 segments and 12 thin spacers in between (Fig 3). The angle to be cut on each end of each segment is 15°. (There are 360° in a circle, and two angles on each of the 12 segments, so the angle required is 360° ÷ 24.)

For me, the easiest way to cut ring segments is to use a home-made cutting sled (Fig 4; see also Fig 2 on page 95). The angle is adjusted through trial and error, using scrap wood to make one or more test rings. Move the end of the stock guide *in* (away from you), if there are gaps on the *out*side of the test ring, and move it *out* (back towards you), if there are gaps on the *in*side of the test ring.

Set the stop block to cut segments 1⅞in (47mm) long. Once you are satisfied with your test ring, cut 14 maple segments for the 12-segment ring – the extras will be used as back-up and to make a jig for drilling holes. Pull the 12 segments together with a hose clamp to make sure that you have a perfect fit. Number the segments 1 to 12 (Fig 5).

Accent spacers

Cut some contrasting veneer 1⁄16in (1.5mm) thick, the same size as the ends of the segments. Glue an accent spacer to the *same* end of each segment.

Drilling the spoke holes

Two sets of holes, 3⁄16in (4.5mm) diameter, are to be drilled into the segments.

The first 12 holes, for the large end of the spokes, are drilled in the centre of the inside face (the shorter side) of each segment. Carefully mark the centre of each maple segment and make an indent using a steel punch. Drill each hole, preferably using a drill press, so that it goes halfway through the finished ring.

The second set of holes on the inside of the wheel is for the 12 decorative finials. These holes will be drilled through the middle of the joint between two adjoining segments. You will have to make a jig that will securely hold the two segments together (Fig 6).

For accuracy, all the holes should be drilled using a vertical drill press if possible.

● Tip

More information on the cutting sled, and on segmented turning techniques in general, can be found in my previous book, *Segmented Turning: A Complete Guide* (Guild of Master Craftsman Publications, 2003).

3 The 12 segments of the wheel rim

4 Cutting ring segments on the cutting sled. The angle of the stock guide (under the operator's left hand) is adjusted by trial and error

5 Test assembly of the 12 segments using a hose clamp

6 A simple jig to hold pairs of segments while the finial holes are drilled

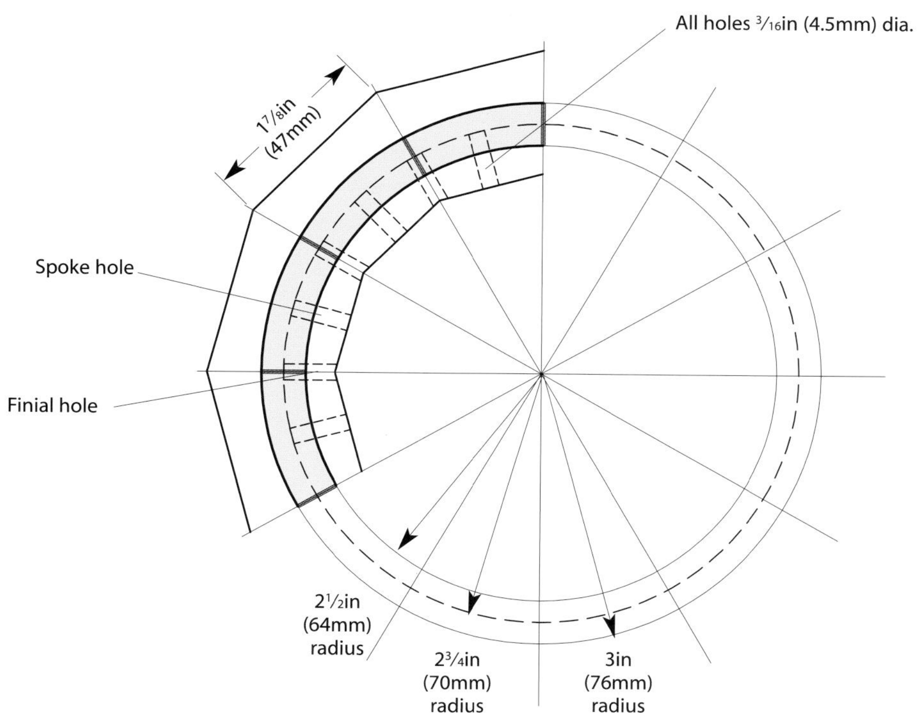

All holes 3/16in (4.5mm) dia.
1 7/8in (47mm)
Spoke hole
Finial hole
2 1/2in (64mm) radius
2 3/4in (70mm) radius
3in (76mm) radius

3

4

WOODCRAFT
Liquid
Storage
Container

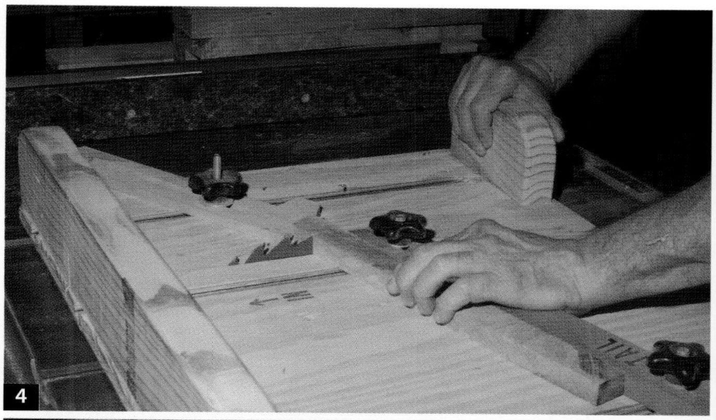

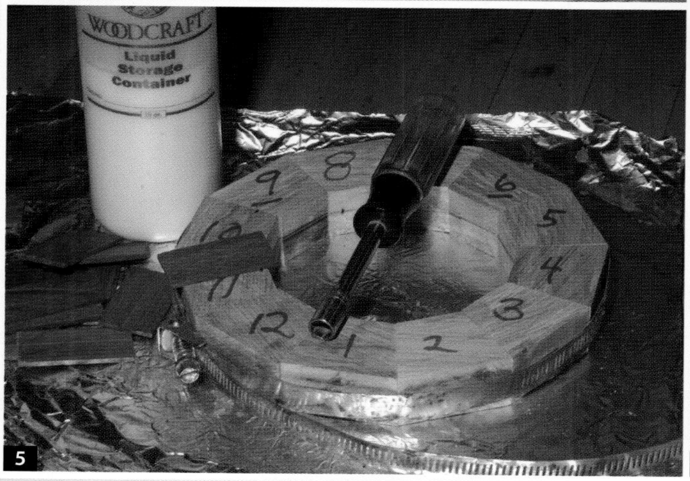

5

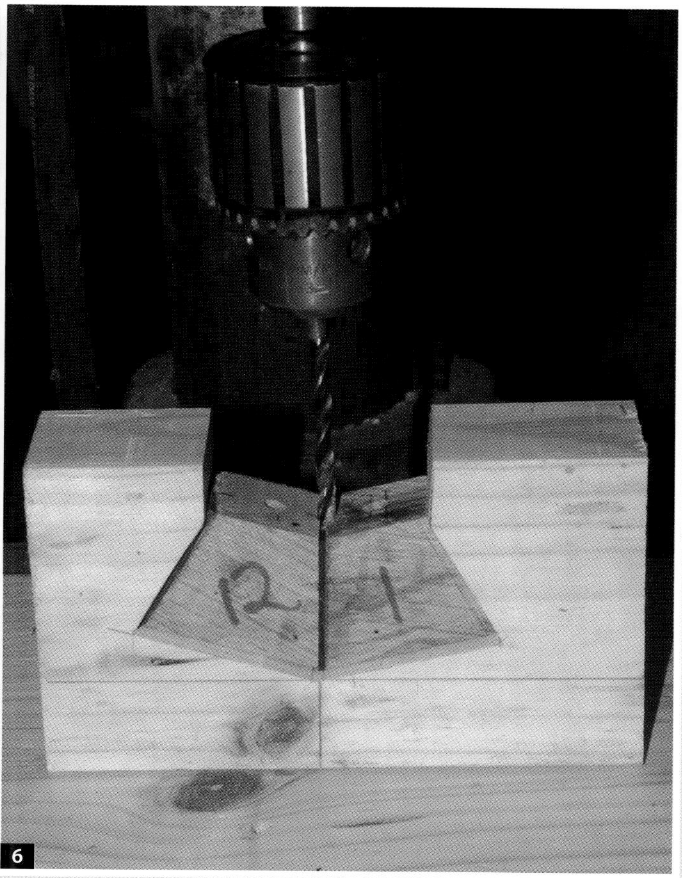

6

Gluing the ring

Each segment already has a thin accent spacer glued to one end. Now glue the 12 segments together using PVA glue. Pull the ring together with a hose clamp and socket drive (Fig 7). Using a cotton swab, remove any excess glue that might have got into the holes for the finials.

Turning the inside

The assembled wheel rim is turned using a jam-fit chuck. Attach a piece of scrap wood to a screw chuck and turn the wood flat, then turn a recess that will hold the big wheel snugly on the outside (Fig 8). True both faces of the wheel rim, reducing the thickness of the ring to approximately 13⁄32in (10.5mm). Ensure that the drilled holes remain in the middle of the thickness of the wood.

Draw three circles on the face of the ring, indicating the inside and outside edges of the rim, and the depth of the spoke holes. Use a parting tool to cut the inside of the rim to the correct diameter (Fig 9) and round over the inside edge of the wheel on both sides.

Turning the outside

Recut the jam chuck, forming a rebate on the outside edge that will hold the wheel on the inside. Use your parting tool to part off the outside of the wheel. Using the very sharp point of a 1⁄4in (6mm) round skew, cut two small V-grooves for the two drive belts to fit into (Fig 10). Sand and apply finish to the wheel rim (Fig 11).

Making the hub

The hub is made of three parts: the spokes are sandwiched between the front and back sections, and the third part is a central plug that fits onto the axle or crankshaft. Once the spokes have been fitted into the back half of the hub, the front half is glued on. A 1⁄8in (3mm) hole will be drilled through the centre for a small screw to join the front and back halves together during the milling stage. Once the hub has been assembled, this hole will be filled by the plug.

Initial turning

Start by turning a piece of stock 3⁄4in (19mm) in diameter. Drill a 1⁄8in (3mm) diameter hole through the centre for a thin wood screw, then part off a 3⁄16in (5mm) section using a thin parting tool. Now place the section that has just been cut off back onto the stock and secure it with the screw. If you look carefully at Fig 12 or Fig 14 you can see the junction between the two pieces of wood.

Marking the spoke holes

Using the indexing head on your lathe (if you don't have one, see opposite), accurately mark 12 divisions around the hub (Fig 12). The 1⁄8in (3mm) holes for the spokes will be drilled exactly on these lines, and exactly on the join between the two sections of wood. Using a sharp knife, make an index mark across the front and back halves of the hub so they can be accurately fitted back together, which is important for the final assembly of the wheel.

7 Assembling the numbered segments. A cotton swab is on hand to remove unwanted glue

8 The wheel rim installed in the recess in the jam-fit chuck

9 Trimming the inside edge to the desired diameter

10 Cutting the V-grooves on the outside of the wheel

11 Applying finish

12 Marking the positions for the spoke holes in the two halves of the hub

Making an indexing head

If your lathe does not have an indexing head you can easily make one using a piece of plywood, a compass and a drill bit the same size as your lathe spindle. Using the compass, make a circle on the plywood about 12–14in (305–355mm) in diameter – or small enough to fit the centre height of your lathe – and mark the centre. Use a bandsaw to cut out the circle.

Now use the compass to lay out 12 sections of 30° each. Work carefully and make minor adjustments until your sections come out evenly. Clearly mark the 12 evenly divided sections. Drill a small hole at each point, the diameter of a coat-hanger or other semi-rigid wire, ½in (13mm) from the edge of the disc.

In the centre of the disc, drill a hole to fit the spindle of your lathe. Mount the disc on the spindle, then attach the faceplate or four-jaw chuck and tighten it in place. The indexing circle will now be secured in relation to the four-jaw chuck.

Drill a hole near one end of a piece of scrap wood (we will call this the indexing plate) the same size as the ones drilled in your plywood disc. Clamp the indexing plate to the lathe bed near the disc. Cut a piece of wire so that one end fits the hole in the indexing plate and the other end drops into one of the holes in the disc. Rotating the disc so that the wire fits into each hole in turn will give you 12 evenly divided segments.

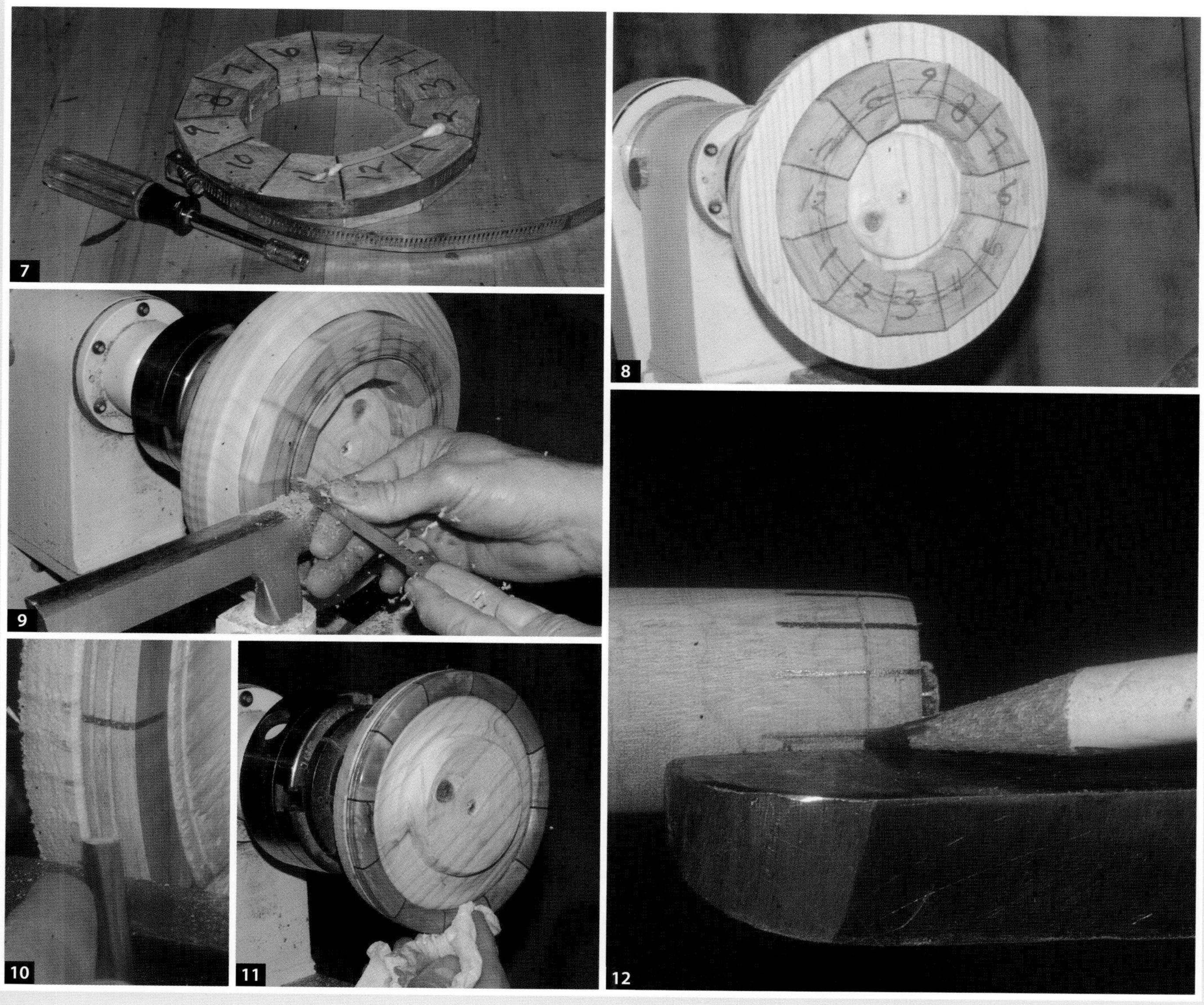
7 8 9 10 11 12

Drilling the spoke holes

Make a jig to hold the hub for drilling. Rout a round-bottomed groove, slightly narrower than the hub stock, into a piece of 2 x 4in (50 x 100mm) stock (Fig 13). This will hold the hub blank while you use a metal punch to make a slight indent at each location. Carefully align a ⅛in (3mm) bit and drill the 12 holes to a depth of 3/32in (2.5mm) (Fig 14).

Return the hub to the lathe and part it off so that the glued joint is in the centre of its thickness. Hand-sand and finish the hub.

The spokes

Determine the length of the spokes (Fig 15) and make four test spokes. Insert these into the rim and one half of the hub. If too long, shorten the spokes on a belt sander.

Turning the spokes

The stock should be ½in square by 3in long (13 x 75mm). To prevent it being split by the pressure of the live centre, drill a small relief hole in the centre of each end and use only light pressure from the tailstock.

Use three sets of callipers. One pair is set to the exact length of the spoke and is not changed throughout the entire procedure. The second pair is set to match the ⅛in (3mm) drill bit used to make the holes in the hub. The third is set to the 3/16in (4.5mm) bit used to drill the holes in the rim. Taper the outer end of the spindle – about a quarter of the overall length – toward the tailstock so that its end is slightly less than ⅛in (3mm) diameter. Taper the other three quarters toward the headstock, down to 3/16in (4.5mm) diameter (Fig 16).

Form the two beads carefully, supporting the small turning with your finger from behind, and cut off the ends to length.

Assembling the wheel

Start by doing a test assembly. Take a flat piece of scrap wood a little larger than the whole wheel, and screw half the hub in the centre of it. Insert the spokes into the rim and lay them in the holes in the hub (Fig 17). Number each hole and keep the spokes in order.

Remove the screw securing the hub to the baseboard. Place a small amount of glue in each of the spoke holes in the hub and rim (but not the finial holes), using a syringe. Insert all the spokes into their correct holes. Then place a small amount of glue into each hole in the top half of the hub, position it according to the witness mark you made earlier, and secure in place with the screw (Fig 18). Lightly tighten the screw to bring the two parts of the hub together. Hold the wheel assembly flat with multiple rubber bands until you are sure that the glue is set.

Finishing the wheel

The decorative finials between the spokes (Fig 15) make the spinning wheel look very ornate. Using a skew chisel, cut a diamond shape at the tip of each finial. Then mark the bottom end of the finial and cut a bead there. Finally, form a long, sloping curve from the bead to the tip (Fig 19). Test-fit each finial, then apply a small amount of glue and seat the finial in its hole.

Drill out the screw hole in the centre of the hub to a diameter of about 3/16in (5mm), being very careful that the drill bit does not grab and spin the entire wheel. Turn a plug that will accurately fit into the centre of the hub. Drill a 1/16in (1.5mm) hole in the centre of the plug for the brass wire axle, then glue the plug in place.

13 A round or ogee router bit can be used to groove a piece of scrap wood to hold the hub

14 Drilling the spoke holes in the hub

15 Details of the wheel spokes and finials

16 Turning the spokes, using one as a pattern for the others

17 Dry assembly of the wheel

18 Final assembly: the screw must be tightened to clamp the two halves of the hub together

19 Shaping one of the wheel finials

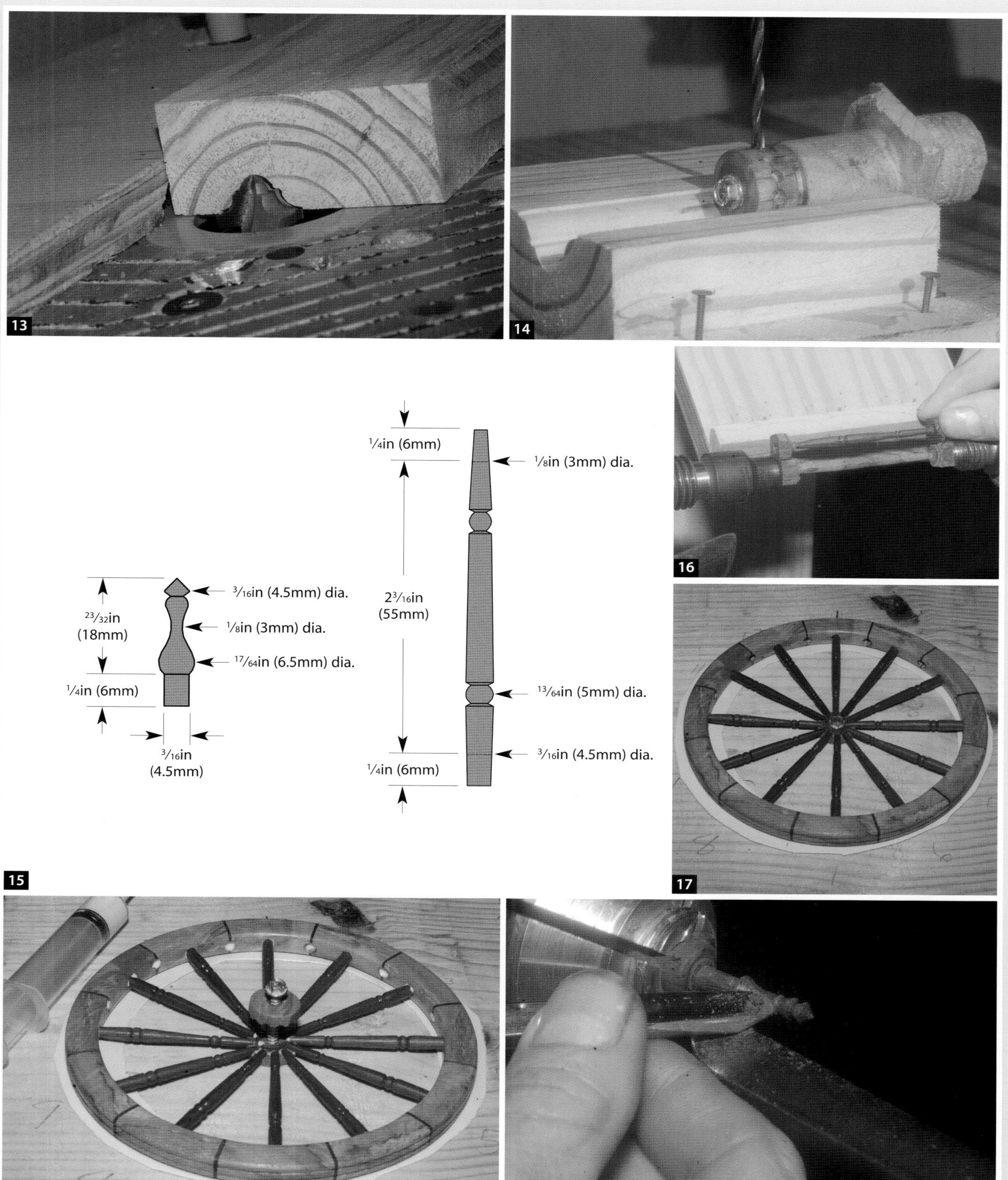
13
14
1/4in (6mm)
1/8in (3mm) dia.
3/16in (4.5mm) dia.
23/32in
(18mm)
1/8in (3mm) dia.
17/64in (6.5mm) dia.
1/4in (6mm)
3/16in
(4.5mm)
2 3/16in
(55mm)
13/64in (5mm) dia.
3/16in (4.5mm) dia.
1/4in (6mm)
15
16
17
18
19

Wheel posts

The wheel is supported by two long posts, which are turned in much the same way as the spokes (Figs 20 and 21). A 1⁄16in (1.5mm) hole is drilled through each post, 1⁄2in (13mm) from the top, to fit the double-cranked brass axle. A tenon 3⁄16in diameter by 3⁄16in long (5 x 5mm) is cut onto the bottom of each post. Stop and check this diameter often.

Making the tables

Lay out the design of the two tables by reference to Fig 22. In the lower (larger) table drill three holes for the legs, 3⁄16in (4.5mm) diameter by 7⁄32in (5.5mm) deep, using a 30° wedge to support the work at the required angle (Fig 23). Use a scrollsaw to cut the tables to shape (Fig 24). Drill three 1⁄8in (3mm) holes through both tables for the three upright spindles which join them together.

The small table has a sliding mechanism which tightens the two drive belts that go around the big wheel and the flyer assembly. Drill a pilot hole 1 1⁄8in (28mm) deep in the end of the small table for a 9⁄64in (3.5mm) brass screw. Use a scrollsaw to cut out the square opening in the middle of the table. Save the piece you have cut out, and remove 11⁄32in (9mm) from one end of it, so that the remaining part will have 11⁄32in (9mm) of travel within the square opening when the screw is turned (Fig 25). Drill a 1⁄8in (3mm) hole in the middle of the sliding part; a dowel will be inserted later to attach the flyer harness to the small table. Use a router with a flush bearing-guided round-over bit to soften the edges of the two tables (Fig 26).

When the time comes to install the screw, the hole in the edge of the table needs to be enlarged slightly so that the screw turns freely inside it. The hole in the sliding part is left slightly undersize, so that the screw cuts a thread in the wood as it is inserted.

20 Details of the wheel posts

21 Shaping the second wheel post, using the first as a pattern

22 Details of the upper and lower tables

23 Drilling the leg holes in the underside of the lower table, using the 30° angle block

24 Cutting out the lower table on the scrollsaw

25 The brass screw which moves the sliding section to tension the drive belts

26 Rounding the edges on the router table

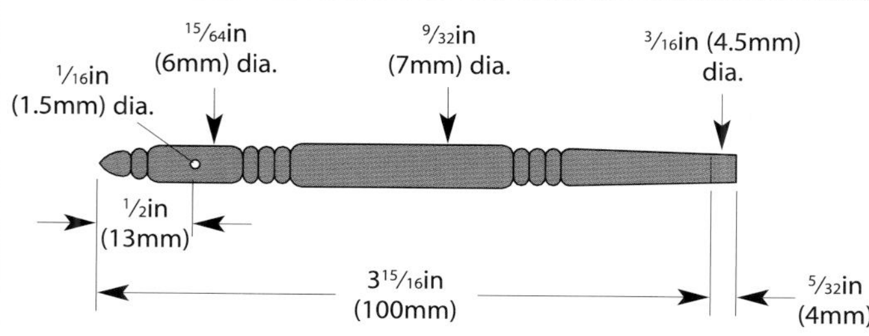

20

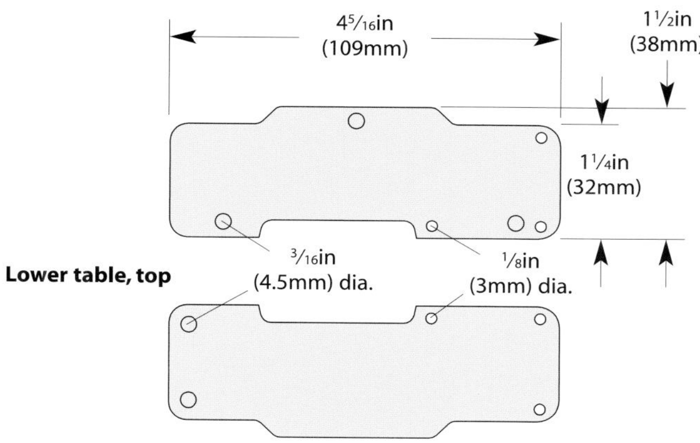

Upper table, top

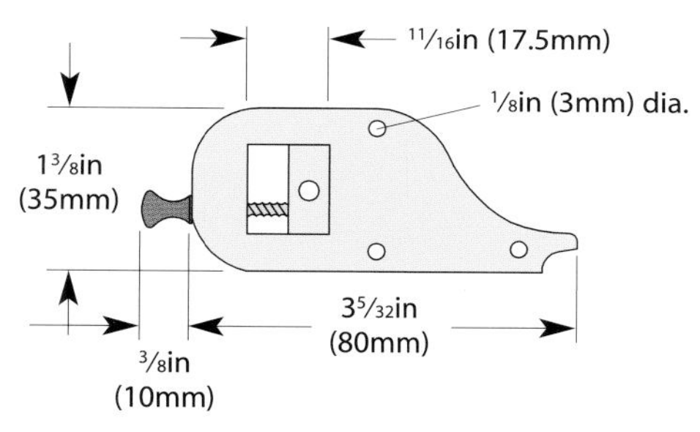

22

25

21

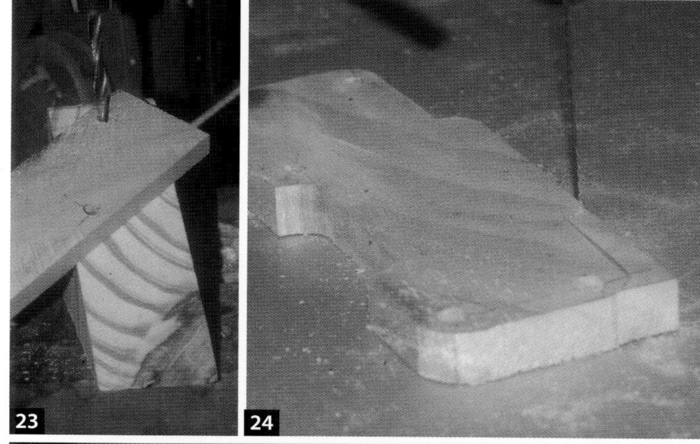

23

24

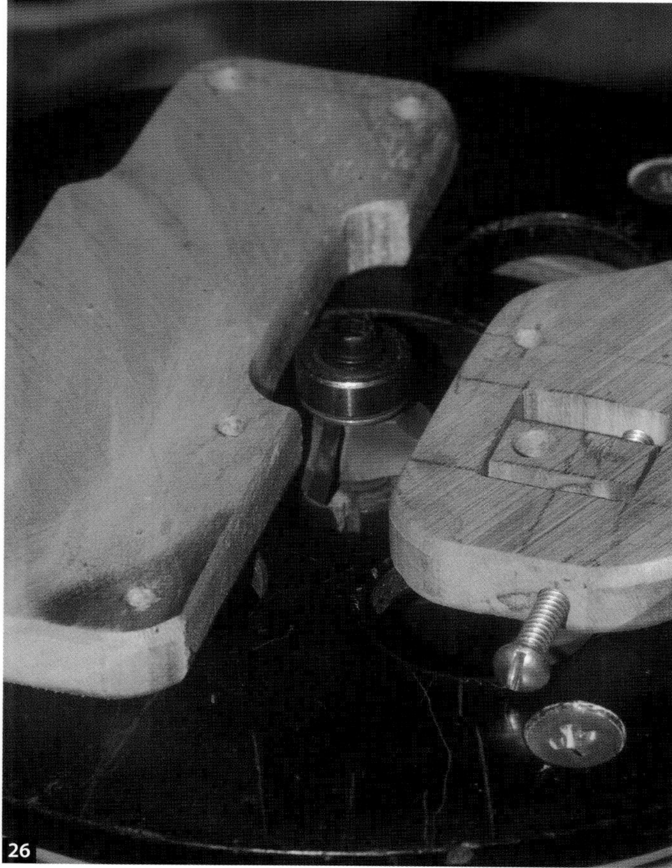

26

Making the underframe

Legs

The three legs of the spinning wheel are set into the lower table at a 30° angle. The two front legs must each have a 7⁄64in (2.75mm) hole drilled 1⁄4in (6.5mm) from the bottom for a stretcher. Drill these with the aid of a 30° wedge as before (Fig 27). Drill the hole 11⁄64in (4.3mm) deep.

Turn the foot down almost to a point. Carefully cut a 3⁄16in (5mm) tenon on the top end of the leg where it will fit up into the table, using callipers to check the diameter. Using a small skew or beading tool, make three small beads halfway up the leg (Fig 28). Use the first leg as a guide for turning the others.

The three short legs to support the upper table are made in the same way as the central section of the main legs (Fig 29).

Stretcher

The stretcher must be made after the table and legs have been completed. Test-fit the two front legs into the table – the long stretcher goes between these legs. Its primary function is to support the two foot pedals that power the spinning wheel. Make a test stick to check the exact measurement between the front legs. Turn the stretcher to shape, starting at the tailstock end to keep unwanted flexing to a minimum (Fig 30).

Foot pedals and floor support

The spinning wheel has two foot pedals (Fig 31). The thick part of each pedal, where it fits over the stretcher, has a 3⁄16in (5mm) hole drilled through the 11⁄32in (9mm) stock. The rest of the pedal is reduced to 5⁄32in (4mm) thickness (Fig 32). The very end of the pedal must have a 1⁄16in (1.5mm) hole drilled vertically through it; this will be used to connect the pedal to the pitman rod, using thread.

The long stretcher must have some support to keep the two foot pedals from breaking it. Make the support from a scrap left over from the pedals (Fig 33). Drill a 3⁄16in (5mm) hole through the support, making sure that the bottom of the hole is the same distance from the floor as the bottom of the stretcher.

27 Drilling the stretcher hole in a front leg blank

28 Detailing the legs

29 Leg, stretcher, supporting leg for upper table, and finial

30 Turning the stretcher

31 The foot pedals, viewed from below to show the thickened part which fits over the stretcher; the upper surface is flat

32 Foot pedal sawn to shape, showing the hole for the stretcher drilled through the thickened part

33 The floor support

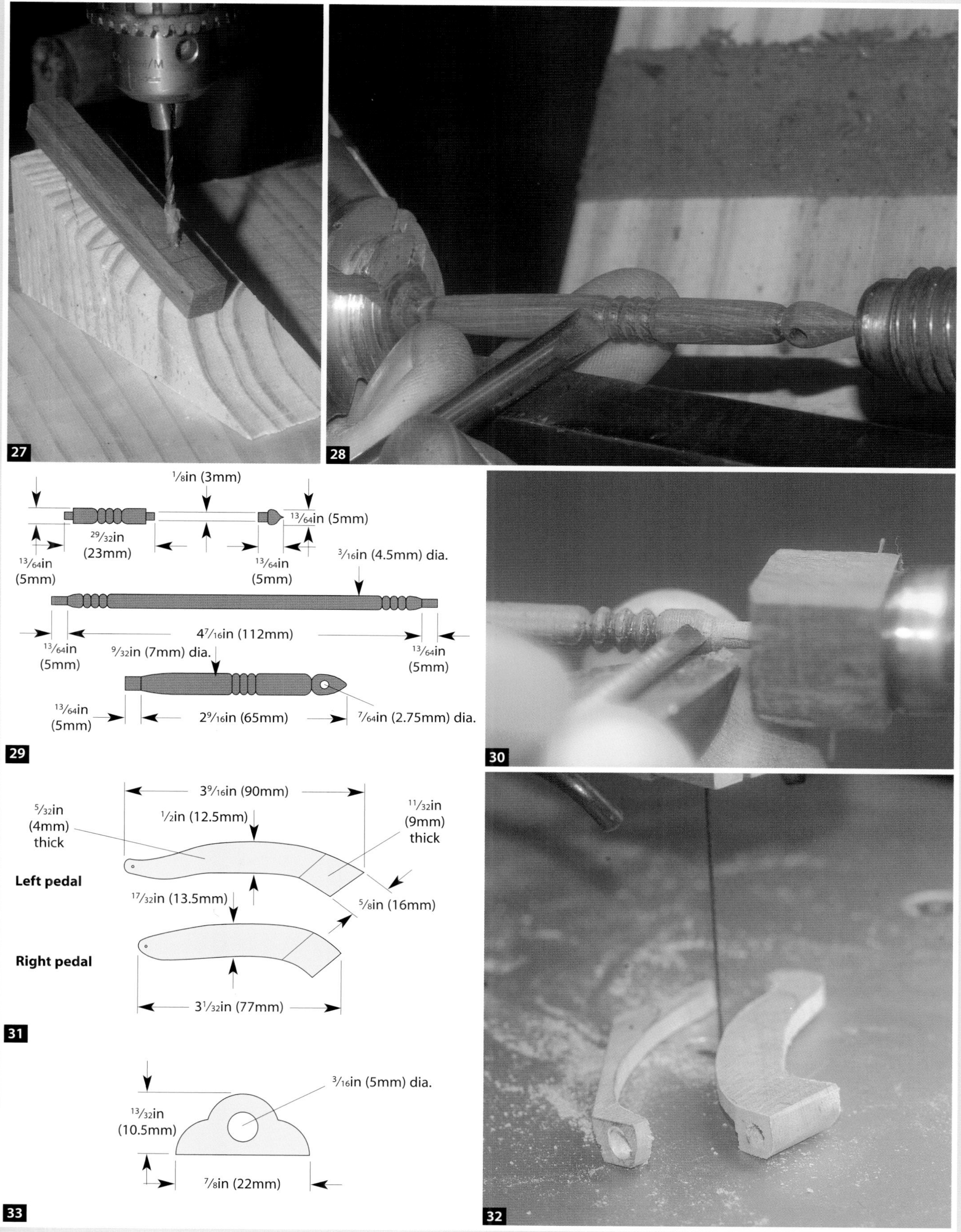
27
28
1/8in (3mm)
13/64in (5mm)
29/32in (23mm)
13/64in (5mm)
13/64in (5mm)
3/16in (4.5mm) dia.
4 7/16in (112mm)
13/64in (5mm)
9/32in (7mm) dia.
13/64in (5mm)
13/64in (5mm)
2 9/16in (65mm)
7/64in (2.75mm) dia.
29
30
3 9/16in (90mm)
5/32in (4mm) thick
1/2in (12.5mm)
11/32in (9mm) thick
Left pedal
17/32in (13.5mm)
5/8in (16mm)
Right pedal
3 1/32in (77mm)
31
3/16in (5mm) dia.
13/32in (10.5mm)
7/8in (22mm)
33
32

The spinning mechanism

The flyer harness

The flyer harness holds the mechanism where the fibre is spun into thread. It consists of a horizontal spindle and two upright shafts (Fig 34). Make the horizontal piece first. Drill a 1/8in (3mm) hole near each end, to hold the uprights (Fig 35). A third hole, to attach the horizontal shaft to the table, will be drilled at a later stage; do not cut off the square ends of the workpiece until the third hole has been drilled.

On each upright, drill a 7/64in (2.8mm) hole right through, 29/64in (11.5mm) from the top. These holes will accept the eyelet-shaped leather bearings that hold the flyer spindle.

The brass spindle

This is a tube 1/8in (3mm) in diameter and 1 3/8in (35mm) long. The hole near one end for the yarn to pass through is made with a small dental drill.

The flyer

The flyer is the narrow U-shaped part, with small pins inserted in one arm, which faces away from the operator. Thread is placed in different positions on the pins of the flyer so that the thread is wound evenly onto the spool. For the sake of strength it is laminated. The middle layer is made from two pieces mitred together, with the grain running at 45° to the midline axis (Fig 36). The top and bottom layers run across the middle layer. Drill a 1/8in (3mm) hole, through the base of the U (the area where the glue line is on the middle piece), for the brass tube through which the thread will travel.

Use a scrollsaw to cut out the flyer and carefully hand-sand to the correct shape. Drill three or four very small holes on the top edge of the flyer, slanting away from the operator, for the small brass rods that will guide the thread (fig. 37).

The leather bearings

The flyer spindle is supported by eyelet-shaped leather bearings. Glue a piece of leather to a thin piece of plywood using a quick-drying rubber-type spray adhesive. For the eyelets, draw two 5/16in (8mm) circles and drill a 1/8in (3mm) hole in the centre of each, then use a scrollsaw to cut out the shape (Fig 38).

From the leftover material make two washers, by drawing a further two 5/16in (8mm) circles and drilling a 1/16in (1.5mm) hole in each. Again use the scrollsaw to cut these out; they will be used on either side of the big wheel.

When finished, the rubber adhesive allows the leather to be gently peeled away from the plywood backing.

The flyer pulleys

The flyer assembly has two pulleys on it. One is glued to the brass tube and spins the flyer which is also attached. The other pulley, which is loose on the brass tube, is made in one piece with the spool on which the spun thread is wound (Fig 39).

The traveller

This is the turned boss on which the flyer assembly sits; it can be seen below the flyer harness in Fig 37. A 3/16in (5mm) hole is drilled through the centre of the boss. A separately made dowel passes through this hole, joining the flyer assembly to the screw block in the small table, and a decorative finial is added at the final assembly stage.

34 The parts of the flyer mechanism

35 The horizontal member of the flyer harness, not yet parted off

36 Mitring the central lamination for the U-shaped flyer

37 The completed flyer mechanism, showing the small brass pins along the top edge of the flyer

38 Cutting out the leather bearings

39 Turning the large pulley-cum-spool

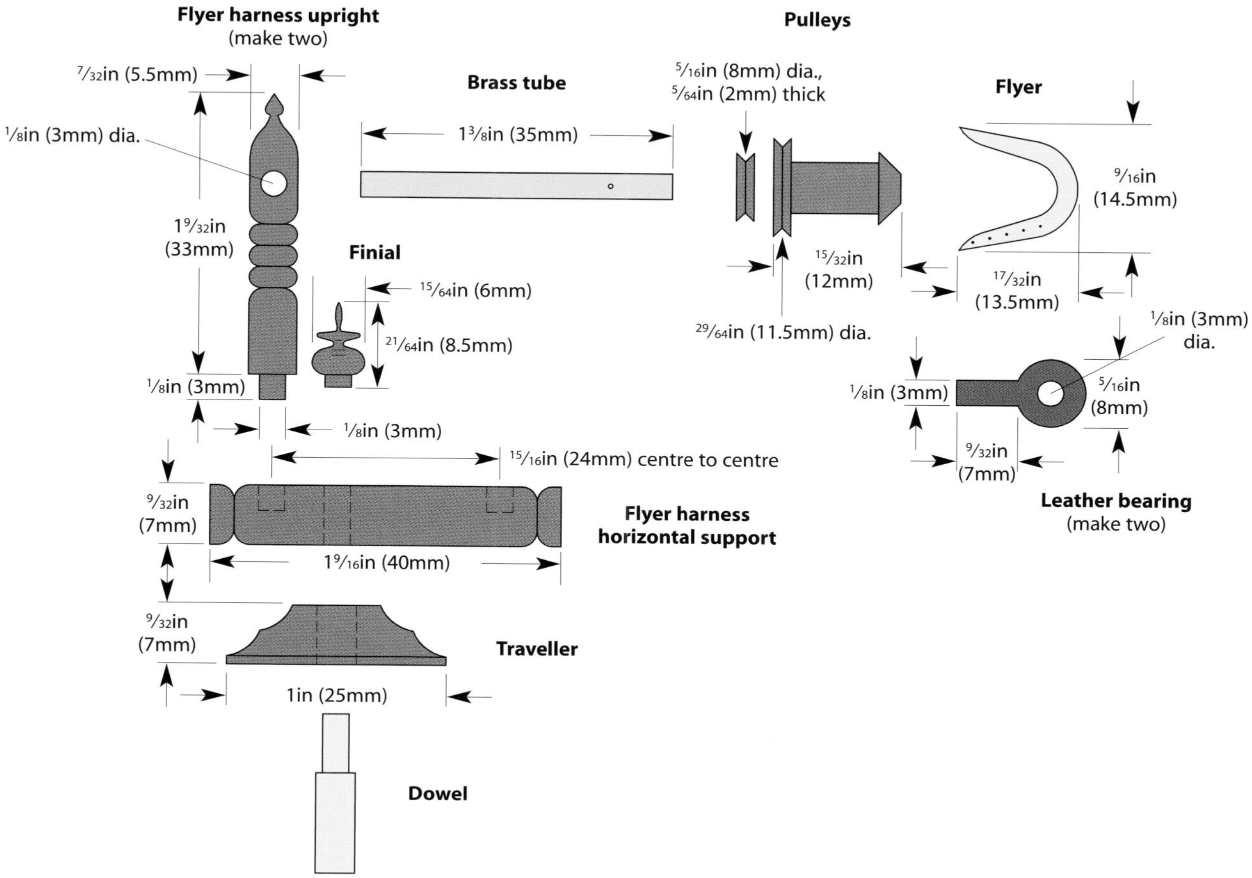

Flyer harness upright (make two)

7/32in (5.5mm)
1/8in (3mm) dia.
1 9/32in (33mm)
1/8in (3mm)
1/8in (3mm)

Finial

15/64in (6mm)
21/64in (8.5mm)

Brass tube

1 3/8in (35mm)

Pulleys

5/16in (8mm) dia., 5/64in (2mm) thick
15/32in (12mm)
29/64in (11.5mm) dia.

Flyer

9/16in (14.5mm)
17/32in (13.5mm)

Leather bearing (make two)

1/8in (3mm) dia.
1/8in (3mm)
5/16in (8mm)
9/32in (7mm)

15/16in (24mm) centre to centre
9/32in (7mm)

Flyer harness horizontal support

1 9/16in (40mm)

9/32in (7mm)

Traveller

1in (25mm)

Dowel

34

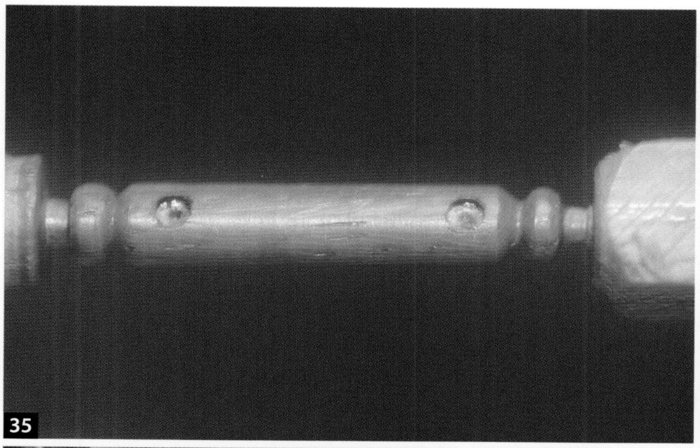

35

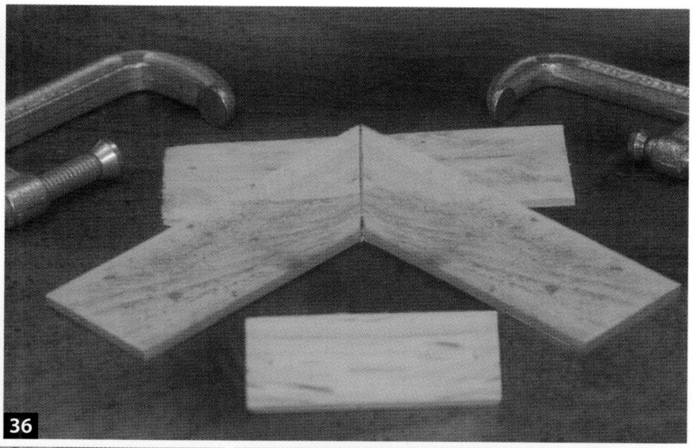

36

37

38

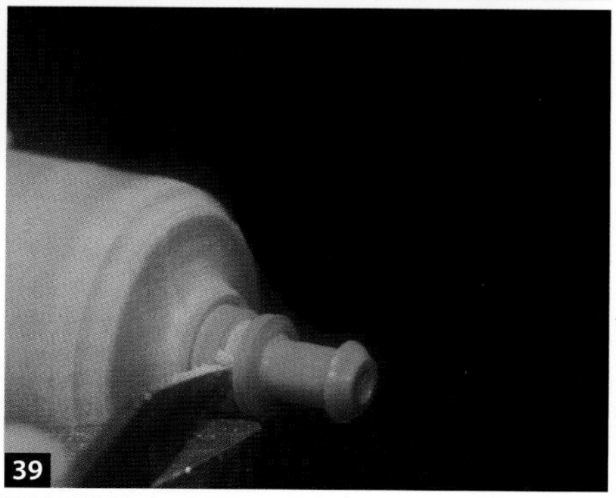

39

Decorative finials

Several small finials are necessary to dress out the spinning wheel. Six identical ones will be needed to fill the holes made for the three upright spindles that support the upper table (Fig 40). By placing a finial above and below each leg, the idea is to make it look as though the leg goes right through the top and bottom tables all in one piece.

A more elaborate finial (shown in Fig 34) is needed to go on top of the traveller which supports the flyer assembly, and a large doorknob-shaped one (Fig 41) to form a handle for the brass tensioning screw. Two small spherical knobs, 5⁄32in (4mm) in diameter, are required for the ends of the axle or crankshaft.

The axle or crankshaft

Make a crankshaft or axle from 1⁄16in (1.5mm) brass rod, which can be found at most craft suppliers. Use needle-nose pliers to make accurate bends as shown in Fig 42.

The pitman rods

Two connecting rods or pitman rods (Fig 43) link the foot pedals to the crankshaft. One end of the rod has a 5⁄64in (2mm) hole drilled through it – just big enough to travel around the bends in the crankshaft, on which the rod is threaded. The other end – which can be made a little smaller if you like – has a hole no larger than 1⁄16in (1.5mm), just big enough for the thin thread that is used to join the rod to the pedal.

The natural world offers many inspirations, especially when it is examined at high magnification. I am a botanist by day and a part-time woodturner in whatever spare time I can glean from the week. My botanical training has served me well in my woodturning endeavours.

Andrea Wolfe

40 Making one of the six finials for the table supports

41 The handle for the tensioning screw

42 The axle or crankshaft

43 Pitman rod (make two)

40

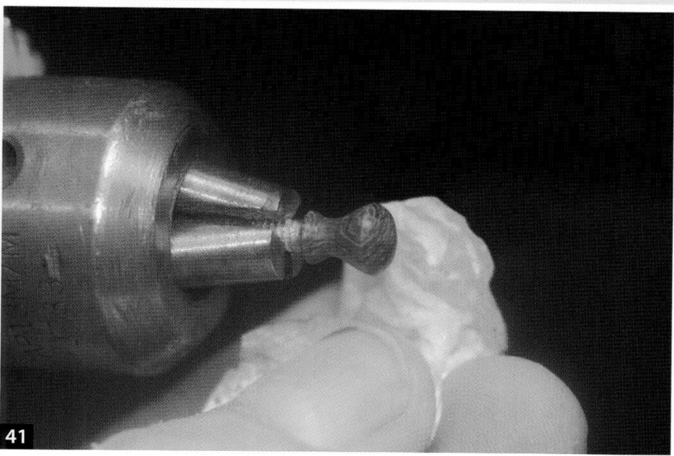
41

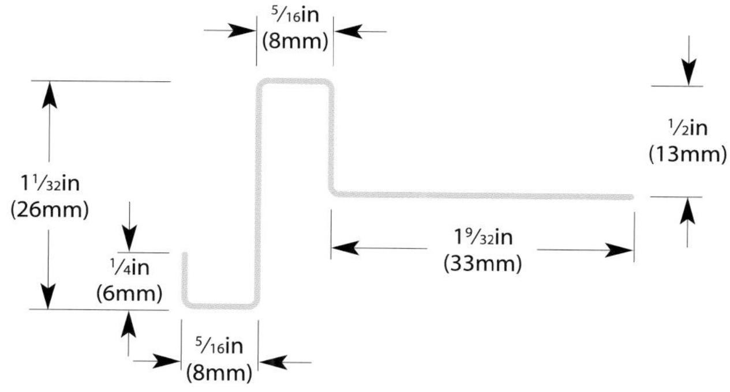
5/16in
(8mm)
½in
(13mm)
1 1/32in
(26mm)
1 9/32in
(33mm)
¼in
(6mm)
5/16in
(8mm)

42

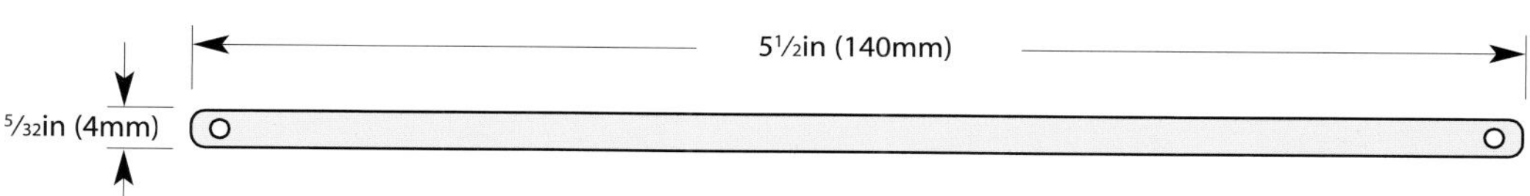
5½in (140mm)
5/32in (4mm)

43

Final assembly

Legs and pedals

Start by threading the two foot pedals and the floor support onto the stretcher. Glue the stretcher into the holes in the two front legs. With the lower table upside down, insert and glue the front legs, with stretcher and foot pedals, into the holes of the table. Then insert the back leg.

Mounting the wheel

Insert the straight end of the crankshaft through the back wheel post. Thread on the big wheel and the two leather washers between the two wheel posts. Gently push the crankshaft through so that $^{3}/_{32}$in (2.5mm) sticks out through the front wheel post. Glue a small spherical finial onto the front end of the axle.

Pitman rods

Carefully thread the two pitman rods to their correct positions on the axle or crankshaft. Glue the second ball finial onto the back end of the crankshaft (Fig 44). Use thin thread to tie each pitman rod to its corresponding foot pedal.

Flyer assembly

Align the two pulleys on the flyer assembly with the two grooves in the big wheel. Keeping the flyer harness firmly fixed in this position, mark the location on the horizontal member of the harness where the hole needs to be drilled so that it can be mounted to the circular traveller and the upper table. Drill a $^{1}/_{8}$in (3mm) hole though the horizontal bar at this point. Now cut off the square ends from the bar, sand and apply finish.

Pass a dowel through the round traveller and glue it to the sliding block inside the small table. The dowel must stop slightly short of the top of the horizontal bar, so that the turned finial can be glued into the top end of the same hole. Glue the two vertical flyer supports to the horizontal bar, making sure the two small holes for the leather bearings are facing forwards.

Glue the two leather bearings into the vertical supports. Pass the brass tube through the rear bearing, with the drilled hole facing the front, and thread on the small pulley. On a working spinning wheel this pulley and the flyer must be made fast to the brass tube. Next, insert the larger spindle-cum-pulley and the flyer, then pass the brass tube through the forward leather support (Fig 45).

The flyer assembly is moved forwards and backwards using the brass screw. The screw will only pull the assembly backwards to tighten the two belts – it will not push it forward.

Make two thin belts from sewing thread, which pass round the grooves in the big wheel and the two flyer pulleys. It is neater and easier to join the ends with superglue than to tie knots in them.

Threading the spool

A length of sewing thread is wrapped around the padauk spool. It then travels up onto one of the hooks of the flyer, down through the drilled hole in the brass tube, and out the end of the tube at the front.

Fig 46 shows the completed spinning wheel from the back.

44 The pitman rods threaded onto the crankshaft

45 The flyer mechanism fully assembled

46 A back view of the completed spinning wheel

44
45
46

Gallery

We woodturners are very fortunate to have a great diversity of accomplished turners around the world who produce beautiful work and are willing to share their artistic vision with us. On the next few pages we see just a small sample of work from some of the world's most accomplished turners, representing five countries and three continents. Studying the art of these masters is beneficial because it helps you to see what is possible and it can be a stimulus for your own creativity. Don't be content to copy, though: imitate other artists only to the extent that this enables you to learn valuable turning techniques. Always be looking for your own unique artistic style or 'voice'. You become a true artist only when you have succeeded in creating a style that is unique and can be easily recognized from across the room as your own work.

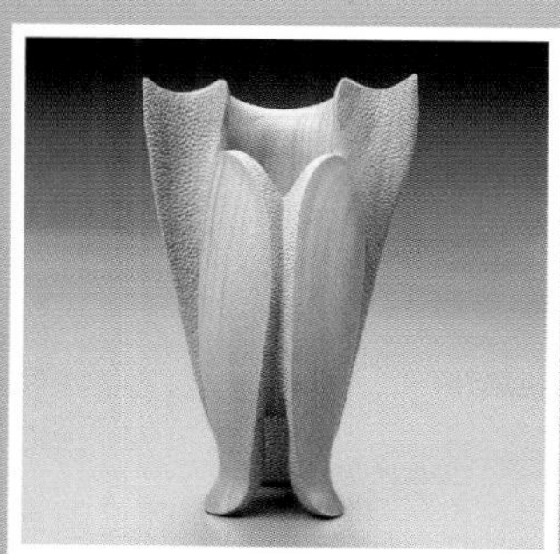

Working with wood is like breaking open a geode and discovering hidden treasure!

Cindy Drozda

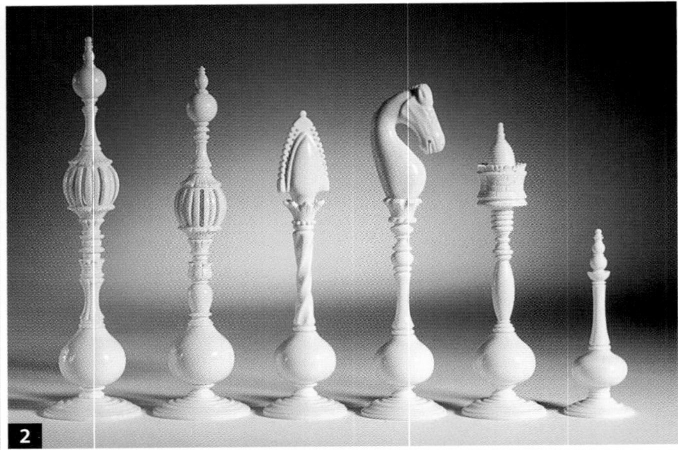

1 David Sengel (USA), *Crab Pot*, 1995. 4in (102mm) high, 3in (75mm) wide. Pearwood, rose thorns, crab claws, black lacquer. Photo: Michael Siede

2 Bill Jones (UK), Indian-style chess pieces. Tallest 7in (178mm) high. Reclaimed ivory

3 Bill Jones (UK), 'Spanish pulpit' chess pieces, 1961. Tallest 4½in (115mm) high. Reclaimed ivory

4 Stuart Mortimer (UK), *Squiggly Range*, 4-start solid twist with tapered double-twist finial. 12in (305mm) long, 3½in (90mm) dia. Blackwood

5 Ray Key (UK), *Cone, Bar and Arch Boxes* (Flavours of the Orient series). 4½in (114mm) high, 2½in (65mm) deep, 4in (102mm) wide. Amboyna, ebony and pink ivory

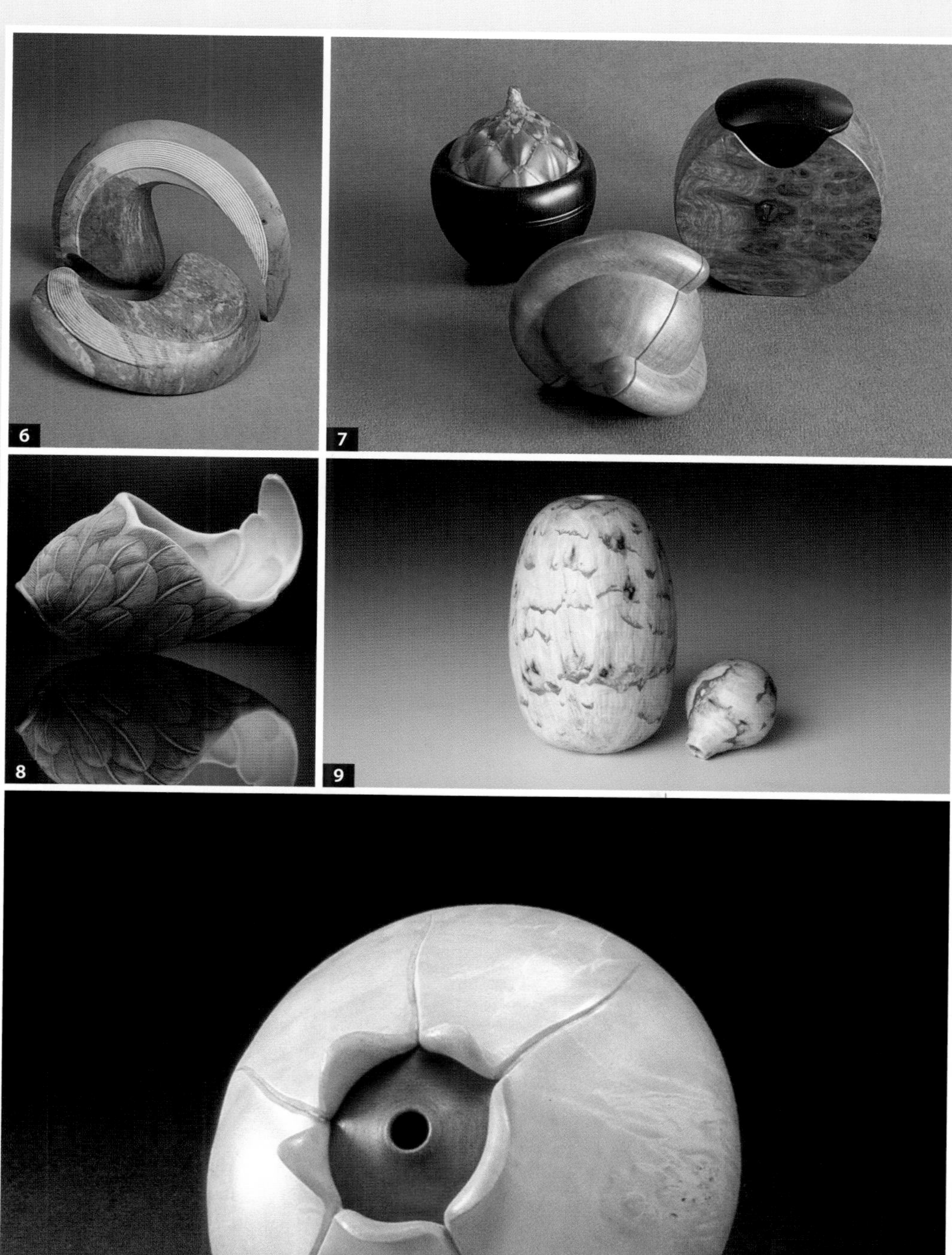

6 Betty J. Scarpino (USA), *Bridge Series*, 1998. 4in (102mm) dia. Spalted dogwood

7 Hans Joachim Weissflog (Germany), three boxes. *Left:* 1¾in (45mm) dia., 2⅛in (55mm) high, American blackwood and raffia palm fruit. *Middle: Third Drunken Box,* 2⅜in (60mm) dia., pernambuco. *Right:* 2⅜in (60mm) wide, 2⅝in (67mm) high, $^{15}/_{16}$in (24mm) deep, amboyna burl and African blackwood

8 Jacques Vesery (USA), *Under an Envious Sea and Sky,* 2004. 6¼ x 3½in (159 x 89mm). Cherry. Photo: Ronn Orenstein

9 David Ellsworth (USA), *Hickory Burl Duo*

10 Trent Bosch (USA), *Vessel of Illusion*. 6 x 6 x 6in (152 x 152 x 152mm). Boxelder and cherry

11 Trent Bosch (USA), *Sienna Series*. 5 x 5 x 5in (125 x 125 x 125mm). White ash

12 Bonnie Klein (USA), threaded-lid box with rose-engine work. 2¼in (57mm) dia., 2in (50mm) high. Cast acrylic

13 John Jordan (USA), English walnut vessel. 4in (102mm) high, 5in (125mm) dia.

14 Andrea Wolfe (USA), *Mahoney*. Approx. 3½in (89mm) high. Maple, pyrography, Prismacolor markers. Collection of Elvie Jackson. Photo: Jerry Anthony

15 Cindy Drozda (USA), ogee lidded box. 6in (152mm) dia., 4½in (114mm) high. Jarrah. Photo: Tim Benko, Benko Photographics

16

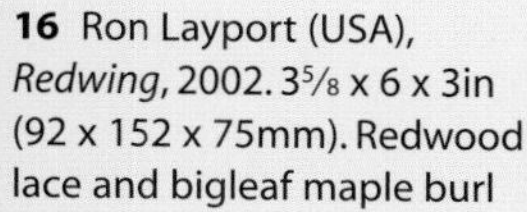

16 Ron Layport (USA), *Redwing*, 2002. 3⅝ x 6 x 3in (92 x 152 x 75mm). Redwood lace and bigleaf maple burl

17 Kip Christensen (USA), *Tower Box Series.* 5¾in (145mm) high, 2¾in (70mm) dia. Russian olive burl, ebony, elk antler. Photo: Don Dafoe

18 Richard Raffan (Australia), small-diameter bowls. 2–4¾in (50–120mm) dia. Woods include forest she-oak (rear), apple box (left), gidgee (centre), coolibah (front right)

19 Art Liestman (Canada), *Luck of the Draw*, puzzling illusion vessel. 5¾in (145mm) high, 4¾in (120mm) dia. Bigleaf maple and ebony. Photo: Kenji Nagai

20 J. Kelly Dunn (USA), vase. 3in (75mm) high, 3½in (89mm) dia. Norfolk pine

17 18 19 20

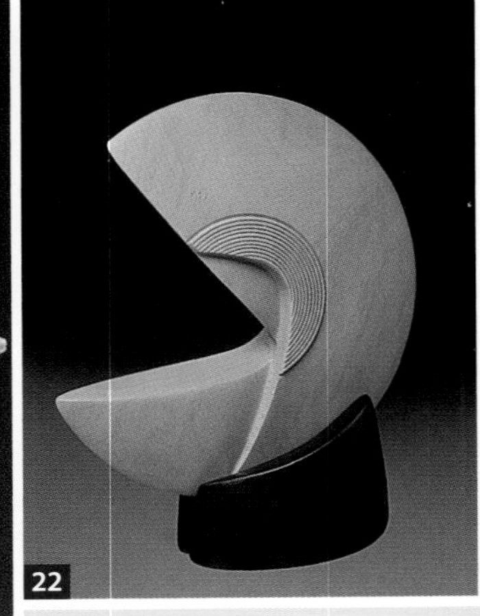

21 Binh Pho (USA), *Winter Night*. 5½in (140mm) high, 3½in (89mm) dia. Maple, acrylic, gold leaf

22 Betty J. Scarpino (USA), *Missing Piece Three*, 1997. 4¾in (120mm) dia. Dogwood. Photo: Cummings

23 Caroline Harkness (USA), *Little Woman* earring stand. 9½in (240mm) high, 3¾in (95mm) dia. Hard maple, purpleheart, yellowheart, Stratabond birch plywood, brazing wire

24 Art Liestman (Canada), *Same as it Ever Was*, dancing men bowl. 2in (50mm) high, 3⅛in (79mm) dia. Bigleaf maple burl. The dancing men spell out the title of the bowl, using a code devised by Sir Arthur Conan Doyle for his Sherlock Holmes story 'The Adventure of the Dancing Men'. Photo: Kenji Nagai

25 Andrea Wolfe (USA), *Saturation*. Photo: Jerry Anthony

26 Bonnie Klein (USA), spinning tops. 2in (50mm) dia., 2in (50mm) high. Hard maple with chatterwork, coloured with felt pens

27 Stuart Mortimer (UK), *Twisted Pink Ivory Range*, 12-bine twist with 4-start twisted finial. 12in (305mm) high, 4½in (114mm) dia. Pink ivory and ebony

28 Ron Fleming (USA), *Awaken*. 7in (178mm) high, 6in (152mm) dia. Mahogany

29 Cindy Drozda (USA), lidded box. 4½in (114mm) dia. Amboyna. Photo: Tim Benko, Benko Photographics

30

31

33

32

34

30 Michael Lee (USA), *Flying Shell Pod*. 6½ x 2½ x 3¾in (165 x 65 x 95mm). Lignum vitae

31 Kip Christensen (USA), boxes and bowls. 1–2⅜in (25–60mm) dia. Elk antler, ebony, pink ivory. Photo: Don Dafoe

32 Caroline Harkness (USA), *Proud as a Peacock*. 6in (152mm) high, 7in (178mm) dia. Russian olive, silver maple, ebony, peacock feathers, turquoise nuggets, dye

33 Binh Pho (USA), *Spring Break*. 6½in (165mm) high, 5in (125mm) dia. Boxelder, acrylic, gold leaf

34 Hans Joachim Weissflog (Germany), three boxes. *Left: Quarter-Circle box*, 2⅜in (60mm) wide, 2 13/16in (72mm) high, 13/16in (20mm) deep, boxwood, ebony and African blackwood. *Middle: What is This? Box*, 2¼in (58mm) wide, 3 1/16in (78mm) high, 13/16in (20mm) deep, boxwood and African blackwood. *Right: Crossing Lines Box*, 2⅜in (60mm) wide, 3 1/16in (78mm) high, ⅞in (23mm) deep, boxwood, ebony and African blackwood

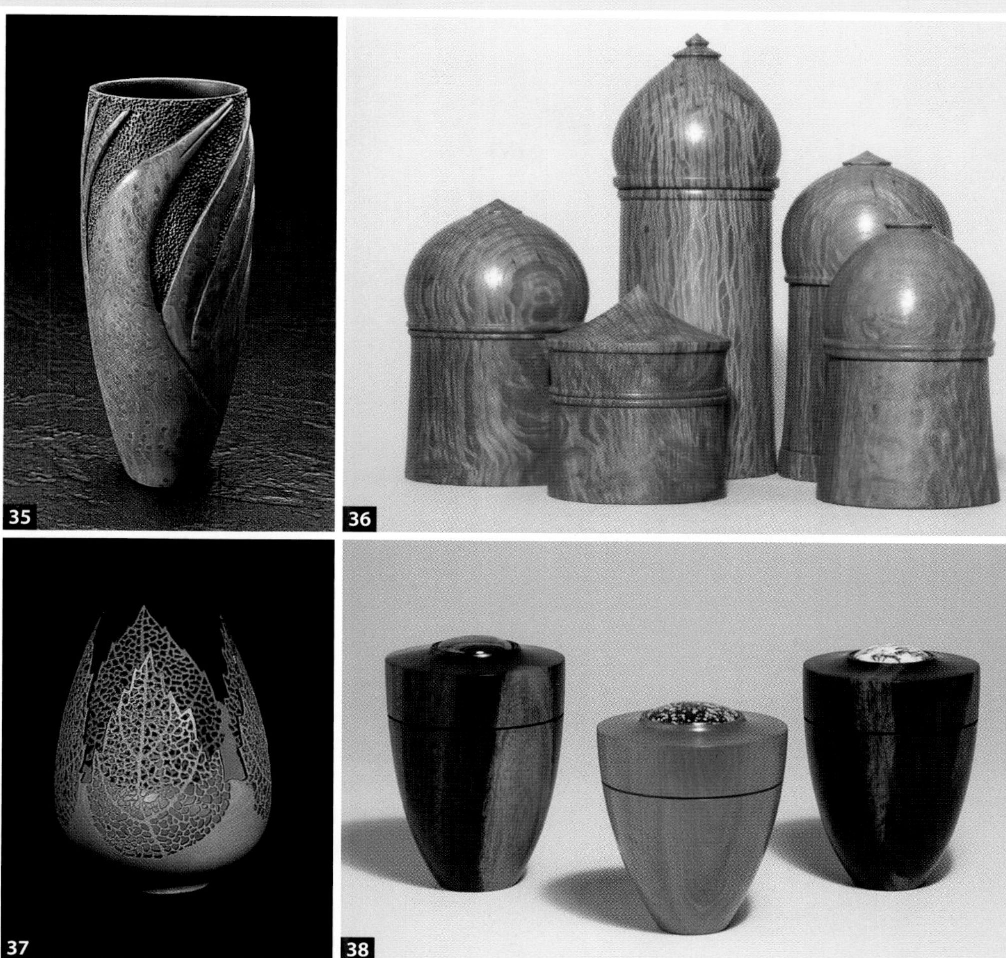

35 Ron Layport (USA), *Northern Dancer*, 2004. 5¾in (146mm) high, 2¼in (56mm) wide. Redwood lace, turned, carved and dyed

36 Richard Raffan (Australia), boxes with suction-fit lids. 2in (50mm) dia. Forest she-oak

37 Frank Sudol (Canada), *Lotus Vase*, 1993. 4in (102mm) high, 4in (102mm) dia. Birch

38 Ray Key (UK), *Cone Boxes*. Largest 3½in (89mm) high, 2½in (65mm) dia. Ebony and pink ivory with stone cabochons

39 Jacques Vesery (USA), *Sister of Envy* (Pleiades Series). 4½in (114mm) high, 3½in (89mm) dia. Cherry, ebony, 23K gold leaf.
Photo: R. Diamante

40 Michael Lee (USA), *Rocking Pod*. 4in (102mm) dia.

41 Jacques Vesery and Michael Lee (USA), *Mai 'Elua Moana, O Ekahi Lani (From Two Seas, of One Sky)*, 2003. 3 x 3½ x 6¼in (75 x 89 x 159mm) Cherry, 23K gold leaf

42 Jacques Vesery (USA) and Hans Joachim Weissflog (Germany), *Rockabye Song Bird*, 2003. 3 x 7in (75 x 178mm). American sycamore (plane) and pigment. Photo: R. Diamante

43 Michael Lee (USA) and Hans Joachim Weissflog (Germany), *Rocking Pod Bowl*. 5in (125mm) high, 5in (125mm) dia. Cocobolo

Metric Conversion Table

Inches to millimetres

in	mm	in	mm	in	mm	in	mm
1/64	0.3969	41/64	16.2719	1 17/32	38.8938	2 25/32	70.6439
1/32	0.7937	21/32	16.6687	1 9/16	39.6876	2 13/16	71.4376
3/64	1.1906	43/64	17.0656	1 19/32	40.4813	2 27/32	72.2314
1/16	1.5875	11/16	17.4625	1 5/8	41.2751	2 7/8	73.0251
5/64	1.9844	45/64	17.8594	1 21/32	42.0688	2 29/32	73.8189
3/32	2.3812	23/32	18.2562	1 11/16	42.8626	2 15/16	74.6126
7/64	2.7781	47/64	18.6531	1 23/32	43.6563	2 31/32	75.4064
1/8	3.1750	3/4	19.0500	1 3/4	44.4501	3	76.2002
9/64	3.5719	49/64	19.4469	1 25/32	45.2438	3 1/32	76.9939
5/32	3.9687	25/32	19.8437	1 13/16	46.0376	3 1/16	77.7877
11/64	4.3656	51/64	20.2406	1 27/32	46.8313	3 3/32	78.5814
3/16	4.7625	13/16	20.6375	1 7/8	47.6251	3 1/8	79.3752
13/64	5.1594	53/64	21.0344	1 29/32	48.4188	3 5/32	80.1689
7/32	5.5562	27/32	21.4312	1 15/16	49.2126	3 3/16	80.9627
15/64	5.9531	55/64	21.8281	1 31/32	50.0063	3 7/32	81.7564
1/4	6.3500	7/8	22.2250	2	50.8001	3 1/4	82.5502
17/64	6.7469	57/64	22.6219	2 1/32	51.5939	3 9/32	83.3439
9/32	7.1437	29/32	23.0187	2 1/16	52.3876	3 5/16	84.1377
19/64	7.5406	59/64	23.4156	2 3/32	53.1814	3 11/32	84.9314
5/16	7.9375	15/16	23.8125	2 1/8	53.9751	3 3/8	85.7252
21/64	8.3344	61/64	24.2094	2 5/32	54.7688	3 13/32	86.5189
11/32	8.7312	31/32	24.6062	2 3/16	55.5626	3 7/16	87.3127
23/64	9.1281	63/64	25.0031	2 7/32	56.3564	3 15/32	88.1064
3/8	9.5250	1	25.4001	2 1/4	57.1501	3 1/2	88.9002
25/64	9.9219	1 1/32	26.1938	2 9/32	57.9439	3 17/32	89.6939
13/32	10.3187	1 1/16	26.9876	2 5/16	58.7376	3 9/16	90.4877
27/64	10.7156	1 3/32	27.7813	2 11/32	59.5314	3 19/32	91.2814
7/16	11.1125	1 1/8	28.5751	2 3/8	60.3251	3 5/8	92.0752
29/64	11.5094	1 5/32	29.3688	2 13/32	61.1189	3 21/32	92.8689
15/32	11.9062	1 3/16	30.1626	2 7/16	61.9126	3 11/16	93.6627
31/64	12.3031	1 7/32	30.9563	2 15/32	62.7064	3 23/32	94.4564
1/2	12.7000	1 1/4	31.7501	2 1/2	63.5001	3 3/4	95.2502
33/64	13.0969	1 9/32	32.5438	2 17/32	64.2939	3 25/32	96.0439
17/32	13.4937	1 5/16	33.3376	2 9/16	65.0876	3 13/16	96.8377
35/64	13.8906	1 11/32	34.1313	2 19/32	65.8814	3 27/32	97.6314
9/16	14.2875	1 3/8	34.9251	2 5/8	66.6751	3 7/8	98.4252
37/64	14.6844	1 13/32	35.7188	2 21/32	67.4689	3 29/32	99.2189
19/32	15.0812	1 7/16	36.5126	2 11/16	68.2626	3 15/16	100.013
39/64	15.4781	1 15/32	37.3063	2 23/32	69.0564	3 31/32	100.806
5/8	15.8750	1 1/2	38.1001	2 3/4	69.8501	4	101.500

Index

About the Author

This is Ron Hampton's fourth woodturning book. His *Mini-Lathe Magic: Big Projects From a Small Lathe* and *A Turner's Guide to Veneer Inlays* are published by Schiffer Publishing of Pennsylvania, and *Segmented Turning: A Complete Guide* by GMC Publications.

A dentist by profession, Ron enjoys writing about turning and teaching turning as a hobby. He likes to learn new techniques and then write articles about them; his goal is to make difficult techniques easy. He has published about 85 woodturning articles to date, in journals such as *Woodturning, More Woodturning, American Woodturner, The Woodturner, Woodworker's Journal, Woodturning Design* and *The Woodworker*. He has also demonstrated at the American Association of Woodturners' national symposium in 1998 and 2000, and for four years at the Texas Turn or Two.

Ron has created a popular woodturning website at Woodturning Plus (http://www.woodturningplus.com). This is a site where turners can come for information or inspiration. Many of the world's best turners are represented here.

Ron lives with his wife Barbara in Texarkana, Texas.

GMC Publications
Castle Place, 166 High Street, Lewes, East Sussex BN7 1XU, United Kingdom
Tel: 01273 488005 Fax: 01273 402866
E-mail: pubs@thegmcgroup.com
Website: www.gmcbooks.com

Contact us for a complete catalogue, or visit our website.
Orders by credit card are accepted.